T0013110

SAY TO THESE
MOUNTAINS

*A biography of faith and
ministry in rural Haiti*

ELIZABETH TURNBULL

Light Messages
Durham, NC

Copyright © 2017, by Elizabeth Turnbull

*Say to These Mountains: A biography of faith
and ministry in rural Haiti*
Elizabeth Turnbull
lightmessages.com/elizabeth-turnbull
elizabeth@lightmessages.com

First Edition

Published 2017, by Light Messages Publishing
lightmessages.com
Durham, NC 27713 USA
SAN: 920-9298

Paperback ISBN: 978-1-61153-229-6
E-book ISBN: 978-1-61153-228-9
Library of Congress Control Number: 2017901017

ALL RIGHTS RESERVED
No part of this publication may be reproduced, stored in a retrieval
system, or transmitted in any form or by any means, electronic,
mechanical, photocopying, recording, scanning, or otherwise, except
as permitted under Section 107 or 108 of the 1976 International
Copyright Act, without the prior written permission except in brief
quotations embodied in critical articles and reviews.

All Scripture quotations are taken from the Holy Bible, New International
Version. The epigraph is taken from the Holy Bible, New Living Translation.

To the people of Haiti, and especially to her Church.

"How beautiful on the mountains are the feet of the messenger
who brings good news, the good news of peace
and salvation, the news that the God of Israel reigns!"
–Isaiah 52:7

PREFACE

WHEN MY GRANDFATHER asked me to write his biography, I initially said yes. Then no. I was too close, I argued. There was no way I could be impartial. Others heard my objections and dismissed them. I didn't need to be objective, they said. After all, my grandfather's story was, in a way, my story, too. Still, I remained unconvinced. For over a decade, I put off the project.

Then I finally read *Lyndon Johnson and the American Dream* by Doris Kearns Goodwin. I was struck by how Goodwin inserts herself into the narrative, sharing intimate exchanges she'd had with Johnson, giving her readers a rare glimpse into the mind and heart of a former president. She wasn't absent from the narrative at all—and the book was stronger for it. I found inspiration in her approach.

Then there was this realization: For years I had watched people write about their work in Haiti—people who had come later and built on the foundation laid by my grandparents. And yet, Wallace's story remained untold. It needed to be written. So I started writing.

While a biographer would ordinarily take years to research a project covering nearly a century of living, I was able to start and complete the book in under two years. This is not a testament to my writing speed but rather to Wallace's extraordinary skills as an archivist. He spent years sorting through his files, meticulously organizing digital and physical documents by date. He also typed up his notes and journals into an informal volume for his family—just in case I didn't get to the project in time. For the biography, I primarily used these notes, as well as interviews with Wallace and Eleanor.

In addition to Wallace's archives, I have relied upon documents from newspapers, websites, and government records to help me fill in the blanks and to corroborate events. Where Wallace is quoted directly, I have endeavored to remain faithful to his own words, editing only with his permission for syntax and grammar.

From time to time, my voice is heard directly in the narrative—to lend clarity, to offer insight, to share what perhaps only a granddaughter might see. I hope this helps the reader get to know Wallace the man, not just Wallace the missionary.

Say to These Mountains is, at its core, the biography of Wallace Turnbull, my grandfather. But it is more than that. It is, by necessity, my grandmother Eleanor's story, too. For as Wallace himself says time and again, "there is no me without her." This book is also a piece of Haiti's story, of her Church, her people, her history—for there is no Wallace without them. Finally, this book is in part my story, for I see now there is no me without Wallace.

ONE
The Beginning... and an End

THE WOODEN SADDLE HIT Wallace's lower back with each step as the mule inched its way down the steep path. Fatigue from the two-day journey had begun to set in—for man and beast—but still they plodded on, the patchwork of the mountains draped around them like a warm blanket, the sun dripping onto their shoulders and rolling down their spines. The same sun had branded Wallace's once fair skin: his ears carved away layer by layer under the doctor's scalpel; the ever-increasing brown spots on his now wrinkled hands; the leathery patch at the back of his once-smooth neck. At 90 years old, Wallace recognized he was nearing the end of his life, but as he rode down from the church dedication in Portino, he also knew that his life had begun on the mission field and, if God granted, would end there as well.

• • •

Wallace's father, John Turnbull, had traveled to India in 1917 to serve as a missionary. He was 29 years old and the third Turnbull to be assigned by the Christian and Missionary Alliance (CMA) to the province of Gujarat in western India; he followed his brothers Walter and Louis, who had arrived in India at the turn of the Twentieth Century in the middle of a devastating famine.

When John arrived, he found a rapidly changing India: the Indian National Congress led by Mahatma Gandhi had called for the self-government of India. The British were fighting wars on multiple fronts as the First World War threatened to topple the empire. Tensions were rising on all sides. Though he never expressed it in such a way, John may very well have found himself in a no-man's-land. Having been born and raised in Peterborough, Canada, he was a British citizen, but as a missionary, his role was to be a friend and equal to the Indians he served. To straddle the ever-higher wall of division, he would have to be three men in one: Citizen of King and Country, Friend to India, Faithful Servant of Christ.

From the very beginning of his ministry, John wanted to raise up local leaders in the Church instead of having new believers constantly relying on foreign missionaries—a passion that would be handed from father to son. So John began teaching promising young men about the Bible, the tenets of Christian faith, and how to be leaders in their churches and communities. Recognizing that even spiritual leaders have physical needs, John sold his shirts from time to time to buy rice to feed his students.

As a bachelor, John threw himself into his service, finding adventure around every corner. The greatest of his adventures were those that led him north to the ancient kingdom of

Rajputana—known today as Rajasthan after the Constitution of 1949. Despite warnings from his brother Louis that it was too dangerous, John persisted in his trips. He was the first missionary to preach in Rajputana. To some, this might seem daring or brave, to others it might seem foolish. But for John, it was a divine calling: he had come to India to preach, and too many of the people of Rajputana had never heard the gospel. This was his duty.

John argued that the Lord would keep him safe from danger. He also likely took a measure of comfort in his red beard, which earned him respect from Hindus as a holy man of sorts. But even holy men weren't exempt from all the perils of an India in turmoil.

One day, while John was on one of his excursions, a Muslim barber held his razor to John's throat, demanding the Muslim declaration of faith. In what John would later term a moment of divine inspiration, he responded, "There is no God but God, and Mohammed was a prophet," rather than saying "his prophet," which to John would have been a betrayal of his own faith. The barber lowered his razor and John was free to go.

John may have escaped the barber's razor, but he nearly didn't survive a more tenacious threat: blackwater fever. One of the most dangerous complications of malaria, blackwater fever is believed by some to be a combination of malaria and typhoid. But in actuality, blackwater fever results from a complication of malaria in which the red blood cells burst, releasing hemoglobin directly into the bloodstream and urine—hence the name "black water." Without proper treatment, kidney failure follows close behind.

Severely weak and ill, John was sent to the cooler area of Coonoor in the hills to recuperate. During his convalescence he was cared for by his nieces Muriel and Marguerite, Louis's daughters. Once he was on the mend, Marguerite introduced John to her Sunday school teacher Maud Smith, whose cheerful, loving nature earned her the affectionate name "Joy." The courtship, which involved chaperones and dinner dates, eventually resulted in a marriage.

John and Maud wed in 1921 in Mehmedabad, and their first son John Louis was born there in 1922. The couple worked to found a church in Gujarat. Some of John's early converts would later travel out of Rajputana across the border to the little church.

As John's wife, Maud remained in the middle of the social circle of missionaries, her joyful nature endearing her to all. Before long, John and Maud had built what they saw as a wonderful life steeped in service, heavy with purpose. They imagined themselves in India for the long haul.

Meanwhile, tensions between the British and Indians were increasing. Gandhi was gaining ground in the Independence Movement. While he arguably led one of history's most successful nonviolent movements, the Revolutionary Movement for Independence argued for armed rebellion. Fear among the British spread after some nationalists began looting businesses and homes and clashing violently with the police and British authorities. John would later tell how for some time when "rebels were on the warpath," all foreigners slept in their clothes, dressed in dark colors, atop their bedding, so they could flee to pre-chosen hiding spots. The men took turns all night at watch during those tense days.

Ever the evangelist, John even visited Gandhi during one of his imprisonments. Gandhi had studied in England, and so John knew he would have at least a modest understanding of the Christian message. He asked Gandhi what he thought of Jesus. Gandhi replied that he agreed with Jesus, but he could not become a Christian: visiting a church in England, he had been asked by an usher to leave because he was colored. The damage done in that moment was irreparable, and one barely dares to imagine *what if*. What if Gandhi had been welcomed? What if he had had been seen as the beautiful creation that he was? What if the usher had truly known and shared the love of Christ? *What if?*

• • •

With tensions building and their family growing, John and Maud chose to travel to the United States for a time. They always expected to move back to India with their family, but they never did. During their passage, Maud undoubtedly carried in her heart countless memories, joys, and sorrows—and in her womb, she carried a child.

Toward the end of Maud's pregnancy, she and the family traveled to Hollywood, CA, to visit John's parents. There, in Hollywood Hospital, Wallace Rutherford Turnbull was born the evening of July 10, 1925.

After Wallace's birth, John went to Los Angeles' Echo Lake and tossed in a handful of lotus seed he'd collected at the Taj Majal. Though his real motives will always remain unknown, I like to imagine that John, filled with joy at his son's birth, wanted to mark the occasion in a way that would share the blessing with countless others, even if they never knew it. Submerged in the waters of the city's largest artificial lake, the lotus seeds would sprout and go on to be celebrated in the annual Lotus Festival, held each year at Echo Park in mid-July, which coincides with Wallace's birthday—a connection unknown to the festival organizers, but one that has delighted Wallace and his family. In his birth, a tiny piece of India had come with him, leaving its mark not just on Wallace and his parents, but on the landscape of the city itself. It would be this way for the rest of Wallace's life—he would seek to leave each place he went a little more beautiful.

Hollywood was where Wallace took his first breath, but his first steps would be in the Holy Land. John had been invited to lead the American Church, an international, English-language church in Jerusalem, after earning a Masters of Arts degree from the University of Toronto in 1926.

The time in Jerusalem would forever mark Wallace and his family, for it would be here that he would cut his first teeth, speak his first words. It would also be where his family would suffer tremendous loss. The innocence of his childhood would end in the historic city.

While John's purpose in Jerusalem was to lead the American Church, he was as much an explorer as he was a minister. In his journals, Wallace writes, "His love for language, evangelism, and adventure led him to find support for trips into the North Arabian Desert with first a Dodge loaded with five-gallon tins of gasoline, and then with a pair of Model T Fords."

For his excursions, John had to obtain the permission of Prince Faisal of Arabia, who later became the nation's king. Prince Faisal required a personal interview with John and decided to grant his request, despite his being a Christian missionary. Less than a decade before, T. E. Lawrence had fought alongside the Arabs of the region in their fight to gain independence from the Ottoman Empire, and at 14 years old Prince Faisal had been the first Saudi Arabian royal to visit London. One can imagine that perhaps John, a Canadian citizen and thus a British subject, might have benefited indirectly from the prince's visit and from Lawrence, who had gained the trust of the people.

To show his gratitude to Prince Faisal, John gifted him a pair of green silk pajamas with gold braiding, which he had acquired on a stop in Japan years before. According to Wallace, the gift "delighted Faisal," and John began his excursions into the Arabian desert—simultaneously becoming the first person to cross that desert by vehicle. Layer upon layer of golden sand stretched out before him. The desert to many is a place of desolation, but to John it must have seemed very much alive. The dunes carved by the winds, patterns in the sand etched by the bellies of sand cobras, paw prints of tiny foxes and even tinier rodents—each sign spoke to a living, breathing world altogether foreign to John who had grown up surrounded by the rolling fields around Peterborough, Canada. Or perhaps he recognized in the landscape the same hues of golds and browns as the wheat, oats, and corn drying in the fields of home.

Blown by the hot winds, the sand of the desert would eat its way under his explorer's helmet, settling deep into his scalp. But the sand was the least of his concerns. What could, under other circumstances, amount to an inconvenience, threatened to turn deadly in an instant: too great a distance between watering holes; a busted radiator; a scorpion hidden in the sand.

"Those exploratory forays were extremely dangerous," Wallace writes.

To mitigate the danger, John traveled with a Bedouin guide assigned to him by Prince Faisal. The trips, which John used as an excuse to seek ways and channels to distribute Bibles and share his faith, were long and remote; there were no mechanics or service stations, and the men would have nothing to rely on except their own skills and the few provisions they could bring with them. The stories would become family legend, to be taken out in a quiet moment and shared with children, grandchildren, great-grandchildren.

On one occasion, the men had been driven to sip tiny bits of rusty water from the car's radiator. They filtered it through a handkerchief before making tea so they could swallow the bitter liquid. "Lost and out of water," Wallace wrote, "they met a caravan of men headed in the opposite direction with cracked lips, also lost and down to their last two goatskins of water. Both parties desperate, they exchanged directions to their last waterholes, and all rejoiced at God's timely provision of guidance."

Along the way, John's Dodge passed through huge flocks of livestock; the guide grew worried when he saw only children with the animals, taking it as an ominous sign. "Passing on the right side of a long, low hill, they saw ahead the high adobe walls of an Arab fortified village," Wallace wrote. When warning shots rang out, the guide ran ahead, waving the right side of his robe, a sign of friendship.

John and his guide had stumbled upon the ancient city of Al-Jaouf, the Arab name for Job. Spotting John, two young men came forward, crying "Abu! Abu!" "Father! Father!" and fell down before him. The young men were two orphans John had befriended in Jerusalem; they remembered his kindness and paid it in full by ensuring his safe and warm reception in Al-Jaouf.

The party of explorers was welcomed in, and the sheik served his visitors a strong, syrupy Bedouin coffee in tiny brass cups. John hadn't yet learned that to signify he'd had enough he must twirl his cup upside down, or his hosts, not wanting to seem stingy, would continue refilling it. In desperation, John spent the evening spotting where his hosts were looking and tossing the coffee on the adobe wall whenever they looked away.

The coffee, it turns out, was the least of John's adversaries. The sheik later told him that his party was fortunate. He had sent thirty men to kill them, but his men had ridden out on horseback by the other side of the long hill, so they had not met. One of John's would-be assassins gave him a *janbiya*, a curved knife, stained with the blood of men it had killed. The knife, Wallace would recall, had a beautiful jeweled silver handle and sheath. John, who was known for his impulsive generosity and lack of sentimentality, would later gift the dagger to a boy in Oregon who collected knives, while to his son Wallace, he gave a donut-shaped stone made from Arabian sand that had been struck by lightning. Wallace regretted the loss of the janbiya, a valuable and notable heirloom. The fact that he had been left with only a glass stone couldn't have been lost on Wallace, though for John it was perfectly within his character to give without thinking of balancing material value.

The exact location of Al-Jaouf, along with countless other pieces of knowledge, had long been lost to Western minds, erased by centuries of enmity from the Crusades. John's brief explorations, and those of other missionary-adventurers, were received with gratitude by the British authorities. For his daring and the information he gained on his trips, John was honored by the Fellowship of the Royal Geographical Society.

While John was exploring the Arabian desert, Maud and her two sons Johnny Lou (later called Jack, at his request as a teenager) and Wallace were occupied with the business of living. Wallace was only a baby, so his memories of these times come from stories John passed down to him throughout the years. It makes sense that the seemingly less glamorous events wouldn't have made it into the family folklore, but one can easily imagine the daily goings-on of an expat pastor's wife and her two sons. They were, after all, immersed in the duties and social life of the American Church in Jerusalem.

For Maud, there would be a household to maintain, people to receive, needs to meet. The mundane chores and dinners would be punctuated with the holy: baptisms, weddings, funerals. And for it all, Maud would have by her side a sixteen-year-old girl called Azizi. A housemaid for the family, she also served as a guide of sorts for Maud—if not into desert forays, then certainly into the equally foreign and difficult terrain of a new culture, a new people to call neighbor, a new land to call home.

On a trip many years later, Wallace would try to find his mother's companion, only to learn that Azizi is a tribal name, widely used. "The Azizis were in Crusader times a Christian people in Medaba who warned Muslim neighbors of a pending Crusader attack," Wallace wrote in his journal, "So they have to modern times been honored by the Muslims."

During the family's time in Jerusalem, Maud conceived and gave birth to her third son, David Walter, on January 10, 1927. The childbirth was difficult. Practicing faith in divine healing, one of the tenets of the Christian and Missionary Alliance of which they were central members, John and Maud refused all medical intervention. Maud would suffer for ten days before succumbing to death. One can only imagine how hard she must have fought to stay with her three boys, how many prayers must have been uttered in absolute faith, and how much grief would wash over the young family, leaving its own stain on each member.

"The rest of his life, though he married twice again," Wallace wrote, "Dad mourned my mother's unnecessary death."

TWO
Transient

AFTER MAUD'S DEATH, John and his three sons, Johnny Lou, Wallace, and infant David, sailed by steamer from Joppa, now Tel Aviv, to New York. From there, they made their way to Nyack, a village along the Hudson River, just north of the New Jersey state line.

Nyack was home to John's brother Walter and his second wife Cora. Walter was the president of the CMA and helped secure John a teaching position at the missions institute. The boys would live with their Uncle Walter and Aunt Cora, whom they would affectionately call Auntie Mother. Walter and Cora were a stable home and must have been fairly well off, for they were able to provide a nanny for the boys in the form of Nurse Rose, who, by all accounts, was also a loving influence for the boys.

One can easily imagine the joy these three boys would bring to Walter and Cora, who had been unable to have their own children. So great was the bond between Wallace and Cora that the couple asked to adopt him, but John refused.

"The house was always a happy place," Wallace wrote in his journals.

There, he formed some of his earliest memories. Like many young children, he was full of curiosity and the joy of discovery, even if it sometimes led to comic outcomes.

"Adult talk is always baffling to tots, and I was always being puzzled by it," Wallace recounted. "We tots heard the expression about trying to lift one's self by his bootstraps, and that started quite a discussion among us. We tried very energetically to do it! Nurse Rose, laughing, said we couldn't do it, and Johnny Lou said that he had already tried it and failed. I tried anyway. David gave up after I did."

Though he was but a toddler at the time, Wallace would forever remember Auntie Mother and Uncle Walter as surrogate parents and their home as a loving one. I can easily imagine that their love and affection must have served as a healing balm after losing his mother to death and his father to circumstance. But the home he'd found would only be temporary. Cora fell ill.

"Auntie Mother's bed was moved into the upper hallway, and she had me called to her," Wallace wrote. "I remember her tearfully telling me that she was going away to be with Jesus. I asked when she was coming back, and she said that she couldn't come back; I'd have to come to her. She wept at that, and they took me away. I was two and a half, looking up at her."

Before his third birthday, Wallace had lost two mothers, and with Cora's death would come another uprooting.

Walter, who himself wasn't in the best of health, felt unable to continue caring for his nephews. John must not have felt able either. Looking back on it from a modern sensibility, it's admittedly difficult to understand how a father would be unable to care for his motherless children, especially when full-time help in the form of a nanny was available. To have even a moderate understanding of what was to come, one must first realize that in John's worldview serving the kingdom of God would go above all else, and he had been called to serve through the Christian and Missionary Alliance. He and his boys would sacrifice their physical and emotional needs as a family to grow God's kingdom.

• • •

After their Auntie Mother's death, Wallace and his brothers would go to live with the Misses Beer, two unmarried women who had, as Wallace described it, "a wonderful yard with a goldfish pool (everyone wanted one in the twenties) and a gazebo out back, a two-story house with a big porch and porch swing overlooking the town below and the river." But as he remembers it, the yard was the only wonderful thing about the Misses Beer. They would prove to be abusive to the boys. Beyond the usual "strictness," as Wallace would put it, the two women could be rather creative in their cruelty. Wallace recounts that they forced two-year-old David to eat his excrement whenever he had a potty-training accident, a horror that caused Wallace nightmares until he was 10 years old. One can only imagine the trauma it left on David.

While the brothers were living with the Misses Beer, John met and married Rhoda, "an airy, tall redhead" who had been a nurse and missionary to the poor in the Appalachian mountains of Georgia. We'll never fully know why, but Wallace does know that John and Rhoda's marriage was met with the protests of family and friends, a protest that would later prove merited.

When Wallace met Rhoda for the first time, he remembers asking, "Are you my new mother?" Five words heavy with longing.

Wallace very much wanted a mother and also to be free of the Misses Beer, but of Rhoda, he wrote, "I wasn't impressed." His mother-to-be did, however, have one redeeming quality that young Wallace discovered. She brought with her a box of chocolates for the young boy, despite her strongly held belief that eating sugar would lead to diabetes. Rhoda prescribed Wallace to eat just one chocolate a day after dinner. Wallace's response would prove typical for his character: "I sat down next to the steps where she and Miss Beer were chatting and ate them all, thereby gaining a lifelong determination to enjoy chocolate." Wallace and Rhoda had drawn their battle lines.

Once John and Rhoda were married, the boys moved back home with their father and new stepmother. Soon, they were settled in the Pardington House, two doors down the hill from the beloved Uncle Walter and his bungalow. The Pardington House, named after Reverend Pardington, an earlier tenant and former CMA president, "was a fascinating place full of memories, with a basement that we children never entered, for its furnace," Wallace recounted. "Its full front porch was draped with honeysuckle that we boys loved to sip."

The home would also become a gathering place of sorts, the hub to John and Rhoda's hospitality—especially for John's students, many of whom would go on to serve as missionaries around the world. "The house was always a place for Dad's students to come," Wallace wrote. "I remember Franck Spain who years later worked night shift operating the Ottawa water works before becoming for many years a CMA pastor in Canada. Also there were Harry and Walter Post—lanky fellows we used to see through the years—and Russell Diebler. These men later had remarkable ministries in Indonesia."

In spite of the occupants' warm hospitality, in winter, the house was drafty and could be bitterly cold. "I used to wake up in winter in our tiny dormer bedroom with snow on my bed," Wallace wrote.

But with the snow also came snow cream, a delightful treat courtesy of his father and Uncle Walter. They would scrape the snow from the windowsills and pour cream and maple syrup on it; the cold from the ice would stiffen the syrup. Wallace, a lifetime lover of ice cream and all its relatives, undoubtedly found this a most delightful dish—especially in the midst of Rhoda's ongoing prescriptions.

"Mother regularly purged us either with flax seed swelled with water to make a glass full of slippery glop, or with a tablespoon of castor oil atop a glass full of orange juice," Wallace recounted. "It was years before I could stomach orange juice."

The castor oil and orange juice, while disagreeable, seem to be the least of the unkindness Rhoda and John would bestow on the young boy throughout the years. Wallace gives us no real reason to doubt that John and Rhoda loved their sons—after all, Rhoda cared for the children day in and day out, eventually serving alongside her husband and son, Wallace, in Haiti; and John, especially, made efforts to connect with his boys, albeit inconsistent ones. But it does seem obvious from Wallace's journals that at the very least John and Rhoda were utterly out of touch about any of their children's needs that went beyond physical requirements or Biblical instruction.

Rhoda was especially abusive with the boys, and beatings were frequent. "Through the years, Mother Rhoda for letting off steam used almost uniquely her large wooden hairbrush on the three of us, breaking a great number. Each time, she reproached us righteously for our great waste in making her break a hairbrush! We got thoroughly thrashed for any notion," Wallace wrote in his journals.

Rhoda instilled a terror in young Wallace, and he would learn to do most anything to avoid a beating. One such occasion was in the summer of 1931 when the family was attending various Alliance summer camps, first at Lake Odessa, Michigan and later in Rumney, New Hampshire. Someone had given Wallace, then 7 years old, a small horseshoe-shaped magnet. During one of the spiritual meetings at the camp, Wallace, who was told to keep silent, leaned out the window to get fresh air. "My precious magnet slipped from my fingers, and fell onto the dragging belt of a woman's dress. Standing close to the window to hear, she kept making little movements, so the magnet clunked against the boards below," Wallace wrote. His parents would hear the noise of the magnet and tell Wallace to be quiet. When he'd try to explain what happened, they'd shush him again. "Terrified of Mother's beatings, I kept shutting up," Wallace retold. "Later that day, Daddy asked me where my magnet was. I told him the full story, and, still not comprehending my real fear of Mother, he said why, I should have spoken up! He made a frantic search for the lady with the drooping belt, in vain. I've often wondered what she thought when she at last discovered my magnet."

Wallace and his brothers' reactions to Rhoda's beating wouldn't always be to keep quiet. In one incident the boys plotted to take to their revenge on their babysitter if not their stepmother. For a time, a woman named Anita Bailey came to live with Wallace's family after her brother Nathan Bailey, president of the CMA, was killed in an automobile accident. To help, Anita would babysit the boys when Rhoda and John attended evening services. "We got so many beatings from Mother Rhoda that we boys, hearing the instructions given to gentle Anita on how to spank us, made a plot," Wallace wrote. "We got out of bed, a no-no, after our parents left for church, and knew that Anita would try to flog us. We all three lit at once into the poor, wailing thing with belt, watch chain, and shoe. She announced tearfully that she'd not babysit those terrors again!"

Wallace remembers, that the beatings typically occurred while John wasn't home. So one day, when Wallace was to be beaten with John at home entertaining company, he decided to use it to his advantage. "One day, Mother decided that it was time to beat me, but Daddy was home, and we had company. I ran from her, yelling, 'No, I've been beaten enough, you mean old stepmother!' Daddy, bewildered utterly by the racket, came out into the yard, asking me what was the matter. I told him that he had no idea what went on when he was not home, that I was not going to be beaten again. He was astounded. The rhythm slowed considerably."

John was so fully engaged with his work at the Alliance that he seemed unaware of how often and harshly his boys were beaten. In fact, John seemed utterly out of touch with any of his children's needs or wants. For example, John would rid the home of items he no longer wanted, whether they were his to discard or not. "Dad used to destroy a toy if he thought it past worth keeping," Wallace wrote in his journal. As a young child, Wallace had a teddy bear that he kept in the bed with him every night; he loved this bear and would even dream about it. "One night, I dreamed that a dozen teddies were playing all over my bed, and I couldn't catch even one of them. I again awoke, sorry that Teddy wasn't alive."

So it's not difficult to imagine how upset he must have felt when he noticed a pile of ashes next to the bed of parsnips and found in them the two glass eyes from his beloved Teddy. His father gave an explanation that the bear had gotten dirty, and he promised to replace it. "He remembered four years later, not noting the time lapse and the age change. The second bear caused much mocking by other boys when they saw it in our car as we traveled," Wallace wrote.

While Wallace lost his beloved teddy, he did manage to hold on to a special gift from his dear Uncle Walter. The two had always shared a special bond; it seems that Walter understood better than his brother how to connect with the young child. Wallace remembers one day in particular when Walter brought them a brass microscope. For the ever-curious, insect-loving Wallace, this must have been a most wonderful discovery. "Uncle Walter caught a fly, and we were all charmed by a little mite running up and down its leg," Wallace wrote. The microscope was a treasured keepsake that Wallace kept for over fifty years, even taking it with him to Haiti.

Not long after Wallace received the microscope, Walter would die abruptly in an accident when the car he was riding in lost traction on loose gravel and slid into the stone pillar of a home. Walter struck his head on the vehicle's doorpost. Walter's death seemed especially cruel, for he had recently remarried and his wife Victoria was four months pregnant.

"One day, we went to Uncle Walter's house," Wallace remembers. "There was adult talk about Uncle Walter being 'in his casket,' and lots of sober people were there. They asked each other 'if he (I) should be allowed to see him,' and decided no. So I waited outside, trying to peer through the glass door to see Uncle Walter and observing that strange long thing on the floor."

Days later, Wallace asked his father why they hadn't seen Uncle Walter. "Very startled, he asked me, 'Why, don't you know? He's dead!' I said no, no one had told me. Dad was horrified." Again, the disconnect is startling. John hadn't even thought to explain to his own son that Walter, John's brother and a beloved uncle, had died unexpectedly.

Later, John would take Wallace to Big Bear Mountain where Walter had died and show him the spot of the accident. Perhaps it was his way of giving Wallace a moment to say goodbye.

Throughout his childhood, Wallace's meaningful interactions with his father would be limited to vignettes like this, with the most precious of them revolving around fishing. Especially ideal summers were those of 1935 and 1936 when John and Rhoda took the three boys camping for several weeks in Canada by Lake Opeongo. John and the boys spent the days fishing and exploring. "We also always caught our limit of five black bass, when we tried," Wallace remembered. "We used wobbly lures that looked like an injured fish, leopard frogs, a small fish, or a piece of fish on a spoon to give it smell. We boys caught a few blue perch too, when left ashore." The summer in Canada was also a time for Wallace to immerse himself in nature, one of his greatest delights. He would remember with fondness the family of deer that snorted about by their tent at night, the porcupine that awakened them as it scattered their cornflakes, the kangaroo mouse that hopped past, and the red squirrel that learned to eat from their hands. "One day she had us all in hysterics," Wallace wrote about the squirrel. "She stole a ripe peach. It was soft and kept falling as she tried to carry it off to her babies. Finally giving up, she stuck it in a crotch of a tree."

It seems no animal was undesirable to Wallace: even the yellow jackets claimed his affection. "A nest of yellow jackets from under a stump always swarmed about as we cleaned fish. A small type of hornet, they can be mean if disturbed. We let them crawl over our hands, fascinated as they carted off bits of fish to their nest."

Fishing and camping was an escape for the exhausted John, who was consumed with what he believed to be work of eternal importance—that of raising support for missionaries and, later, building up churches to win souls. Times like the ones at Lake Opeongo, while brief and far between, provided a respite for a tired man as well as time for him to connect with his sons who were rapidly growing into men. John may not have been the most engaged father, but there is no doubt that he loved his boys in his own way.

• • •

A year after Walter's death, the Depression was in full swing, and the CMA was feeling the effects. "One day students from all over the world, including a very dark chap from India, came with wheelbarrows to get most of Dad's books. He had a library of 3,000 books, including all the works of A.B. Simpson, his father's friend. He never was attached to things though he enjoyed them," Wallace wrote. "Dad with his salesman's gift had been asked to travel about, urging church folks to support the CMA missionaries overseas."

John bought the first one-wheeled trailer from its inventor, exchanged the family belongings for camping gear and embarked with his family on a whirlwind fundraising tour, a process well known among missionaries as deputation. The grueling schedule would take them through all 48 states in two years. The most stability Wallace and his brothers would know would be in one-semester blocks as they'd stay put in a town for the school term, using Christmas and summer breaks to move on to the next destination.

Wallace's first grade would be spent first in Nyack, NY and then in Los Angeles, California. Second grade would be divided between Asheville and Portland, Oregon. Third grade began back in Asheville and ended in Upper Darby, Pennsylvania, where the family would reside for eight years as John worked with the CMA to start a main church in Upper Darby and two outstation churches in neighboring towns. In Flourtown, home to one of these outstation churches, the chapel was converted from a stable. Wallace remembers helping to clean out the stable and prepare it for service.

To this day, Wallace has harbored resentment against the idea of deputation, calling it a "begging horror," and one can't help but wonder if his feelings aren't rooted in this time on the road. Wallace, a great lover of people and an even bigger lover of nature, would encounter many marvels on the family's expedition, but at what cost? "By the time I finished high school, I'd attended 19 schools," Wallace tells.

During their travels, the family would seek permission from landowners to set up their tent and cots in pastures. When those were unavailable, they'd camp in what Wallace describes as "wild places" on public land.

"One morning, we awoke to find a cattle drive around us next to an icy Rocky Mountain stream of snow melt," Wallace writes. "We boys were delighted to see real cowboys, their horses, and their gear. Jack and I momentarily escaped close watch by Mom. A cowboy warned me away from the rear of his horse. I wondered why it'd kick a friendly kid. One chap gave me a forbidden white bread ham sandwich. Mom hollered at us to leave our new friends and gave David my sandwich as punishment for wandering off."

As they traveled, they found the Depression's tentacles spread throughout the country; her victims could be spotted everywhere. The site of Okies crossing the great white sandy desert with their cattle would stay with Wallace for the rest of his life.

For all their faults as parents, John and Rhoda were unusually hospitable and generous, taking nearly every opportunity to be of service to those in need. Throughout his life, Wallace would bear witness to and help serve countless people coming in and out of his house—for meals, for gifts, and even, on occasion, to stay. Many of these people would embed themselves in his memory, and even now, the people he has met are some of his greatest joys.

"God has been so good to us, sending all kinds of people our way," Wallace has told me many times. "From the very lowly people to even a vice president of the United States. And it isn't because of us. God has done it all." What is perhaps most remarkable isn't just the vast range of people Wallace has met in his life, but rather the incredible clarity with which he remembers many of them—regardless of their social rank. What endears (or vilifies) a person to Wallace isn't money or power or perceived importance; he remembers people for what sometimes appear to be the most trivial details—traits of character or habit that etch them into his mind.

From his first grade spring semester in Los Angeles, Wallace remembers with particular clarity a traveling salesman. "One day, a man came to our back door, with a square of corrugated cardboard. On it were stitched a wonderful collection of pencil sharpeners shaped like people's heads—cowboys, Indians, policemen, etc. The man said that he was selling them for a nickel. Mother said that she really didn't need one, but would he like something to eat? He gratefully accepted and said that he had not eaten in two days, having sold nothing. I was fascinated with his performance; he ate peas with a table knife, not dropping any! Mother shooed me away, said that it wasn't polite to stare. Finished, the man, extremely grateful, insisted on giving me a sharpener. I chose a cowboy's head."

Over 80 years later, after having shared only a brief moment with him, Wallace remembers this man with fondness. Though Wallace can recount how the man ate his peas, he doesn't seem to remember, or care, what the man looked like, what he wore, or whether or not he seemed respectable. The man was interesting—he managed to eat his peas with a table knife—and he had been kind to the young boy—gifting him a sharpener.

This is the lens through which Wallace would see the world for the rest of his life. Not by "the trappings of this world" but by the traits that make us each individual creatures of God's creativity—rich or poor, human or nonhuman.

• • •

The family's years on the road would come to an end in Pennsylvania where John would lead the CMA evangelistic outreach in Philadelphia. Renting a hall on Market Street in Upper Darby on the city's west side, John held meetings to preach, pray, and spread the gospel.

"Those meetings, held nightly for several years, were greatly blessed," Wallace wrote. "Every night, souls were saved, responding to the invitation at the end of services, and folks were healed of many kinds of diseases. Dad had the Alliance's standard tiny vial of olive oil in his pocket to touch to his finger and then on the forehead of the sick person before praying."

The family's years in Upper Darby would be the most stability Wallace and his brothers would know in their youth, and even then the roots were shallow. "We moved several times, twice close to another grammar school still in Upper Darby," Wallace writes. "Looking back, there were special things for me to learn in each place, to give ideas for ministry further down the line."

At one of the schools, Wallace's teacher sent him home and said he couldn't return until he had glasses. "My years of not seeing distant objects were over; a new world opened. Mother was greatly chagrined that her faith and divine healing had not prevailed," Wallace writes. "With glasses I was put in the class next door for faster pupils. Our teacher was excellent. We learned the multiplication table in six weeks, and a lot of other stuff."

At another Upper Darby school, where Wallace spent the fourth grade, Mr. Woodward would give him his first taste of carpentry and building. "In those days, crates and baskets made of thin wood slats were used for fresh produce. He sent us to get two-sectioned fruit crates discarded behind the grocery store called the A&P (The Great Atlantic and Pacific)," Wallace remembers. "We made wonderful little chairs by cutting half off the sides and removing one end, and tables by nailing the sides of one crate atop another crate standing on its end." Wallace traces the beginning of his interest in building to those crates. Decades later, that simple project would go on to multiply itself into hundreds of church and school buildings and thousands of school benches and desks in Haiti.

During his time in Upper Darby, Wallace also deepened his joy of stamp collecting. It's hard to know if his lifelong love of correspondence and countless pen pals he'd maintain throughout his years was born of his love of stamps, or if his letter-writing fueled his stamp collecting—in the end, the two probably went hand in hand, until email would take over in Wallace's later years. Over the course of sixty years, Wallace would amass an impressive collection of stamps from around the world. I remember as a child leafing through the books with my cousins, sitting on the floor in Grandpa's office, his face alight with a smile as he fussed at us to be careful. His stamp collection would end in the hands of the same organization which, in many ways, was responsible for its beginning. "I collected stamps from age six to sixty-six and gave some thirty thousand to the Christian and Missionary Alliance to raise funds for missions. I'd had no time to spend on them since arrival in Haiti, thank the Lord!" Wallace wrote. "Today, I still collect and donate and encourage others to."

Upper Darby is where Wallace would finish his elementary school and where he would turn 10 years old—a memory that seems as vivid in his nineties as on the day it happened. "On my tenth birthday, Dad took me alone for the day to Atlantic City," Wallace writes in his journals. "We dared the old wives' tale about not mixing seafood and dairy products—ate soft-shelled crabs followed by ice cream from a chest on the boardwalk, outside the restaurant. Dad was delighted to meet fellow CMA pastor, Erb, a short Pennsylvania Dutchman from Wilmington. So they chatted while I ate ice cream. We didn't get sunburned, and that was my happiest birthday."

As his granddaughter, I would venture to say that most of Wallace's happiest memories involve ice cream, but in this case I think the happiness is rooted in a detail much more meaningful: His tenth birthday was a rare moment of quality time spent with his father, at the ocean, a place they both loved. This was a moment carved out of time to be savored between the two of them.

Wallace and his family would remain in Upper Darby through the ninth grade, moving three more times—including into a one-bedroom apartment "to save rent." Their last move in the area was into a house John bought that served as the parsonage until the shrinking CMA sold it to the Presbyterian Church years later. The house was the oldest in the area, built on land that had once been the city dump.

If Wallace felt the weight of his family's economic struggles, he didn't say. His childhood interests seemed to lie not in whatever place they called home but rather with the outdoors and its wonders.

One of the homes Wallace and his family lived in was near the woods. During winter, Wallace would walk among the skeletal trees looking for cocoons and birds' nests. He would bring home the treasures, and in the warmth of his bedroom, the cocoons would turn into moths. Wallace's interest in the insects was more academic than affectionate; he mounted the specimens and added them to a growing collection that he could study. Eventually, when he moved to Haiti, Wallace donated his collection to Marion College.

Camping one summer in the Poconos is an especially fond memory for Wallace. There, he, his brothers, and Rhoda, who would eventually be replaced by a friend to chaperone, set up camp to pass the long days. The three brothers spent their days fishing from lines of string with a hook attached, marveling at the salamanders and foraging for berries. "There were tall bushes of extra-tiny blueberries. God made them that way, to keep little boys busy and out of mischief," Wallace writes. "That summer was idyllic."

When he wasn't exploring and collecting treasures in the outdoors, Wallace found equal enjoyment in building. So much so that when he managed to earn a little money of his own by selling a collection of old papers from a neighbor, he bought his own set of tools. Nine years later, he'd take those same tools with him to Haiti, along with leftover screws from a church building project—a humble beginning to a work that would eventually impact a nation for generations.

• • •

Upper Darby would be a formational part of Wallace's childhood, but his time there was far from stable. John and Rhoda consistently put their ministry first and family second, believing, perhaps, that service to God far outweighed any other earthly responsibilities. Though John would never abandon his children completely, he also wouldn't allow them to stand in the way of what he believed to be a calling from the Lord.

So when an opportunity came for John and Rhoda to create a new tool that would spread the good news, they seized it. "As movies had heretofore been seen only in theaters, considered off bounds by evangelicals, Dad got a radical idea. He said that movies would be a great tool for raising missionary support, instead of slides," Wallace writes in his journals. So John, who was nothing if not a savvy fundraiser, scraped together the necessary funds for the missionary movies project and "took-off for at least a year of visiting Alliance fields, 16 millimeter movie camera and lots of film in hand," Wallace wrote. "They farmed us boys out."

David went to the Westervelt Homes for missionaries' kids at Batesburg, South Carolina. Johnny Lou, who now felt he was old enough to be called Jack, went to the Academy of Houghton College, Houghton, New York. Wallace was to stay in Upper Darby with the interim pastor and his wife, but when she became ill soon after, he joined David at the Westervelt Homes. All three boys would end that year marked in ways the family, two generations later, is still seeking to understand.

If Wallace had thought Rhoda heavy-handed, he would soon learn that others could be much crueler.

According to Wallace, Mrs. Westervelt believed her charges "must all be prepared for difficult conditions as overseas missionaries. They must be used to spartan fare, and it must be vegetarian. Our protein intake thereafter was limited to occasional beans, or a quart of peanut butter (for eighty people) added to the white sauce served with our evening big plate of grits." The plate of grits would become the staple of Wallace's diet for the entirety of his stay.

One happy exception that Wallace remembers is his first meal at the Westervelt home. "For the eight people at the table, there were nine little meatballs. Everyone seemed satisfied with their measures, and I was still hungry from my travels. Mr. Westervelt was startled when I finally asked if, since the meatball was not desired, I might eat it. He smiled yes, not telling me that was the last meat ever to be served at the Westervelt Homes."

If Mrs. Westervelt required that her charges be mostly vegetarian, it seems clear from Wallace's recollections that not everyone in the household abstained from meat. "There was a pen of ill-fed leghorns out back. When one was killed in a scrap, its bones went in our Wednesday night 'soup.' All the clear pot liquor (water in which vegetables are boiled) was saved for the 'soup.' There was great mirth if, once or twice in the year, someone recognized an accidental toothpick-sized sliver of leghorn that had been boiled with the bones. We never knew who ate the leghorn."

To this day, Wallace expresses disdain for vegetarianism, as I quickly learned when I became a vegetarian for several years in my twenties. My grandfather would explain often Peter's vision in Acts when he is told to "kill and eat" from all kinds of animals, and that we are not to "call anything impure that God has made clean" (Acts 10:15, NIV). I would then argue that the way God intended animals to be raised and slaughtered had nothing to do with the factory farming often employed today. And around we would go in circles, neither one gaining ground with the other.

Had I known then what I know today about my grandfather's time in the Westervelt Homes, I would have realized that his aversion to vegetarianism was rooted in a place much deeper than concern for his granddaughter's nutrition—it was at some level a reminder of a painful year in his life. I would have seen that arguing was futile, as it often is with Wallace, and I would have, I hope, responded with a greater measure of compassion and understanding.

"Eating anything but our meals was forbidden," Wallace said. But that didn't stop the children from searching for a way to stop the hunger pains. Wallace and the other children would forage for food and eat, surreptitiously, from the gardens. Forbidden fruits included "runty melons" and pea pods snitched from the beds, wild blackberries, wild persimmons, scuppernongs, and even sprouting pecans buried by a squirrel.

Perhaps the most infamous of the children's adventures comes not from Wallace himself, but from a few of the girls living at the home.

"The Westervelts became indulgent and arranged with the mill owners for us kids to spend a week camping at the pond. We enjoyed sweet wild blackberries, except when a little stink bug was hiding on the underside from the hot sun! Each day, we boys watched a four-foot water moccasin swim across the pond. Next week, the girls went. Meat-hungry, Marjorie Trout and other missionary girls from Africa ate it. Back in the dining hall, I was mystified when Mrs. Westervelt ranted at the *horrible* thing the girls had done. Later, laughing boys told of the girls' culinary treat."

Looking back, it seems hard to laugh at the hunger that led to such a desperate act. But one can hardly blame the girls or Wallace or any of the other children for seeking out extra food, for it's clear they weren't fed nearly enough.

"I lost 35 pounds and gained six inches in my 12 months in the institution," Wallace wrote in his journals.

The malnutrition was just one of the burdens Wallace and his brother would carry during their stay at the Westervelt Homes.

To this day, Wallace's feet are deformed from his being forced to wear the same pair of shoes all year long, despite his tremendous growth spurt. He speaks of it with forced levity, as he does many hardships, referring to "my wife's present amusement at my funny hammer toes," but one can only imagine the pain endured during the deformation.

Added to this is the fact that when not in school, Wallace and the other children at the Westervelt Homes spent most of their time working the gardens and doing other manual labor on the property.

"We boys learned a lot about farming. We grew bumper crops of stuff. We hoed long rows of spinach, corn, and whatnot. Planting was in holes in which we mixed manure from Prince, a spirited young horse that the Westervelts' son used sometimes for plowing or for a playmate," Wallace writes.

When the farming season ended, the labor did not. "We were put to work in cold weather, when gardening was impossible, at cleaning out the woods on the big property," Wallace remembers. "We pulled many wiry, thorny vines out of trees and dug up stumps of trees that had been logged. The biggest stump was a poplar, at least six feet across. Too big to be uprooted, it was rolled into a huge hole, hand dug next to it, and covered."

No matter the arguments that the Westervelts might make for preparing children for hard lives as missionaries, it's hard to see their "home" as anything other than a labor camp, one which Wallace and David were all too happy to leave when John and Rhoda finally returned from their filming adventure.

• • •

John and Rhoda's travels ended around 1938 shortly after the Japanese invaded China and the war in the Pacific intensified. Home again with three square meals a day, their sons began to recover, though the mark left by the home would never disappear completely. "Back on a nourishing diet, we found that our enormous appetites that permitted us to devour a quart bowl of cereal and feel unsatisfied rapidly shrank to normal. A touring group of young folks from the Westervelt Homes stopped by, and we found that they had the same experience, having been fed proper meals along the way."

With the Second World War now in full swing, the plans John and Rhoda had of visiting international mission fields would have to wait, but any measure of stability in the boys' lives would be tenuous at best.

Rhoda's beatings and emotional abuse were relentless, and the strain it put on the boys didn't go unnoticed. "We were pounded so much by Rhoda that I learned just to be numb, waiting," my grandfather told me. "We children were offered homes by observing friends, but my father never witnessed the situation, and he never had any interest in anything medical, so he was blank and refused the help."

Years later, commenting on the abuse she'd observed, "Aunt" Marie Green, a family friend, told Wallace she thought he'd have been the first one of the brothers to "crack." Wallace didn't crack—at least not in the way of a mental breakdown—though he'd carry the consequences of the abuse for a lifetime.

While Wallace and David were at the Westervelt Homes, Jack, then about 14 or 15 years old, was at the Academy of Houghton College in Houghton, New York. And just as his brothers would return marked by "the Westervelt experience," Jack would also undergo a transformation of sorts when once again under the harsh rule of Rhoda—only his change would be much darker and have far bigger consequences for the family.

According to Wallace, Jack grew increasingly reclusive and paranoid after they all returned from their year apart. "He refused to come out of his room when adults were around, even barricading his door with the furniture when they insisted." Instead of seeking medical help for his troubled son, John turned to the police.

"The officer who came with Dad was very touched by Jack's state and said to get him to the state hospital for care as quickly as possible," Wallace wrote.

The state hospital in question was Norristown, known more commonly by Upper Darby residents as "the asylum." Fortunately for Jack and his family, the hospital at the time was under the care of the renowned Dr. Arthur P. Noyes. During his tenure at Norristown, Dr. Noyes started the Psychiatric Residency Program, which gained national prestige for its many innovations in therapeutic treatment. To this day, Dr. Noyes' *Modern Clinical Psychiatry* is considered a classic text in its field. While it undoubtedly wasn't perfect, Norristown was a far better environment for Jack than state prison or even any of the nation's other asylums—and sadly, it was an immense improvement for the boy from his own violent and toxic stepmother.

Indeed, for a time it seemed that Jack was improving and maybe even thriving in the structured environment. "Jack was put on the kitchen detail, as he was a diligent worker and responded to the therapists," Wallace recalls. But any hope surrounding Jack's mental state was soon put out.

"He was accidentally locked in the kitchen one night, while cleaning-up," Wallace writes in his journals. "Next morning, the attendants found the kitchen a shambles. Jack has never spoken since, but once." That one time would be years later when Wallace took his wife Eleanor and their young son Wally to visit. "He was brought out to us from his ward. I said, 'I'm your brother Wallace.' He became awake, looked surprised, said, 'Oh, I didn't realize!' Though he has never spoken since, he has come out very easily, to stroll on the grounds." Jack would remain at Norristown for 60 years; he was 77 years old when he died.

When Jack was admitted at Norristown, Wallace lost a brother and a dear friend. As is to be expected between brothers, Wallace had looked up to the older boy, following him in and out of mischief. Yet, what Wallace mourned most from his brother's illness wasn't his own loss of a brother but rather the fading away of Jack's bright spirit. "The loss of a cheerful storyteller has been a great sadness, but has helped in empathy with families of others," Wallace writes.

Perhaps what is most telling about Wallace's grief surrounding Jack is the fact that I never knew of his existence until I began reading my grandfather's journals. And when I mentioned that to my father, Wally, who had visited Jack as a toddler, he said that he was an adult before he knew of his father's brothers. One thing that is clear from his writings and from the questions I've since asked my grandfather is that he never abandoned his brother, even if he didn't talk about him. Wallace maintained a regular correspondence with the nurses at Norristown and followed Jack's life from 1,500 miles away in the rural mountains of Haiti.

• • •

In spite of Jack's mental breakdown, or perhaps in part because of it, Wallace strove to have as normal a high school experience as possible. "Upper Darby Junior and Senior High School were a pleasure after the Westervelt experience," Wallace writes in his journals. He joined the cross-country team in tenth grade and enjoyed his studies as much as any teenage boy is apt to do. But in the context of Wallace's life, perhaps the most remarkable part about these years is how unremarkable they were, Jack's admission to Norristown aside.

With one son in the asylum, and two more sons carrying the weight of abuse at home, John remained oblivious to the toll his decisions were taking on his sons. According to Wallace, the missionary movies John and Rhoda had made while he was at the Westervelt Homes were "a marvel to the Alliance churches." They had John on the road much of the time, and he was highly successful in his fundraising.

Back in Upper Darby, John still had a church to care for. In the same way that he'd leave his sons and home entirely to Rhoda's supervision, he left the church in the hands of an interim pastor. Eventually, the deacons called for John's resignation, citing all the time he spent away. "This led to a very trying situation," Wallace writes. "He gave the films to the missionaries in them, but the deacons were adamant." John had to leave.

In 1941, as Wallace was entering the eleventh grade, John was once again unemployed and uprooting his family in search of the next ministry. "We abruptly moved to Hialeah, where Mom had an old school chum, Beva Baxter, married to Al, a chap who worked in the racetrack stables," Wallace recalls.

Wallace, David, John, and Rhoda would temporarily move into a small flat in the upstairs of an old wooden home, but they wouldn't stay together long. "Dad was a hustler, looking for a ministry opening," Wallace writes in his journals, "so he put us boys to board with an old retired Alliance missionary from India—Miss Pritchard, in northeast Miami."

Miss Pritchard must have been a kind woman to the boys, for Wallace and David went out of their way to help her and show their appreciation. "She had rented half of her bungalow to an FBI man, with his wife and little boy. Her half, with the garage shed, was a veritable junk pile, and grimy," Wallace recalls. "One day, we cleaned the place up, scrubbed it down from top to bottom. Coming home, she was too shocked at the improvement to thank us and said that we should have let her do it! Asked where we had put the junk, we said across the street, hidden among the palmetto scrub, if she wanted to recover any of it. She didn't."

As is the case with much of his childhood, most of Wallace's memories from his time in Florida center on a handful of people and a consistent escape into nature. David and Wallace would spend nearly all of their free time fishing and swimming in the canals near Miss Pritchard's home. The fish were a welcome source of food, but more than anything, fishing was one of a select few happy memories Wallace shared with his father and consequently was a way to keep John close, no matter where he was. The boys sitting at the water's edge in hopeful anticipation, the elusive catch swimming just below, became a sort of metaphor for Wallace's childhood. Happiness seemed to move right below the surface, nibbling at the bait, teasing the line. Just as it seemed all hope would be lost, there it was—a catch, a fleeting moment of glee and satisfaction.

• • •

In one year, the family would move three more times, with John hopping from one interim position to the next: first Tampa, Florida then Knoxville, Tennessee, and settling for a time in Fort Wayne, Indiana, then Flint, Michigan. Before long, David was drafted and sent to the Philippines while Wallace went on to begin formally his pastoral training. "Because I'd soon be drafted if I didn't prove my ministerial intentions, old Doctor Bob Jones Senior admitted me to his schools in Cleveland, Tennessee," Wallace wrote in his journals.

The trip from Fort Wayne to Cleveland would forever sear itself into Wallace's memory. Throughout his life, Wallace would travel by foot, jeep, donkey, boat, and any number of other methods, each of which he'd view as an adventure, guzzling in the opportunity to observe people or take in the scenery. But his memory of this trip by train is one of the few times I've heard him complain about a journey. "I rode the Chattanooga Choo Choo to Chattanooga from Fort Wayne, then got a bus to Cleveland," Wallace recalls. "Standing eight hours at night in the smoke-filled passenger cars was a horror. I never have endured such heavy, lung-searing smoke. I'd go out into the cinder-filled air between the cars for a quick gasp of something else, no better."

The trip, however unpleasant, would pay off a thousand fold in the ministries to come. Wallace graduated high school from Bob Jones Academy on May 19, 1943, and then began his college training.

Wallace's time at Bob Jones, while fruitful, wasn't without its trials. "I was perhaps the poorest one on campus," he writes in his journals. "I did laundry and pressed clothes for other students, never spent a nickel in the snack shop." As he would prove time and again, Wallace was nothing if not creative in his problem solving. "The water in our dormitory washbowl was so hot that I used it to make tea, with a few soda crackers and jelly as a snack for the four of us in the room. Mom sent homemade cookies at times, a welcome treat."

Wallace was a hard worker, but he wasn't always the most focused student, preferring instead what one might call *hands-on activities*. "I learned in Greek class that in forty-five minutes, using my sharp-pointed Boy Scout pocket knife, I could drill a hole in a penny so it could go on a keychain," Wallace recalls. Geometry fared even worse than Greek. Wallace failed geometry the first time he took it, claiming that he has difficulty memorizing, a fact I find hard to understand since Wallace's recollections from decades ago are still crisp, clear, and usually supported by independent verification. I might posit that perhaps memorizing wasn't the difficulty so much as bothering to learn. Even if he wasn't the most studious alumnus Bob Jones can boast, the school would be hard pressed to find a graduate who put its classes to more practical use than Wallace. That geometry class he repeated? He used it in building time and again, eventually helping to build over 400 rural churches and schools with no formal construction training.

As it is with all teenagers, Wallace's high school graduation was an important milestone in his life. And yet, as they had been with so many other milestones, Rhoda and John were notably absent. "Mom sent me a new fine wool navy blue pinstripe suit that cost $75, a fortune for our family, my first suit." Wallace writes in his journals. "My folks couldn't come. We wore our dark blue coats, and white pants. I wore that same suit for my wedding in Haiti five years later."

His year at Bob Jones was perhaps one of the happiest of Wallace's youth. He formed friendships and got in and out of mischief as most teenagers are prone to do. Here, he was fed well and, most importantly, nobody beat him. Bob Jones was the place Wallace transitioned into adulthood.

Even so, Wallace's college years would prove little more stable than his childhood. He began his studies in 1944 at Fort Wayne Bible College, working as a janitor in the dormitories and fourteen hours on Saturday—and snatching bits of pickled pig feet at the Fort Wayne Junedale Meat Market—to help pay his bill. He soon moved on to Marion College, where he studied until 1946. Here, Wallace returned to his fallback as a dishwasher to help cover the costs of his schooling, but it wasn't enough. Wallace took on extra jobs such as working in a factory making rubber aprons, clerking at JC Penney's, and working a graveyard shift at the VA psychiatric hospital—experience that would prove useful later in his ministry when he would have to interact with people who had a mental illness.

At Marion, Wallace began his BA in history and social sciences, but he would never finish, a fact I learned only recently. And in typical Wallace fashion, the revelation came not as a confession at all, but as a matter-of-fact, casual statement in an email about something only tangentially related.

How could a family not know such a thing, one might ask. The thought simply never occurred to any of us. On Wallace's office wall hung myriad diplomas, awards, and recognitions. He talked of his college times, and we just assumed he'd graduated. In truth, we never asked. Wallace's college diploma came not from Marion but from Webster University in general studies, which he completed via correspondence. Eventually, Wallace would even receive two honorary doctorates—but that would come nearly a lifetime later.

An engagement at Marion College ended poorly and added to his quick departure. Wallace and his fiancée met through Wallace's dishwashing job at the college. "Hand-holding in the suds was an entertainment to the crew, led to engagement in 1945, but the girl's parents had no stomach for her marrying a missionary and going to Haiti, so we fortunately broke-up," Wallace writes. With the perspective of 60 plus years of marriage to a strong, vibrant woman who would serve as his ministry partner and advisor as much as any wife ever has, Wallace can easily see God's hand in directing him to Eleanor. But to the twenty-one-year-old Wallace, the heartbreak was real. Though he has never said so himself, throughout the years the family has deduced that his departure from Marion College was as much tied to the broken engagement as to any other factor.

Out of school and hurting, Wallace was eager to join his father on the mission field. His hurt, unbeknownst to him, would eventually lead to physical and spiritual healing for thousands—and to the love of his life.

• • •

While Wallace was attending college, David continued to move with the family, hopping from one place to another. During a brief time in Flint, Michigan, David learned to play the trombone "with excellence," Wallace proudly notes, and it's a talent that Wallace has held onto when remembering his brother—likely because everything else would soon be taken from David. He was barely out of high school when he was drafted and sent to fight in the Philippines. He would return home "with his mind completely confused and sedated," and would be admitted to a Veterans' Facility in Battle Creek, Wallace recalls. Though David's condition would improve with the right medication, he'd remain in supervised care for the rest of his life. "The shock of David's illness was hard, as we had been close as boys," Wallace shares.

"Hard" doesn't even begin to describe what I imagine my grandfather truly felt. David was more than a brother to Wallace; he was the closest living link to their mother, whom he resembled, and she had given her life to give David his. With the benefit of time and perspective on his side, Wallace has been able to gain a lesson from his loss, a lesson he has applied to almost every hardship he's endured. "Again, I was given a hard experience and situation, to help me to empathize with other hurting people."

Empathy. For all his character flaws, and there are more than a few, Wallace would always have a gift for connecting with the hurting, the scared, the weak, the rejected. He would be grossly insensitive on more than a few occasions, hard-headed on a regular basis, and harsh in his words, but always, even in his worst moments, he'd know what it was to suffer, and he would use that day after day in his ministry.

• • •

With Wallace in college and David overseas, John had been busy moving on to the next venture.

After John was forced out of the church in Upper Darby, he eventually made his way to Fort Wayne, having been asked to oversee the missions work at the Fort Wayne Gospel Tabernacle, which was pastored by Clifford Hollifield. Clifford was "a big, jolly preacher from Chattanooga, Tennessee," Wallace recalls, and his church was one of several permanent congregations established by Paul Rader, an evangelist and the first "radio preacher" in America.

With evangelism as its primary focus, the Fort Wayne Gospel Tabernacle had a growing interest in missions and was helping to fund a Cuban preacher working in the island nation of Haiti. John, who had primarily focused his ministry efforts on the Middle East and India, now turned his sights south, to the tropics.

Shocked at multiple reports that the preacher was a fraud, Clifford asked John to go to Haiti to investigate. John believed he verified the fraud and pastors told of the man's depredations, but the man continued working in the mission field. Wallace admits the man did use funds from Fort Wayne to "build a fine campus on a hill overlooking Port-au-Prince." That campus now houses the Séminaire de Théologie Évangélique de Port-au-Prince, or the Evangelical Theological Seminary of Port-au-Prince, referred to commonly as STEP. The seminary has produced some of Haiti's brightest evangelists and pastors and has been a strong ministry ally to several missions.

Shortly after John returned from Haiti, Clifford fell ill with meningitis; the strain of the illness caused heart failure, killing him in a matter of days. The Cuban pastor's work in Haiti was turned over to the Unevangelized Fields Mission. But John's heart had been moved by what he witnessed in Haiti; he was determined to begin his own mission in the country.

While on his first trip to Haiti, John met Zenas Yeghoyan, an Armenian who had fled the civil war and genocide of his homeland. Zenas and his wife Novart met as refugees in Cuba, where they were waiting in hopeful anticipation for passage to the US. Unsuccessful, they moved to Haiti; there, Zenas taught Spanish as a way to feed his family.

Touched by Zenas' circumstances and his stories of faithful Christians slaughtered in the Armenian War, John implored Zenas to join him in the budding work in Haiti. Zenas agreed and John had his first missionary. Though the Yeghoyans would eventually move on to another ministry, they remained lifelong friends of John, Wallace, and the family, who would with great affection tell stories of "Uncle Zenas."

John's initial attempts to establish the mission in Haiti met constant obstacles, not the least of which was missionary recruitment. As John was trying to build a mission in Haiti, a global war was coming to a bloody and gruesome end. In the context of the Normandy invasion, the atomic bomb in Japan, and a continent in ruins, a nascent evangelical effort in a forgotten island of the Caribbean could easily seem irrelevant.

As Wallace would put it, John had a mission with no missionaries. More than 30 men and women had come and gone to serve with John in Haiti, all but two blaming him for convincing them to go to "such a place." No longer in school and with no meaningful ties keeping him in the US, Wallace agreed to join his father in Haiti.

From the time he was four years old, Wallace had said he was called to the mission field. Missions had consumed his family. In a way missions had taken both his mother and his father from him, for Maud died on the mission field, and the ministry meant everything to John: his family would always come second or third or fourth, but never first. One could argue that in seeking out the mission field, Wallace was looking for something else altogether, a way to fill the void that had been created by Maud's death, John's absence, and Rhoda's abuse. One could be tempted to argue that perhaps Wallace wasn't running *to* God's calling at all but rather *away* from the life he'd known. Or that in seeking to be a missionary Wallace was making the ultimate play for John's approval, hungering for a tangible connection to his father. The potential for analysis is endless when one thinks of Wallace's childhood, but that would deny the divine calling he has claimed nearly all his life. Indeed, the life and ministry that were to unfold go far beyond any human imagining.

God called, Wallace answered, and grace crept across the nation as a morning light, easing over the mountains, soaking the folds of valleys with its rays, bathing quilted fields in its warmth.

THREE
Building Blocks

THE MOUNTAINS WERE SHROUDED in an afternoon cloud as Wallace arrived with the first truckload of belongings in the land that was to be his new home. John and Rhoda had stayed behind at the docks with the rest of the supplies that couldn't fit on the truck. Disoriented from the fog, exhausted from the trip, and with no knowledge of the language, Wallace began his first task of setting up house. The cabin that was to be their home had been built from scrap materials by Philippe Brun, who built the American ambassador's house. The cabin had never been intended to be a full-time home but rather a mountain escape from the heat and pressures of the city—a castle in the clouds for a working man.

"Peasant men with long machetes in scabbards hanging from their belts appeared out of the cloud, chattering excitedly," Wallace recalled of his first impression. One can only imagine what they thought of him: a skinny, pale man who gestured wildly in an effort to communicate. "One little man, whom I came to know well as Isaac, asked if they could carry the things up there for us. I heard the word 'poteé' (*portay*). I replied '*Wi*,' and went up to receive the things."

That afternoon, Wallace received his first impromptu lesson in Haitian Creole. "It seemed that each piece was deposited upside-down," Wallace wrote in his journal. So he used gestures to show the men how to turn over the crates. "To their '*Woulé-l? Mété-l laba?*' (Roll it over? Put it over there?), I'd reply, '*Wi. Woulé-l. Mété-l laba.*'"

Haitian Creole is beautiful in its simplicity and clean grammar. Completely phonetic, with no verb conjugations and no gender rules, it's an easy language to learn. The deeper one digs, the more one finds astounding depth in the deceivingly simple turns of phrase and colorful proverbs. Living immersed in the language and faced with an absolute necessity to communicate, it took Wallace only three weeks to develop an ear for the language, using what he referred to as "the help of Canadian Marie's 1938 French phonetics, and my sleepy early-morning college Spanish."

Wallace, John, and Rhoda had arrived in Haiti by ship, plane, and automobile. They had driven from Indiana to Tampa and on to Miami, visiting churches and collecting supplies, which they packed in old tobacco crates from the cigar factories in Tampa. From Miami, they flew to Jamaica and then took a ship to Haiti, the voyage lasting over 22 hours. But when Wallace unloaded the first crates on the fog-covered mountain, he knew they were just getting started.

In a way, Wallace and John hadn't chosen this particular patch of mountainside to begin their ministry; rather, as is often the case with the things that matter most, it had chosen them.

When Clifford Hollifield died, John's heart had already been pricked for the people of Haiti. Struggling to build momentum for the fledgling ministry there, John met with the Haitian president, asking where a mission was most needed. President Lescot directed him to the area of Kenscoff, a village less than 20 miles southwest of Port-au-Prince and whose surrounding mountains are peppered with desperately poor and isolated communities known as *habitations*.

In response to President Lescot's request, John purchased a plot of land in Fermathe from Philippe Brun. Though owned at this point by Brun, the land had originally belonged to Ostellus Veillard, an *oungan*—Vodou priest—and soldier in the Haitian revolution. For his service in the revolution, Ostellus and all soldiers were granted plots of land by Alexandre Petion, the nation's first president.

The land John purchased, just three miles below the town of Kenscoff, was believed to be haunted by the spirit of Ostellus and others. People told of a donkey that appeared at night with candles on its ears. While none of us ever ran into a mysterious donkey, there were clear signs of Vodou on the land. Years later, when excavating for a building, Wallace would find the remains of Ostellus' house and his buried Vodou charms along with a mass of yellow dahlia roots where the home's doorway had been, confirming the story of Ostellus' service as a Vodou priest. The yellow dahlias were likely planted to honor Papa Loko, the highest Vodou *lwa*, whose colors include white and golden yellow; he is also the *lwa* who bestows the sacred rattle of the Vodou priesthood.

A Vodou stronghold claimed for Christ. Eventually, hymns of praise would ring out where drums once beat their steady rhythm; Easter lilies would take the place of yellow dahlias; and the feet of churchgoers on a dirt floor would erase the marks of spirits who had governed. The clustered buildings would be like Abram's altar in Shechem, a testament to God's faithfulness. *To your offspring I will give this land.* But even as he built, Wallace knew his true battle was one for hearts and souls, not earth and rock.

• • •

Wallace and John set to work right away. Their first project would be to build a church combined with a traveler's shelter on the newly acquired mission land in Fermathe. The walls of the church had been built by Philippe Brun before their arrival, but the structure still needed a roof, doors, windows, shutters, and other finishing details.

The building crew was patched together from willing, if not highly skilled, laborers. One consistently smelled of *kleren*, the equivalent of moonshine, and another, who was to be the roofer, couldn't read the plans; in fact, he couldn't read at all. With the cobbled-together crew, one can imagine that it was only a matter of time before someone would get hurt. Jean Baptiste was the first casualty of the construction project, and through him an entirely new ministry was born.

Early on in the building of the church, Jean Baptiste badly injured his ankle when, unloading supplies, he slipped under the hitch of a loaded trailer. Wallace and John sent him to the cabin to see Rhoda, who was a registered nurse and would know how to treat the wound. "He desperately asked if he was fired," Wallace writes in his journal. "I repeated that his ankle needed a rest. He didn't stay away and was soon squatting close-by, watching. He became our most enthusiastic helper."

Once Rhoda tended to Jean Baptiste's ankle, word spread quickly through the mountain communities that there were "white people who tended to people's injuries." Wallace recalls that people came "in gruesome shape."

"People began to come in crowds to our door every morning for medical aid," Wallace recalls in his journals. Rhoda, who had never been on the frontlines of hard labor, was overwhelmed. But she could see the need and came up with a solution. "My folks wrote to Mrs. Holdeman in Tampa, who they remembered had been a practical nurse and mountain missionary. She must have gotten the next plane out of Tampa. In her old tobacco crates, she brought all kinds of castoff things, including a hammer and a saw."

Indeed, Bertha Holdeman had been waiting and praying for just such an opportunity. Though she was 59 years old when she arrived in the mountains of Haiti during the summer of 1947, Bertha had been longing to serve in the mission field for most of her adult life. Her husband "Doc," who was nothing if not colorful, had wanted nothing to do with missions—and indeed he would have been a less than ideal missionary though his skills as a rural doctor would have undoubtedly come in handy. By the time Bertha received the Turnbulls' letter, Doc had divorced her, her son Ross was building airplanes, and her daughter, Eleanor, was preparing to serve as a bush pilot in Africa. Bertha had no more obligations in the US and was free to go wherever she was called.

Bertha's experience serving in some of the poorest communities of the Appalachian Mountains would be used and stretched in every moment of her time. Never having had access to proper medical care, the rural people had developed their own methods and lore around treating injuries and disease.

One commonly held belief about widespread infection was that "it has to rot before it can heal." In fact, the thin thread between a simple malady and a deadly complication was so woven into the fabric of daily life that it was embodied in proverbs, the language of the rural men and women. When referring to how a small problem can easily become complicated, people would say, "pimples bring sores; sores bring leprosy"—and they were right both literally and figuratively.

But sometimes a small problem can grow into a much bigger blessing, as was the case with Jean Baptiste. A relatively small injury led to a constant stream of people seeking help for their own wounds and sores, which led to Bertha joining the Turnbulls, which eventually led to Eleanor. Bertha's daughter Eleanor would be the single biggest influencer in Wallace's life and ministry as well as spearheading many of her own projects. Overnight, a medical ministry had been born from a simple accident. Beginning with a medical box and bandages, it would grow into a full-service, 100-bed hospital with two operating rooms, a maternity ward, a tuberculosis clinic, and a mobile clinic. But the thought of a formal hospital wouldn't even begin to form until the arrival of Bertha and later Eleanor, who in spite of having no formal medical training would become one of the most respected hospital administrators and medical influencers in the country.

• • •

With their initial efforts floundering, John and Wallace both realized quickly that they needed better help, especially until they could fully grasp the language. That help came indirectly from A.F. Parkinson Turnbull, a Methodist pastor from England who was serving at a church in Port-au-Prince. Despite the curious coincidence in last names and callings, A.F. Parkinson was otherwise unrelated to John and Wallace. But in the yard of the church he pastored, there lived several English-speaking families, including Joseph Swan, "a cheerful little man with a Haitian wife named Sylvia," and Mme. Megene Lacossade, who was of Jamaican descent and had been born in Jérémie. Joseph would serve as John and Wallace's interpreter; Mme. Lacossade would work first with Rhoda and later with Bertha.

The communication was now easier, but the path was still bumpy, and John wasn't always easy to work with. Joseph and John would argue often and John would always get his way, "even if disastrous," Wallace recalls in his journals. "Dad and Joseph, an absent-minded pair, eventually came to an understanding" after Joseph wandered off in Port-au-Prince one day, leaving John stranded without an interpreter. "After waiting forty-five minutes, Dad drove off without Joseph, who hours later arrived up the mountain out of sorts and out of breath. That cured Joseph of that trick."

As is to be expected, the hurdles for Wallace and the others in the early days of the ministry weren't just the obvious language barriers but also a cultural barrier. Few men and women were available to teach him the ways of the people, to guide him in avoiding potential missteps. Instead, he learned through classic trial and error seasoned with a heavy dose of prayer.

In Wallace's world, for example, a builder was a person with a clear set of skills, skills that included being able to interpret diagrams and building plans. So when John hired a builder in Fermathe, it didn't even occur to him that the man might not be able to read, let alone follow a set of plans. When Wallace realized the mistake, he knew he'd have to take over. "I had never built a building, so I prayed," Wallace writes in his journals. "I sat down in the corner of Samson's forest of poles, which were his proposed roof supports, and took up sticks to whittle model timber joints. Soon, I had a plan for joists and braces of tree trunks, and roofed the church with *vetiver* grass. It took three hundred big bundles brought in with vines and sticks on people's heads, at five cents a bundle."

The new Fermathe church celebrated its first service on January 5, 1947, just a few days after the New Year and Haiti's Independence Day. While January 1 is the day Haitians celebrate their independence from France, Wallace sought a different kind of freedom for the people he was beginning to call his friends and neighbors. He wanted for them a profound spiritual freedom—one that would liberate them from fear, from superstition, from illiteracy, from discord—and he knew that just as the political revolution had been born of the people, so, too, must this spiritual revolution. He could say little to change their minds and hearts—but there was plenty he could do.

The morning of the first church service must have felt like an enormous accomplishment to Wallace. After all, here was a building he had roofed through divine inspiration. Next to his new countrymen, he had labored to finish the sanctuary. Now, he and his father were calling all to come hear the Word and to worship side by side.

That Sunday morning, there were three Haitians in attendance.

If Wallace felt discouraged, he didn't remain so for long. The next Sunday the church was packed with men and women climbing in and out of the windows and others leaning in to catch a peek. They didn't yet understand the promises of the gospel, but they definitely were curious about the new structure and the newcomers. In the remote area of Fermathe, entertainment was scarce, and offering what the people surely saw as a Sunday show of music, speaking, and exotic strangers was enough to draw a crowd—as long as there wasn't something more interesting happening elsewhere.

"The hardest part of beginning in 1946 was to find the first few *serious* illiterate, barefoot disciples," Wallace writes in an email.

Today, terms like "illiterate" and even "barefoot" could be considered derogatory, but for Wallace in the context of his early days on the field, they were simply facts of life. The people he was serving could not read or write, and they were so desperately poor that many of them had never worn a pair of shoes. Yet, these were to be the men and women who would form the foundation of the Church. They were to be the first lay preachers, the first missionaries back to their own *lakou*. In the same way that God once called a motley crew of fishermen and outcasts nearly 2000 years before, He was now calling the illiterate and the barefoot to change a nation.

However Wallace felt that first day, it's clear now that God was just getting started, planting the very first mustard seeds of faith. *"Some fell on rocky places, where it did not have much soil. It sprang up quickly, because the soil was shallow. But when the sun came up, the plants were scorched, and they withered because they had no root. Other seed fell among thorns, which grew up and choked the plants. Still other seed fell on good soil, where it produced a crop—a hundred, sixty or thirty times what was sown"* (Matthew 13, NIV). Three churchgoers in 1946 eventually became over 350 independent church congregations organized into a single association led by trilingual seminary graduates.

• • •

Wallace's approach to evangelism, while now common practice, was unconventional in the early days of his ministry. In fact, he avoided typical evangelism all together.

"I never evangelized in Haiti," Wallace writes in an email, saying he didn't want people to profess conversion just to see what he might give them. Instead, he offered himself freely and hoped they would see Jesus through the actions. This isn't to say Wallace wasn't quick to share the gospel or talk about Christ, but rather that he didn't want to push conversions; above all, he avoided any link between accepting Christ and receiving physical aid.

In the early days of world missions, hearing the gospel was often tied to receiving a reward. Something along the lines of, "First we go to church, then you receive the aid you're seeking." Or even, "We hire only Christians" as a way to support and reward the converts. While perhaps well-intended, these methods all too often led to false conversions and planted bitterness in the hearts of the people. After all, nobody likes to be coerced.

From the very beginning, Wallace resisted these methods, choosing instead to embody the gospel in action and compassion, sharing but not preaching, inviting but not compelling. He conducted parallel but clearly separate ministries. Aid wouldn't be tied to church, workers wouldn't be hired on professions of faith, and whenever possible, Haitians would share the gospel with Haitians: it wouldn't be the message of the white man.

Wallace was criticized by many for his approach, but he stuck to it, believing firmly that a false conversion would be worse than no conversion at all, for it would undermine the very foundation of the fragile, nascent church. As a result of

Wallace's methods, the church grew slowly at first, but it grew steadily, soul by soul, one kind act followed by another.

Countless times, I've heard my grandfather say with a knowing smile, leaning forward as if to share a great secret, raising his index finger, "It wasn't us. God helped us, you see. We didn't know anything, but He showed us."

• • •

That very first service on January 5, 1946, Wallace faced a nearly empty church. He'd come in a distant second, it turned out, to the burial of Veillard Veillard, the local patriarch and grandson to Ostellus Veillard. And so, Wallace did what any of us might do—he went to check out the competition.

"We went to pay our respects, as we had known him, and had hired some of his relatives. The assistants played cards or dominoes, sang and danced to the beat of Vodou drums, drank *kleren*, and chatted. Sometimes some would stop to do ceremonial wailing, supposed to convince the departed that he was mourned so he would not become a haunt," Wallace tells in his journals.

Even that first service was evidence of the conflict the Church would consistently face. From the very beginning, Wallace's mission to build up the Church would create a tension with Haiti's most entrenched religion. The pull of grace pitted against the ties of ancestors; a Christ sacrificed for all contrasted with endless sacrifices to the spirits; one God versus dozens of deities.

Throughout the years, Wallace would get to know countless Vodou priests and followers; he would pray with some as they sought the Lord, and he would mourn those he could never reach. Some would try to curse his family; others would praise him; and others still would bring their children in the night to be healed, not wanting to let their neighbors know the traditional methods had failed.

"I was not as kind with sorcerers as I should have been," Wallace says, reflecting on his younger self. "I grew up with actions that I learned—all three of us boys would mock falsehood—so instead of being kind toward a person, I mocked them. I wish now that I had not. That's not the way to treat people."

Janwa, however, was one Vodou priest who managed to see past Wallace's gruff language. When Janwa converted to Christianity, he became an ally to Wallace, asking him to eliminate all evidence of Vodou from his property. Together, they scraped the walls, removed nails, and burned all relics. Because the priesthood is hereditary, Janwa told Wallace that he didn't want his son to find "a trace" of Vodou. The line ended with him.

• • •

In the first few months, Wallace and John had a particularly hard task ahead of them. Not only were they beginning a work from scratch with little money, but they were also having to undo the misdeeds of some who had gone before them. As history has proved time and again, too many men (and not a few women) have seen the Church as a way to profit for personal gain. Their lies and cheating eventually catch up to them, embittering the communities against not only the charlatans but also against the faith as a whole. As they made their first movements into some of the mountain communities around them, Wallace realized this had been the case with a few of the churches in the area. So he set about undoing the wrongs and rebuilding trust with the people. His strategy was to live the scriptures—not to preach them.

Before long, the mountain people saw he was different. They could tell that he cared about them, that he never asked for anything in return, that he was genuinely present to serve. "People began to be saved, and many lives were changed," Wallace writes in his journals. "Among them, three men stood out: Nicolas, Hermann, and Juser."

Like many of the first disciples, Nicolas was an unlikely candidate for the church: an alcoholic who could neither read nor write. "God took away his desire for alcohol and gave him a good mind with a gift for soul-winning," Wallace remembers. "He learned and used in witnessing many hymns and passages of Scripture."

The Faithful Three, as Wallace referred to them, would bring to the Fermathe church the Vodou relics they collected from new converts. As a response to their young faith, new Christians would first destroy in a fire all relics of their old faith, a symbol that they were cutting ties with the past and placing their trust in Christ. "Many of these charms were burnt in bonfire celebrations at the church, the new Christians helping to throw things in the fire," Wallace recalls. "This encouraged their faith, and many more proceeded to win neighbors." The fire served a symbolic purpose as well as a pragmatic one: it was a sign of a complete break from the old religion, destroying all evidence of the relics that were once believed to hold great power. Following tradition, the act of burning the sacred Vodou charms should have also brought a backlash curse on the believers, but it never did—a sign to the others that their Christ was stronger than any Vodou deity.

The superiority of Christ's power was central to Wallace's ministry throughout the years. He never denied the power of Vodou or its deities. Like the Israelites of the Old Testament, he sought to prove time and again that his God was more powerful, more benevolent, and eternally loving.

Motivated by the enthusiasm of new believers, the Faithful Three and other converts would go "on long trips into the mountains, to share their faith," Wallace writes in his journals. "Thus, five other churches were founded." Within a few years, the thatched roof Fermathe church had helped to found churches in the communities of Choffard, Grande Source, Quit Croit-Bongar, Bolosse-Roche-a-Legoua, and Rangement.

FOUR
Eleanor

AT WHAT POINT does someone become the single most important person in our lives? Can we boil it down to one event, or is it a process compiled of insignificant moments that, when stitched together, amount to a fabric so tightly woven we can no longer see in the pattern where we end and the other begins?

Wallace and Eleanor. *Pasteur and Mme. Wallace.* Grampa and Grandma Turnbull. The names have become so synonymous, so linked together that it is impossible to think of one without summoning to mind the other. And yet, they both had lives distinct and utterly separate from one another—until they didn't.

• • •

Eleanor was born Eleanor Jane Holdeman to Bertha and Roscoe "Doc" Holdeman in rural Tippah County, Mississippi, near the town of Ripley. "Tippah" is derived from a Chickasaw word meaning "cut off," and in many ways they were "cut off" from the outside world—though Eleanor would spend her adult life building connections.

Her father was the country doctor and her mother the nurse—together they cared for a large rural population. Doc, as he was known to most, was not an easy man. Many who knew him said with a deep laugh, "if it was a drink, he drank it; if it was a card, he played it; if it was a skirt, he chased it." Eleanor is quick to defend her father, as most daughters are, and protests this unfair characterization of him. But even she would agree that her father's ways were wilder than Bertha, an old-fashioned, righteous woman, had hoped for her husband.

Doc was, by all accounts, an excellent doctor—his claim to fame being that he delivered Elvis Presley, and, he'd readily add in his colorful tone, the family never paid the bill! One might argue, however, that the story, which has been repeated countless times from generation to generation, was payment enough.

The strong personalities of Eleanor's parents left their mark on her; she grew up equally strong and independent, equally colorful, or more so. While Eleanor and her mother would be inseparable, Doc was more removed from Eleanor and her brother Roscoe or "Ross." Doc rarely called his children by their names, referring to them simply as Boy and Girl.

"Girl, help your mother." "Boy, come here."

Boy and Girl grew up with a fierce sense of competition between them. Eleanor was determined to match her brother step for step. Sibling rivalry is a story as old as humankind, and the source of it is often the same: vying for a parent's affection. Doc overtly invested more in Ross, his son, whom he expected to go into the world and make something of himself. His daughter, on the other hand, was expected to grow up, get married, and live a pleasant life—she didn't need as much training. Whether he knew it at the time or not, Doc was right. Eleanor did grow up, marry, and live a pleasant life. As for the training, she was perfectly capable of training herself. "She has always been one to say, 'whatever you can do, I can do better'—even as a young girl," my father once told me. Her brother learned to drive; she would drive faster. Her brother worked with airplanes; she would fly them. Her brother served his country; she would change a nation.

Perhaps it was this same fierce competition that led to a devastating accident when Eleanor was a teenager. Or maybe it was the result of one accident opening the door for another.

When Eleanor was ten years old, her family home burned down, and to this day the exact cause of the fire remains a mystery. Seeing the smoke, neighbors came to help rescue what little they could from the flames: the family dining table, a hutch full of dishes, a handful of photographs. In the rush to push the hutch to safety, it caught and tipped. Dishes crashed to the floor, and a large serving platter was the sole survivor. That platter had been passed from Elizabeth Halstenberg to her daughter Bertha who passed it to her daughter Eleanor who, having no daughters of her own, passed it on to her daughter-in-law, my mother. Each year, that platter, which survived flames and missionary barrels alike, is piled high with roasted turkey as we gather to give thanks: for family, for friends, for food, for home.

In a story of resilience as old as fire itself, Eleanor's family did the only thing they could: they started over. Perhaps this is why there was a sawmill on the family farm: to produce the timber for building.

Eleanor has never told why she was in the sawmill that day, and none of her family has ever bothered to ask. It seems the most natural thing in the world to think of her where the most commotion is, and it stands to reason that on a family farm in rural Mississippi, that might be in the sawmill. Whatever the reason for her being there that day, Eleanor cut off the last three fingers on her left hand in a gruesome accident. She gathered the fingers and was taken to the hospital where doctors managed to sew them back on. The fingers never functioned again, though the nails continued to grow.

When my grandmother was younger, most people would have been hard pressed to notice the slight deformation from the fingers fixed in place. She was agile and adept, determined not to let an accident of her youth mark her for the rest of her life. When she wanted to learn to play an instrument to help lead worship services, the piano was not an option, nor was the flute, a personal favorite of hers. So she learned to play the trombone with excellence because it was one of the few instruments that didn't need dexterity in the left hand. Those who know Eleanor well can think of few instruments that better suit her than one which is a little unwieldy, a little too loud, and so very joyful.

Over time, the lines of age would carve deep paths on Eleanor's hands. I'd like to think each one recounts a journey up and down a mountain, a wounded man bandaged, a meal cooked for the unexpected visitor, a wedding cake iced with care, a baby washed, an infant rescued, a grandchild cuddled. The wrinkles grow deeper with each passing year, running from her arm to the tips of her fingers, stopping at the three fingers she once severed. These fingers ceased aging that day and have remained young for more than three quarters of a century. As the rest of Eleanor has grown a little less nimble with time, they have begun to regain their feeling. Now, in her nineties, Eleanor can move them the slightest bit.

"God heals all with time," my grandmother once told me when I asked her about it. "Do you think the fingers will ever heal completely?" "In Heaven, yes."

• • •

After graduating from Stetson, Eleanor had earned her M.A. in Christian Education from Columbia Bible Institute—now Columbia University—in South Carolina and was teaching Bible in the public schools of Ware Shoals, South Carolina when her mother Bertha moved to Haiti.

Eleanor's plans were far loftier than a classroom—quite literally. In 1945, she had earned her pilot's license—a feat so rare that her license number had only a few digits. Eleanor was working toward serving as a bush pilot in Africa with Missionary Aviation Fellowship (MAF). Like her mother, she had a strong desire to serve in international missions; she, too, wanted to do something different, something eternally meaningful. Though she'd never put it quite this way, Eleanor wanted—needed—to live a life outside of the domestic sphere that had swallowed up her female peers.

When her mother accepted John and Rhoda's invitation to serve in Haiti, a shift began to take place, a barely perceptible move as part of God's divine plan. And it began, as many stories do, with the love of a young man.

After Bertha's arrival in Haiti, John and Rhoda returned to the US to raise funds for the growing mission. Left alone in the small cabin and without much else to do in the evenings, Wallace and Bertha would pass the time talking and sharing stories. Wallace was especially inquisitive about Bertha's daughter.

"I had been seeing a photograph of a fine-looking young lady on Mrs. Holdeman's dresser. She told me that it was her daughter Eleanor," Wallace recalls. In the photograph, we see her in profile, gazing at an unknown point in the distance, her chin slightly raised, her lips only hinting at a smile; a thin, single braid forms a wreath around her hair. She is beautiful, yes, and, from the high collared shirt and single strand of pearls she wears to accentuate her slender neck, we can tell she is elegant. But there is more to the woman in the photograph than only youthful beauty. She is also thoughtful, serious, and fiercely independent.

In 1947, just over a year after he'd arrived in Haiti, Wallace would have the opportunity to meet the woman he'd come to know—and maybe even love—through her mother's stories. "At Christmas vacation time, we were happy to receive Eleanor, and her fellow Bible teacher, Lib Weeks," Wallace writes in his journals.

On their way to Haiti, Eleanor and Lib stopped in Havana, Cuba for a night, making sure to visit the glamorous nightclubs that have since become the stuff of legend. "We had a great frolic," Eleanor says, recounting the time in Havana and, on the return trip, in New Orleans. After all, Eleanor might be ready to lay down her life in service to Christ, but she wasn't about to stop living. The time in Cuba and New Orleans were lighthearted bookends to what would be an otherwise heavy trip.

When Eleanor arrived in Haiti with Lib, she found her mother healthy and safe, albeit in rather primitive conditions. There was no running water in the tiny cabin and no electricity.

Only a rudimentary divider separated her mother's sleeping quarters from the young man's. But Eleanor and Lib hadn't traveled to Haiti for a vacation. They'd gone to see Bertha, to learn about her work, and to see some of her new homeland.

"Mrs. Holdeman and I took the women on a mobile clinic trip to Bassin General in Dumay, and I enjoyed taking Eleanor on a horseback trip to Fort Jacques, getting a good sunburn sitting atop the fort, to get acquainted," Wallace writes in his journals.

Wallace doted on Eleanor throughout her visit. Seeking opportunities to serve her and make her stay in the rustic conditions more comfortable, Wallace found a rather pragmatic way to show he cared for Eleanor. There was a bucket used to collect and hold water for the household, and it had become quite a point of contention between Wallace and Bertha, who was forever scraping the bottom of the bucket for the last of the water before Wallace would fill it up again. But throughout Eleanor's visit, the bucket was always full. Bertha took note, though Eleanor never caught on—at least not directly.

To Eleanor's credit, her first visit to Haiti was so utterly overwhelming at 23 years old that she might hardly remember to drink water let alone observe its level in a bucket. When I asked her about that first trip, Eleanor recounted vividly the horrific conditions of the people she met during her mother's clinic hours. The suffering she witnessed marked her and changed the course of her life.

• • •

In 1947, Haiti and much of the tropical world was plagued by yaws, a flesh-eating spirochete protozoa. Without medical treatment, yaws would eat away indiscriminately at men, women, and children, often leaving gaping holes in their faces, legs, and arms. Gangrene and other infections would also take root, leading to a painful existence and even more painful death. As Eleanor was encountering yaws for the first time, a man named Dr. François Duvalier was working with the World Health Organization to help control the spread of tropical diseases, including yaws. His work earned him the once-affectionate nickname of Papa Doc, a name that would later be whispered with fear.

The first time Eleanor worked alongside her mother during the clinic hours, she had never heard of Papa Doc and she couldn't possibly have imagined the role he would play in her life. She was too overcome by the stench of infection and the gruesomeness of the wounds to think of anything else. The worst were the gaping sores caused by infestations of burrowing fleas, known as *shik*. The insects would burrow into the skin and lay eggs, causing the flesh to fester before the eggs would hatch and spread. To help stop the maddening itching, people would cover the wounds in warm ashes, which quieted the fleas. The smell of the infection was as horrific as the sores themselves. "I had to turn away and wretch," she told me. More than seventy years later, she still cringes at the memory.

Eleanor soon curbed her sensibilities, however, and spent a large part of her visit assisting her mother in the clinic. In those moments—bandaging a woman's half-eaten face, caring for a severely malnourished child, offering comfort to a man plagued with tuberculosis—God began the whispers of a new calling for Eleanor, one that would take her not to the skies, but to heights far beyond anything she had imagined.

Eleanor's early days in the makeshift clinic with her mother would inform the rest of her life and impact the health of tens of thousands of individuals. With no formal medical training, Eleanor would go on to found not just the *Hôpital de Fermathe* through the Baptist Haiti Mission, but also the nationwide Association of Christian Hospitals, which would establish guidelines and best practices for the major hospitals of other missions across every department of Haiti.

At Christmas in 1947, neither Eleanor nor Wallace knew what God had in store for them, but Wallace did know he wasn't ready to say goodbye to Eleanor. He asked her permission to write to her, and she granted it, knowing full well his intentions but perhaps not yet understanding her own. Throughout the first half of 1948, Wallace and Eleanor exchanged what he characterized as "a laconic correspondence." And, in fact, one might extend that term to their lifelong communication with one another: they would never be great communicators, but whatever they spared in words, they shared in mission, dedication, and hard work.

Wallace, in his typical fashion, kept the nature of his letters with Eleanor close to his chest, intentionally leaving her mother's curiosity unsatisfied, for few things bring my grandfather more pleasure than goading what he believes to be silly behavior. "Mrs. Holdeman used every scrap of paper to wrap pills for her patients," Wallace writes in his journals. "I gave her all my used envelopes, including one a week from Eleanor, with no comment. Weekly, as I made no comment on the correspondence, Mrs. Holdeman got meaner." When another missionary visiting Wallace and Bertha asked if he knew why Bertha was so upset with Wallace, he answered candidly. "I laughed, and said yes, because she thought that I was going to marry her daughter. She asked if I'd like to, and I said yes, but I didn't know if Eleanor would have me."

As the summer neared, John wrote to Eleanor and asked if she'd return to Haiti to spend the summer running a children's program, but Eleanor knew the invitation carried extra weight. Years later, Eleanor told me she knew what "would likely happen" if she returned. Going back to Haiti that summer would mean she'd probably never be a bush pilot in Africa; it meant giving up a dream that she had believed to be her life's calling. Though she's never said it so explicitly, Eleanor was likely not in love with Wallace when she received his invitation—at least not in the typical way we think of romance. But she saw something in Wallace that appealed to her even more deeply than a fairytale love story. "I could serve alongside him," she once told me. "I wouldn't have to walk behind him. We could be partners."

So Eleanor did return that summer, and Wallace soon took his opportunity to propose. "I felt that she was *the* one," Wallace says, remembering their courtship. "I've always felt that. In Haiti, they talk about Pastor Wallace and 'Kay Wallace'—the mission—but Good Lord, she's half of it."

Taking Eleanor's hand for the first time, Wallace walked with her up a small hill on the property. He was tall and lanky, his hair combed to the side; thin, round wire frames perched on his nose. He'd donned his suit coat and bowtie; he chose his white pants because they were his most fashionable, and he'd polished his shoes. He clutched his explorer's helmet in his hand, for the tropical sun was merciless, even in his Sunday best. Sitting on the stump of a mango tree, just a few yards from the site that would become their home, Wallace summoned the courage to speak. "If you will marry me, I will always try to make you happy."

Eleanor's answer was as pragmatic and unsentimental as she is. "Well, I suppose that's what we should do," she responded.

After Wallace kissed her, she said simply, "We should tell Mother."

Eleanor never did move to Africa, and she never again flew a plane, but if she's ever wondered what might have been, she doesn't say. When I asked her about this, she acknowledged that she understood what she was giving up when she chose to move to Haiti, but she also said that in her heart what she really wanted, and what she believed God was calling her to do, was to serve as a missionary. "Looking around me, I knew that this place needed missionaries every bit as much as Africa," she told me.

When asked why she went to Haiti and stayed so long, her answer is always clear. "People say, 'Oh, you must really love the people of Haiti,'" she has recounted multiple times. "And yes, I do. But that isn't why I'm here. I'm here because of obedience. God called me here, and I must be obedient to Him."

In truth, Eleanor had always said she never expected to marry, though the idea of loneliness in old age didn't sit well with her. "It was obvious to me that this was God's will," she says now, reflecting on her decision to marry Wallace. "There was a Divine, sacred, pre-ordained plan here. And no Christian wants to make a choice contrary to what you feel is divinely ordained." Eleanor says that instead of "looking for happiness" she chose to "follow after holiness," and in her journey, she found more happiness than she could have ever searched out on her own.

With her mind made up to marry Wallace, Eleanor didn't look back, not even to return to the US to put her affairs in order. "As we had no funds to spare on travel, Eleanor had her father send her hope chest that he had made," Wallace recounts. Moreover, the couple would marry soon. When Eleanor decided to stay in Haiti until her wedding day, Bertha told her, "If you're going to marry him, you should do it quickly. Don't wait."

Eleanor, Bertha, and Wallace were all living in the same house. With common law marriages more common in the mountains than legal marriages, Bertha was concerned about tainting their witness. She wanted the people to know that as a family, they lived as they encouraged others to live. So, a wedding date was set for August 8, just a few months away.

Eleanor's wedding dress was made for her as a gift by Mrs. Rosebrough, the mother of her closest friend Margaret, who lived at the time in Deland, FL. The floor-length dress was made from a white satin with a beautiful lace veil. Simple but elegant—much like Eleanor herself.

• • •

With the details falling into place for the wedding and John and Rhoda scheduled to arrive for the event, Wallace set to work building a home for his bride. Wallace believed strongly in using the local building methods, certain they were best suited to the topography and climate. In his case, that meant using hand-cut limestone carved from the mountains as the building blocks and a mortar made from limestone marl and slaked lime also called hydrated lime.

The process of making the mortar requires heating limestone in a wood-burning kiln until the stone reaches an intense heat over the course of several days to remove all traces of moisture. The heat generated by the fire is so strong that one cannot stand in front of the kiln. Wood is added through an iron pipe that serves as the mouth of the kiln; the wood is then pushed with a long rod into the fire. Once all of the water has been cooked out of the limestone, it's allowed to cool. While resting in the kiln, the stones still look whole, but they can be crushed with a simple squeeze of the hand; the moment one adds a few drops of water to them they dissolve into a white powder. That lime mixed with limestone marl, sand, and gravel is then used to set the hand-cut stones one on top of the other, building a strong, solid rock wall.

Because the lime mortar is labor intensive and requires a huge amount of cooking fuel—usually wood—it has since been replaced by what we know as Portland cement, which is superior in its durability and strength.

Stone by stone, side by side with Haitian workmen, Wallace set to building a simple home perched on the mountainside. A cement slab roof covered the tiny bath, kitchen, and the airy room the doubled for bed and dining. The conditions were rustic, he knew, but it was the very best he had to offer the woman he loved. Lacking both funds and access to materials, Wallace invented creative solutions, repurposing materials he could scrape together. "I bought crates from the Bazar National, the capital's only grocery, and made window shutters and doors," He recounts. "Lacking boards for the back door, I propped a sheet of corrugated roofing in it. When married, we warmed a five-gallon square lard can of water on the kerosene stove and bathed in a basin in the corner."

The house completed, the next project to tackle was the church roof. The grass they'd used to roof the church over a year before had begun to rot, and Wallace wanted to replace it before the wedding. Eleanor worked beside him throughout the project.

"Eleanor had put on blue jeans, and passed roofing up to me, as I worked alone, frantically trying to get a new roof on the church," Wallace writes in his journals.

While Rhoda disapproved of Eleanor's unconventional clothing and foray into construction, I can only imagine how proud Wallace must have felt and how determined Eleanor must have been. Wallace has always praised Eleanor's spirit and grit, marveling at her energy. Eleanor agreed to marry Wallace because she wanted a man she could serve alongside—and Wallace was madly in love with her for it.

With the house built, the church roofed, and John and Rhoda present, the wedding was a go. On August 8, 1948, Wallace and Eleanor's friends from Port-au-Prince as well as the people of the Fermathe area crowded in to watch them be married. For many of the mountain people, this was the first church wedding they had ever witnessed and was certainly the first between two foreigners. It was the social event of the year.

A young American woman Wallace's parents had brought with them to Haiti stood as Eleanor's maid of honor, and Pastor Ruben Marc, a close family friend, served as Wallace's best man, a request Wallace admits he made hastily "when he appeared." Pastor Marc was the first man Wallace was introduced to upon arriving in Haiti. "We found him with his wife, son, and daughter sitting around a little table prepared to eat big plates of fresh-ground cornmeal and green peas," Wallace recalls. "Wishing that my dad would take me somewhere to find some, too, I went out to the car and picked up seeds of the royal red flamboyant tree common to the city." Wallace later planted the seeds, and nearly seven decades later, one remains, "a lovely reminder of Pastor Marc."

A young man in his only suit. A woman in a satin gown. Vows spoken in a dirt-floored church under a half-roof. And exotic guests of all shades and social levels. The setting likely conjures up images of a fairy tale wedding. But as with all fairy tales, we need only scratch the shallowest bit below the surface to see the grit of real life. Within that bucolic setting, Eleanor spent the service using the toes of her heeled shoes to grind out fleas that lived in the dirt. And the service itself came to an hour-long halt when John, who was presiding, realized he had forgotten the rings and went in search of them. "This is part of the process," Eleanor remembers thinking to herself as the ceremony and chaos unfolded around her.

The reception was equally colorful. Bertha had prepared a drum full of cookies and another of herbal tea to serve to the mountain guests after the ceremony. For the more intimate friends, a private reception was planned to be hosted near the house. "The simple board doors that I had made for Dad's house were laid-out on sawhorses as a long table, to receive city guests," Wallace recalls.

Bertha baked a multi-tiered wedding cake for the celebration. The cake fell over and she scrambled to make a second cake the night before the wedding. "We feared for it as a storm roared the night before the wedding, threatening to again blow off the roof, but roof and cake survived!" Wallace writes in his journals.

The storm the night before the wedding was a prelude to "a minor hurricane" that was to make landfall on their wedding night, testing the strength of the stone house Wallace had just built for his bride. The storm "blew water in, around the sheet of roofing in our back door, which Mrs. Holdeman held against the wind. We were grateful for her efforts to keep our things dry," Wallace writes.

With Bertha to hold down the fort, quite literally, the newlyweds retreated to the *Châtelet des Fleurs*, a bed and breakfast a few miles up the mountain in Kenscoff.

Their first full day as husband and wife, they hiked to Découvert at the top of the mountain. There, Wallace took a photograph of Eleanor sitting on a boulder. The name of the setting means "uncovered" because as one reaches the spot, it uncovers the view of the mountain below. With Eleanor bathed in the soft mountain light, the morning after her wedding, one imagines that the place has taken on a new meaning for Wallace and Eleanor, a new sort of uncovering as husband and wife grew in intimacy and love.

The setting of the *Châtelet des Fleurs* was also incredibly beautiful, filled with flowers and views of the mountains, but the hostess who had invited them left the couple feeling jostled. "She moved us morning and night from room to room, saying each time that she needed the place for a guest." Within a few days, they tired of the nomadic stay and returned to their stone cottage, but not before meeting Maarten De Vries, whom Wallace describes as "a nice young Dutch man." Maarten's fiancée Johanna was arriving shortly from Holland, and her mother insisted the couple be married immediately to avoid scandal. "He asked if I could perform their wedding," Wallace recalls. "I had not yet performed a wedding, but said I'd be delighted."

Still immersed in the newness of marriage, Wallace and Eleanor paid forward the blessing. Wallace performed the ceremony and Eleanor baked a multi-tiered wedding cake, the first of many she would make throughout the years. "The wedding was a happy occasion of singing Dutch folksongs accompanied by a lively accordion," Wallace remembers. Maarten and Johanna would be the first of thousands of couples Wallace would marry, and they'd remain good friends through the years.

Decades later, Wallace's family would sit around the dinner table telling stories of how he would wear his "wedding suit"—a suit hemmed extra short for hiking along muddy trails—to marry couples in isolated communities dotted throughout Haiti's mountains. On one occasion, Wallace brought me along, his worn leather Bible in hand, his black socks poking out below the hem of his pants. As we arrived to a small clearing carved out of the mountainside, hidden by trees and bushes, he called out to the patriarch and matriarch of the *lakou* and told them to gather their family: Today, they would be married. The couple were well into their seventies, and as they called out for the family, more than a dozen people gathered around, including several great-grandchildren! Laughter and smiles set against the backdrop of the patchwork mountains proved more lovely than any gilded altar or taffeta garland. Standing before three generations of witnesses, the lines of age etched into their faces, man and woman promised to love one another, to honor each other, in sickness and in health, in riches and in poverty, for better or for worse—a vow fulfilled even as it was just beginning.

My grandfather later told me that though they were Christians and wanted to officially be husband and wife, the couple had never gone through with a wedding because of the widespread Haitian belief that to marry one must first be able to meet a series of demands, which can range from a gold ring to furnishing a home properly to hosting a real reception and celebration. Given that this couple were poor mountain people with barely an income to live from, they'd never be able to meet those demands. Since they wouldn't go to the church to be married, Wallace brought the church to them.

Wallace would go on to marry nearly a thousand couples throughout his ministry, including two of his sons and four of his grandchildren; he even presided over several mass weddings, one of which included 30 couples and witnesses—120 people in all—crammed at the front of the church to say their vows.

Wallace and Eleanor's own wedding and honeymoon could serve as a metaphor for their life together, begun under the shadow of a hurricane. On the surface, their marriage and family would seem to conjure the most saintly images of service to God and humankind, an idyllic union of souls seeking to unite other souls. But one need only peer through the smallest crack to know that just below the myth live the very human marks of hardship and heartbreak. If Wallace and Eleanor's marriage and life of service is to be considered remarkable, let it not be for how saintly it appears to outsiders but rather for how flawed it is, even from the beginning; for the miracle of God's grace lies in the way they have lived and served, not without brokenness but in spite of it.

FIVE
Growing

ON A JUNE MORNING IN 1949, Eleanor sat on the edge of the bed holding her newborn son and weeping. In addition to the bed and a few meager furnishings in the tiny two-room home, a bassinet had been added for the infant—a woven basket made by a local artisan, lined with the satin cut from her wedding dress.

Wallace and Eleanor had yet to celebrate their one-year anniversary and already the remnants of their chaotic wedding day were slowly being consumed by the rigors and necessities of daily life. The introduction of a newborn and all that entails couldn't have been easy—Eleanor's pregnancy certainly hadn't been. For the first four months, she could barely get out of bed. Her mother tended to her, of course, and Eleanor was visited by Dr. Yvonne Sylvain, Haiti's first woman doctor, who would check in on her. Yvonne and Eleanor remained friends after that, even working together on several healthcare projects.

Wallace, in his own way, also did what he could to care for his wife. "Each day, I supported her on a forced march for exercise, up to the latrine, site of the present mobile clinic office," he writes. Eleanor, when asked about her pregnancy, remembers how terribly sick she was. "Your grandfather, who went without good shoes for a time, you know," she'll tell me, "would sit on the edge of our bed every morning and inspect his shoes. He'd jostle the mattress as he moved them this way and that and then bend forward to put them on. I remember the whole world spinning and him inspecting his shoes." She also remembers the bananas—so many bananas! Every morning, Wallace would eat a bowl of bananas with powdered milk. "It was a long time before Eleanor could stand bananas!" Wallace remembers. Then, as if to make sure I understand, Eleanor adds to the end of the stories, "He didn't do it on purpose, you know. He didn't really know how sick it made me." Truth be told, the nausea isn't what would have bothered Eleanor the most—it was being bedridden, a curse she's had to endure only a handful of times in her life, but one of the few trials she doesn't bear with grace and ease.

Soon enough, the difficult first trimester passed and Eleanor was back on her feet. Scarcely 10 months after their wedding, on June 2, 1949, in a little clinic in Port-au-Prince, they welcomed their firstborn son, Wallace Rutherford Turnbull, Jr., and dubbed him Ti Wally. His birth brought with it a second christening. Bertha Holdeman became "Granny," and she was called such for the rest of her life by all who knew her, from the housemaid to the President. In fact, on one occasion she even received a letter from the US addressed to "Granny. Haiti."

On this particular morning, as Eleanor remembers, she was overwhelmed by the fragility of her baby and the harshness of the life she had chosen. Everything in this country was hard—even walking took extra energy to move up and down the hills. And resources were scarce as they had little food or money to spare. Eleanor remembers looking down at the face of her firstborn, Wally, and thinking, "What have I done bringing a child into this place? I can't even buy milk for him."

And then, Eleanor's problem-solving nature kicked into full gear. She couldn't flatten the mountains of Haiti into easily traversed plains and she couldn't soften the edges of this rough land, but she could buy a cow and that would give her milk.

Eleanor sent word through their neighbors that she wanted to buy a cow, and before long a farmer appeared with one. "She was scrawny, but I was told she had milk," Eleanor recounts. But Eleanor was aware of tricks that farmers could pull by feeding their cows specific herbs to increase milk production for a day or two. "So, I told the farmer that I would buy her but that if she stopped giving milk, I would return her to him and he'd have to give back my money." A deal was struck and Eleanor was delighted. The problem had been solved and, even if just for a moment, it looked like everything might be okay.

One early morning shortly after buying the cow Eleanor went out to milk her. "It wasn't fully light yet," she recounts. The cow had gotten loose, so Eleanor, wearing nothing but her white nightgown and flapping bathrobe, went after her. "I held on to her rope as she pulled me all over that mountainside. In my nightgown!" Eleanor tells with a wry smile. I can picture the incident so clearly in my mind. Eleanor, having paid for the cow, was not going to lose her—nightgown or no nightgown.

"As she flew down the slope in long leaps, her bathrobe flapping, I was in stitches," Wallace says. "I hollered, 'Let go of the rope!' She did, and the cow stopped just short of me and began to eat grass." The incident itself was one of great glee for the mountain people and a wake-up call for Eleanor. She might be many things in her life if she put her mind to it, but she was no dairymaid. "I decided that was enough of that and returned the cow to the farmer." When I asked her what she did to get milk for Wally, she answered matter of factly, "We made do."

With a growing family and a ministry spreading faster than they had the funds to support, they would learn quickly and always to "make do."

• • •

With little money coming in, Eleanor's last paychecks from the South Carolina public schools proved a great blessing to the growing family. The money she had earned teaching provided, over the course of several months, a kerosene stove, a mahogany bed, a table, chairs, and a hutch with drawers and glass doors. The table still sits in their apartment in Haiti, a reminder of the family friend Madeleine Price Mars.

In truth, Madeleine was Wallace's friend before she was Eleanor's. While Bertha and Wallace lived in the "rough bungalow" with thatched roof that John had built, Wallace developed the custom of "receiving curious neighbors who became friends." he recalls. "There were a group of us young folks 19 to 25 years of age who enjoyed socializing. We visited together either in my place or in the home of the big family of our friend Senator Emile St. Lot." Among the group was Madeleine, who was renowned for her beauty and by 19 had been chosen as queen of Port-au-Prince's carnival. She lived in a small bungalow in Kenscoff with her father, Dr. Louis Price Mars, Haiti's leading writer. Though he was arguably one of Haiti's most celebrated authors, Wallace and Eleanor came to know him "as a kindly elderly gentleman whom we enjoyed dropping in to see or to ask a bit of practical advice."

Shortly after Eleanor and Wallace were married, Madeleine also married. Her husband was a young Jewish American. "He set up a furniture manufacturing shop on the main city street, and I approached him," Wallace writes in his notes. "I said that I had seen an ice chest that had lids that slid over and under each other. The number of our guests varied, and I wondered if he could make us a dining table with parts that could slide under or out to extend its length." Madeleine's husband had plans for such a table and soon delivered it.

Not long after, the birth of the country of Israel was declared, and Madeleine's husband went there, never to contact Madeleine or their daughter Elizabeth again. Madeleine never remarried. Her friendship has been a source of consistent joy and help to Wallace and Eleanor throughout the years—even lending a small shelter in her yard to their first three pedagogy students. The table, at which hundreds of visitors have dined, remains a gathering place, a communion altar of sorts where all are welcome to nourish body and soul regardless of creed, language, or social standing.

• • •

Having traveled for the wedding, John and Rhoda stayed for a while. John's lifelong passion for what Wallace terms "pioneer evangelism" was reignited when a small group of believers from Haiti's *Nord Ouest* (Northwest) Department arrived in Port-au-Prince looking for a pastor. "He made several forays to visit the tiny groups of lonely Christians," Wallace recalls. "I went with him to Jean Rabel. It turned out that about twenty believers gathered at the home of their leader four miles by foot trail up in the hills." At the time, Eleanor's pregnancy left her unable to go anywhere, especially along rough, winding mountain roads, though later she would match him stride for stride.

Elima Henry, one of the Northwest Christians, convinced John to travel with him to Anse Rouge, a place Wallace describes as "an awful hot little seaside port in the desert south side of the Nord Ouest peninsula." Along the way, Elima "rode a horse ahead of Dad's little canvas-topped red Jeep, cutting with a machete thorny branches of mesquite that crowded the market bridle trail that ran from the big town of Gonaives to Anse Rouge and on across to Port-de-Paix on the north coast."

In Anse Rouge, the difference between John and Wallace's approach to ministry would again become apparent. While both felt a passion and commitment to share the gospel, Wallace would take a long-term approach, seeking, in a way, quality over quantity. One sincere convert would mean more to him than a hundred hasty professions of faith. John, on the other hand, was a true traveling evangelist, charismatic in his preaching and consistently receiving flash conversions, many of which would die out as quickly as they were made. John, however, rarely stayed long enough in any one place to know the difference. "Many people made pretense of conversion, to see what they could get out of the new religion," Wallace writes in his journals of that trip to Anse Rouge. "Dad never knew Seda, his only convert."

• • •

From a place of privilege and education, it is easy to speak of the romance of Vodou, to claim the ancestral rhythms and embrace the mythology, to dance to the beat of drumming echoed in the footprints of elephants and the roars of lions.

But for those who live at its mercies, there is little romance in the reality of the religion. The financial burdens of sacrifices alone were often insurmountable for those already living hand to mouth. And should one have the grave misfortune of falling under a curse, an entire family could be ruined—for if they were lucky enough to survive the curse itself, they might just as easily be crushed by the financial cost of getting out from under it.

Wallace saw the heavy burden carried by the practitioners of Vodou. And while in many ways he has made it his life's work to woo followers away from the ancient faith, it isn't because he believes it to be fake but rather because he knows just how powerful it is. He also knows the power of his own God and Savior and the liberating power of grace—a gift of salvation freely given, freely shared, the ultimate sacrifice paid once for each and every person. He has seen how this grace, when shared, brings not curses and fear but instead rallies men and women and children to build up one another in love. Grace, not fear: that has been his message for over half a century.

Among the lore and legends of Haiti's Vodou, perhaps none is more famous or mythical than that of the zombie, the one who is brought back from the dead through the use of black magic. As with most legends, they begin with a grain of truth. The zombies of Haiti are more than fiction, but their deaths and resurrections are the result of dark science not black magic.

A powder, whose formula is a closely guarded secret among Vodou priests, is at the heart of the zombie legend. This fine white powder is usually mixed into food and ingested. The powder contains toxins from the liver of the puffer fish that slow down the victims' metabolism, heart rate, and breathing such that they appear to be dead, especially when diagnosed without the benefit of modern medical equipment. Without a way to preserve bodies in the rural areas, funerals usually follow within 24 hours of a person's death. So, under the spell of the powder, the person is typically entombed quickly only to be abducted in the darkness of night. With family and loved ones believing the victim to be dead, he, or more typically, she, is never missed.

Once in the hands of the priest, the victims are revived, but only enough to function as slaves. The priest or other abductor then regularly administers a milder dose of the toxin to keep the them unaware of their situation and unable to think clearly enough to escape. The victims' cognitive abilities often remain impaired for the rest of their lives, resulting in the legends of the undead zombie.

Many zombies never come back from the undead state, but sometimes they do. Seda, John's only faithful convert from Anse Rouge, was one of the lucky few.

Seda, who was born to a desperately poor family in Jérémie, was placed to live with a family in town, a tragically common occurrence. But shortly after joining the family, she was kidnapped and made into a zombie. As a captive, she lived in confusion and despair. "After some weeks she must have eaten some food with salt in it," Wallace writes in his notes, referring to the idea that zombies must be fed a diet without salt, which is reputed to restore their cognition. "Finding her way by a little corridor out of the back of the establishment to the street, she was helped by passers-by to find her way to her adoptive family."

Years later, as a young adult, Seda traveled by sailboat from Jeremie to Port-au-Prince where she met a man. He took her to Atrel in the Northwest, and they were married until his death a few years later. Seda supported herself by living in a room of an Anse Rouge salt producer and harvesting salt for a few cents a day. Salt had saved her once before; this time it was leaving its mark. "Salt crystals scratched her shins as she waded in the mud of the drying basins, and her hands were raw," Wallace remembers.

Seda had only known poverty in her life. School was a luxury she couldn't imagine; even so, she had learned to read a little. Seda was bright, Wallace remembers. And she was hungry— for redemption, for grace, for love. "She wondered how she could ever reach Heaven after such a life," Wallace writes. "She asked the priest who told her to attend mass, which was in Latin in those days, and to say her rosary. She already did that. A traveling Catholic evangelist came through. He gave her the same unsatisfying answer."

When John preached, Seda heard a different message. She heard one of repentance, grace, and forgiveness. "He told how to pray the penitent's prayer, and her heart found peace," Wallace recalls.

After the birth of their firstborn, Wallace and Eleanor took Seda to live with them in Fermathe as Wally's nursemaid, freeing Eleanor to work. During her time with them, Wallace, Eleanor, and Bertha worked to teach her basic first aid, including how to dispense worm medicine and malaria pills and how to bandage sores. "After a short while, Seda became restless," Wallace remembers, so she returned to Atrel near l'Arbre, where she had lived as a young, married woman.

Years later, Seda developed glaucoma. She faithfully administered her own treatment of pilocarpine for years but eventually stopped and went blind. It was her turn to receive the care she'd so lovingly given to so many.

"The whole countryside heard the gospel through *Sè Seda* when they went to her for help," Wallace writes. "She remained a pillar of the rapidly-growing church, 'till her death."

• • •

In the following years, with Ti Wally in tow, Wallace and Eleanor continued their trips to the Nord Ouest, nurturing the growing communities of new believers in Porrier and Atrel. Traveling 100 miles took 8 to 10 hours by road: the conditions of the region were particularly grueling, as one might imagine from the poorest department of the poorest country in the Western Hemisphere. Extreme heat, desert conditions, and a lack of clean drinking water were just a few of the challenges they faced.

Wallace and Eleanor's journeys to Porrier and Atrel may have started with the intent of spiritual encouragement, but they soon evolved into a ministry with a physical component as well, just as it had occurred in Fermathe and would occur time and again throughout their lives. "We discovered much illness, so we got to taking along a few bottles and vials of medicines," Wallace writes. "Often, we treated the ills of several hundred people a day. We sat them down in illiterate batches, diarrhea in one group, chills and fever in another, to recite their prescriptions so if one forgot another would help them remember." Neither Wallace nor Eleanor had any formal medical training, but they undoubtedly received guidance from Granny on which basic medications to prescribe for which symptoms.

On one of their trips, Ti Wally, who was still just a baby, became their most urgent patient. Wallace, Eleanor, and Granny were in Baie de Henne when Ti Wally developed a severe fever and diarrhea. As his symptoms grew worse, Wallace and

Eleanor grew increasingly alarmed, as one can easily imagine. "We thought we might lose him," Eleanor told me. "I knew I had to get back home to a doctor."

Leaving Wallace and Granny to continue their work with the budding church, Eleanor set out on her own to make the long and winding trip back to Port-au-Prince. She hoped doctors there would be able to save her son. The trip would take two days, requiring her to stop along the way.

Spending the night in Granny's cottage in Anse Rouge, which was dark, hot, and stuffy, Eleanor reached for the curtain to pull it back and invite a breeze into the room. A scorpion was hiding among the folds of the fabric and stung her arm.

The Haitian scorpion is a pale brown, almost translucent arachnid, and while not as deadly as some of the species found in the Middle East, they carry a potent sting that can lead to fever, infection, and other complications. Eleanor was now alone, in the middle of the night, with an infant son who could be dying and her own fever to battle. When I asked her what she did, she said, "I prayed."

The next morning, Eleanor boarded a small sailboat with Wally to sail along Haiti's coast to Gonaives where she hoped to catch a ride with a truck going to the capital. Eleanor, who could fly planes and, some would say, cars, has never been able to stomach a boat—in fact, she even gets queasy standing on a wharf. She added seasickness to her growing list of ailments.

When Eleanor and Wally finally saw a doctor, his condition was serious, and hers wasn't much better. Eleanor prayed for Wally's healing, asking the Lord to spare him. Tenderly she nursed him back to health, bathing him in prayer, while she awaited Wallace's return. In this case, the Lord spared Eleanor the immense grief of losing a child; it was to be a grief delayed not forgone.

• • •

In spite of the rough conditions, the distance made greater by rough and winding trails, the threats, and the incredibly limited resources, Wallace and Eleanor persisted. They prayed. They nurtured. They encouraged. And the Lord blessed their efforts.

With congregations numbering in the hundreds, the home-based churches needed a larger space to gather, so the new believers "worked with all their might to gather materials for church buildings," Wallace remembers. "We bought corrugated roofing, cement, boards, and nails. To build a church, I worked weeks at a time with a Haitian carpenter and a couple of masons, while the Christians supplied sand. They also carried hardware, roofing, cement, and lumber many miles on their heads and gathered stone and hardwood poles."

Wallace has always believed firmly that a church must grow from within a community. While he's eager to spread the gospel message, he has never been aggressive in church planting, choosing rather to nurture the natural growth of a church in a community. As the gospel message takes root in a community, men and women naturally long for their own space to gather and worship. Learning of their desire, Wallace would then work alongside the congregations to help them build their own sanctuary. Throughout the years, the Baptist Haiti Mission would provide the skilled labor and purchased materials, but the congregants would help to carry the materials over long distances, to make the building blocks out of cement, and to gather the sand and other local materials available to them.

From the very beginning through today, building a church has been an act by and from the community that church would serve.

Surprisingly, this approach hasn't always been well received by outsiders, and Wallace has had his fair share of critics decrying his methods. If the people are so poor that they can barely feed themselves, how can he ask them to sacrifice to build a church? Isn't the sole purpose of missionaries to build churches? More than a few critics would argue that he should raise all the money needed for the church instead of taking advantage of the poor to supposedly promote his own agenda.

These are arguments with which Wallace and Eleanor would become all too familiar, but they wouldn't give in to pressure to do things as they had always been done. Neither Wallace nor Eleanor wanted to come in as white saviors; they had no interest in forcing a church to grow where it wasn't wanted. "A church must come from the local believers," Wallace would say time and again. "When people build their own church," he'd continue, "it becomes a part of their common treasure; they take care of it; they value it."

Regardless of how popular his methods were at the time, God certainly seems to have blessed and multiplied Wallace's approach throughout the years. "The group of twenty believers gathered at Porrier and the eleven at Atrel have grown into thousands in forty-five scattered congregations," Wallace writes in his journals.

Even as the congregations blossomed in the Nord Ouest as well as in the areas surrounding Fermathe, Wallace and Eleanor knew that listening to sermons wasn't enough. "As we believe that the Lord's children should read His Word, we encouraged literacy from the beginning," Wallace recalls. Once they were able to read and write, the new believers desired the same gift for their children, "so new literates became the church's first teachers," Wallace writes. The churches, built by the hands of new believers, were now community schools, too.

Seventy years later, more than 350 schools would serve 68,000 children a year. At one point, about twenty percent of Haiti's rural school population attended schools the mission supported. In nearly three quarters of a century, hundreds of thousands of men and women from rural Haiti have received a solid education from one of these schools. The children of illiterate parents went on to be teachers, pastors, lawyers, doctors, nurses, engineers, and even politicians.

From the very beginning of the French colonization and slave trade in Haiti, illiteracy and ignorance had been perpetuated in a perverse power struggle designed to keep "the people" in their place. Teaching men, women, and children to read one scripture passage at a time, the churches had turned on a light in the darkness, and there was no turning back.

As true pragmatists, Wallace and Eleanor were likely unaware of the subversive effect of their actions. They wanted to see hearts turn to God, but in doing so, they also helped to unravel the first knots in a centuries-long oppression. Building churches at the invitation of rural communities led to parents who wanted to read their Bibles, which led to them desiring the same for their children, which led in turn to establishing small schools, which led to an education breakthrough Haiti had been unable, or unwilling, to achieve in hundreds of years.

Through even the most basic education, the rural people began to experience an incredible change in their communities. They were still poor, they still struggled for survival, but their world had grown beyond measure. Children would go to school in the morning and then sit by the dying fire at night to share their lessons with their parents, to read to them, to contemplate scriptures as a family, and, perhaps, to sit in wonderment that for the first time in generations, they had access to new knowledge.

While the churches created a desire for schools, the schools built up good will toward the churches. Congregations sprung up and grew quickly in many of the rural communities, especially in the Northwest where Wallace and Eleanor had the best access to communities. Despite the proximity of the mountain communities around them in Fermathe, the lack of roads and the steep, barely visible footpaths made reaching those communities more difficult than reaching the ones in the Northwest. Eventually, they'd touch nearly every community around Fermathe and Kenscoff and as far as Nouvelle Terrain and Berly, but that wouldn't happen until later.

• • •

While growth can be expressed by numbers on a page, it doesn't come without tangible brick and mortar. Buildings don't build themselves, and cement blocks don't transport themselves. As the churches and schools continued to grow, Wallace and Eleanor were faced with substantial hurdles, not the least of which was the utter lack of infrastructure in and around the communities they served. Perhaps with unlimited funding and a fleet of civil engineers, the challenges might not have been so daunting. But Wallace and Eleanor were living on a shoestring; often they relied on gifts of produce and livestock from the mountain people to feed themselves. Nearly every penny the couple had was put back into the ministry, but even then it wasn't enough. If they were going to build—with almost no money—churches and schools in some of the most isolated communities, then they would have to get creative.

Their saving grace would come a few years later—in the wake of a conversion and a hurricane.

SIX
Becoming Baptist

Now THREE YEARS into their marriage with a growing toddler and dwindling finances, Wallace and Eleanor agreed at the urging of their friends and family to take a break from the mission field. "We flew to Miami with little Wally, an almost two-year-old cherub," Wallace recalls. "In Hialeah, he charmed our hosts by climbing fully dressed into the first bathtub he had seen, and turning on the water. We all agreed that it would be great to take his clothes off and put the plug in the drain. He loved it."

Using a car John left for them in Hialeah, Wallace and his family drove from South Florida to Flint, Michigan where his parents had lived. Along the way, they visited friends and shared about the work they had been trying to start in Haiti. In Flint, they stayed in John and Rhoda's "tiny bungalow with a backyard full of fruit trees." Spotting ripe cherries for the first time, young Wally exclaimed in a mix of Creole and English, "*Gadé*! Strawberries *monte*!" "Look! The strawberries climb!"

From his notes, it's clear that this was a time of unusual familial joy for Wallace. Perhaps for the first time since his marriage, he was able to truly see his wife and child, to delight in them and the simple happiness of family. From moment they were married, Wallace and Eleanor had been pushing forward in their work, giving everything they had to everyone they could. This time away afforded them the gift—however fleeting—of resting in the presence of one another as husband and wife, father and mother.

Even with a break from the daily strains of ministry, Wallace's time in Michigan was far from a true vacation. Penniless and needing to support not only his own family but also a rapidly growing ministry, Wallace went to work. He took odd jobs "one-after-another" in the factories of General Motors, driving to work in John's old car.

During their time in Flint, Wallace and Eleanor attended the Flint Bible Temple, which Wallace describes in his notes as "a fundamental Bible-preaching church that had left the Methodist church a generation before because of modernism. White-haired, handsome old Pastor A.G. Frost was a member of Dad's mission board of Flint area men."

Eleanor, who has never been one to keep idle, agreed with Pastor Frost to take care of his mother and his wife who suffered from dementia so that he could do more pastoral work. But it didn't take a very hard look to realize that Flint Bible Temple was in trouble: "...there were only a small handful of young folks in his withering congregation," Wallace notes. And so, Pastor Frost, Wallace, and Eleanor began to look for a way to keep the church alive. "We discussed a denominational affiliation with him, and he and the deacons invited state representatives of the Baptist Churches to present their groups to the members. Feeling the Conservative Baptists to be more kindly and biblically outreaching, we swung the church to join the latter," Wallace explains.

And just like that, Wallace and Eleanor became Baptists—by choice, by circumstance, and by an appreciation for the biblically-based doctrine of the denomination. The move was more of a formalizing of beliefs than a true conversion, but it was to prove a turning point in their mission work.

Whereas Wallace and Eleanor had been working as missionaries loosely associated with the Christian and Missionary Alliance, they had been largely on their own, sharing and living the basic tenets of their faith. Now, they had an entire network of evangelically minded Baptists to encourage and support them. And Ray Hein, the CB state representative in Michigan, would be the first to help them connect their mission to supporting Baptist churches.

"Ray Hein... discovered that we had been working—Eleanor for our meals, and I for cash—to prepare to return penniless to Haiti. He had previously visited Haiti and gained a burden for Haiti's struggling church and a vision of helping its growth. Ray introduced us to four other Michigan CB pastors and a Christian lawyer. He got each pastor to put in with him to offer our first regular support. Their ten dollars apiece made fifty dollars a month, the encouragement needed to head back to Haiti."

With the promise of support in hand, and a small savings from his work at the General Motors factories, Wallace and Eleanor began gathering supplies and making the journey south to Florida and back to home in Haiti. Wallace purchased a four-wheel-drive Jeep pickup and built a "Haitian-style" cover on the bed of the truck. He added two iron folding cots from the Salvation Army to close the sides of the bed and loaded the Jeep with cardboard drums containing an electric hand drill and a Sears Roebuck table saw along with "miscellaneous gifts from well-wishers." "Wally's tiny repainted tricycle topped the load," Wallace notes in his journals.

During their months in Flint, Eleanor had decided it was time they had a second child, and as they prepared to return to Haiti, she was well advanced in her pregnancy. "The trip south in the middle of sleet storms covering the Eastern Seaboard was a nightmare," Wallace recalls. With little money to pay for hotels, they drove slowly for 15 hours a day. "Little Wally had very little space on his mother's dwindling lap as the baby's development progressed."

When the family finally arrived in Hialeah, they found refuge and encouragement from their close family friends, "Aunt" Beva and "Uncle" Al Baxter, who took up a collection to help Wallace and Eleanor finance the trip. "We gave pickup and drums to the shipping company and flew home. From that moment, we have never looked back."

SEVEN
The National Stage

WALLACE GALLOPED THE STURDY mountain pony, his two-year-old son Sandy draped across his arm like one might carry a coat. Born Walter Sanders Turnbull on March 19, 1952, Sandy was undoubtedly used to the adventures and misadventures of his parents, as was his older brother, Wally. Since John had surrendered the work entirely to them in 1952, Wallace and Eleanor had spent nearly half their time in rural communities scattered across most of the island, as they would for the next decade or more.

From the tiny, isolated clusters of homes dotting the patchwork mountains that overlooked their home in Fermathe to the dry heat of the *Nord Ouest*, Wallace and Eleanor spent days on foot or horseback and nights on folding cots, bringing a message of hope, of love, of grace and forgiveness, like a glass of cool water to a traveler in the desert.

Their message was carried as much in their actions as in their words: bandaging wounds, building schools, carving roads. These actions would often be criticized by other missionaries and foreigners as overstepping the traditional bounds of missions. Though it might be hard to fathom when viewed through the modern lens of cross-cultural missions, in the mid-twentieth century, building anything other than churches, tending to the sick, and creating income-producing jobs was counted as social work, better left to the government than to those who should be preaching God's Word.

Of course, neither Wallace nor Eleanor had ever been one for maintaining practice for the sake of tradition. Truth be told they rather liked goading those they thought to be overly self-righteous—though paradoxically they had also done a rather impressive job of settling in to Haitian society, interweaving themselves from the lowest to the highest classes in a way that had perhaps never been done before and that, even today, is rare. Wallace and Eleanor's friendships haven't come by machinations or ambition, but rather through a genuine interest in the individuals they meet.

Perhaps one reason for this can be found in Wallace's upbringing. Though it came at the expense of constant uprootings, Wallace's transient life as a child planted the seeds of a lifelong curiosity about people and an openness to those who crossed his path. Perhaps it was because he never had long to get to know someone before moving on, or perhaps it's a divine gift, or, more likely, it's a little bit of both; but whatever the reason, Wallace has yet to meet a stranger—and neither has his wife. Both Wallace and Eleanor are practitioners of extreme hospitality, opening a door for people in need no matter how low or high their station. The couple's openness has led to lifelong relationships with some of the country's most influential and controversial people. "We didn't go looking for friends in high places; they just came to us, and we would receive them," Wallace says. "We were friends with everyone—still are!"

Those friends would forge paths that Wallace and Eleanor could never have created on their own. Antonio DeMatteis, the son of an Italian ambassador who married a Haitian woman, produced lumber and what Wallace calls "the best cement blocks in Haiti," without which Wallace could not have built schools or churches. This close friendship led to other connections who would themselves become friends. Jean Claude Leger, a lawyer, lent untold hours of legal advice. And Dr. Louis Roy, who founded the Red Cross in Haiti, ushered them into a world of disaster relief that propelled them to an international stage. In each case, service led to trust, which in turn led to friendship, which brought more service.

• • •

On this particular outing, Wallace did finally catch up to Eleanor, Sandy still slung over his arm. He stood his toddler on the tiny, bucket-shaped saddle. Designed to carry only one slender person, the saddles made traveling with young children especially difficult, hence the unorthodox arrangement of rider and passenger. Sandy, having bounced relentlessly across his father's forearm, was understandably winded from the effort, and as he stood up, gasping for breath, he exclaimed, "Mamma! I smell tired!" It took his mother a moment to figure out that what he'd meant was "I *feel* tired," but since the word for smell and the word for feel is the same in Creole—*santi*—Sandy had transposed the two in his young mind. That would be how it went for Wallace and Eleanor's sons throughout their childhood, moving between two worlds and languages, tripping only on occasion across the thresholds of transition.

The boys wouldn't always be able to accompany their parents, and they were often left behind in the loving and capable care of Granny. But for the most part, Wallace and Eleanor kept the boys with them. They wanted a hand in raising their own children, in part, I believe, as a response to Wallace's own frequent abandonment by his father, and also because they believed it best that their children live "among the people"—a phrase I've often heard my grandparents use—learning to live the gospel even from the crib.

The conditions that the family traveled in were far from comfortable; neither, in most cases, were they hygienic. In one instance, Eleanor and Wallace had been awakened several times in the night by the quaking ground: their cots shook, and the rafter poles of their hut, which were tied with vines at the roof's peak, creaked. "Stretching lazily at dawn, Eleanor exclaimed, 'It must have rained in the night; the roof is dripping,'" Wallace writes. "I spotted the white belly of a rat overhead, and she suddenly came to life and leaped out of her cot as the rat finished on her forehead."

Fleas were another common pestilence that lived in the dirt floors and thatched roofs. But perhaps no pest was more trying than the aggressive bedbugs that plagued the nation, an unintended side effect of the US-Haitian anti-malaria campaign.

"All buildings to a certain altitude were sprayed with insecticides," Wallace explains. "The idea was that after first filling with blood, a female mosquito would go to rest and get killed by the insecticide." That part worked fairly well. "The hitch was," Wallace writes, "that all other insects died, including ever-present ants which feed on, among other things, the eggs and newly-hatched baby bedbugs. So, having nothing to limit their numbers, bedbugs filled every building, including the national palace." Wallace and Eleanor's home in Fermathe was above the altitude that required spraying so they were saved from the bedbugs in their own home. But they had to avoid accidentally transporting them from the lower altitudes.

Wallace, who is allergic to most insect bites and suffers huge welts as a result, was desperate to find a defense against what he called "the trial by fiery darts."

"We tried insecticide powder," he writes, "but the bugs marched through it, even though they died later. Our best defense was cloths soaked in diesel fuel tied around the cots' legs." That stopped most of the bedbugs, though some were especially relentless and "climbed the walls and advanced to the attack by way of the strings holding up our mosquito nets."

To avoid taking the bedbugs into their own home, Wallace and Eleanor learned to put all of their belongings in tall drums and fumigate the bugs using a spoonful of carbon bisulfate. "We often removed outer clothing also, for the same treatment," Wallace remembers. With a bit of tongue and cheek, he writes in his journals, "Now the bugs are few (as a result of the light of the gospel?) since the spraying stopped." The gospel's light has solved many an ill in the world, but I'm not sure even Wallace can credit it for ending the bedbug invasion—though if he could, I'm confident he would find a way.

On the morning that Wallace rode with Sandy draped across his arm, they were riding out of Anse Rouge, but the exact location scarcely matters. They might just as easily have been riding to the high plateau of Seguin in the south of Haiti where, remembering the temperature dips of the winter months, Wallace writes, "We froze at night, lacking proper shelter, and found the ground covered with frost in the mornings." Or they could have been on their way to Bassin Général across the Rivère Gris, which drains the mountains east of them. But on this occasion they were most likely heading to Porrier, an isolated spot in Haiti's *Nord Ouest*, a few miles up the mountain from the Port-de-Paix road. Porrier had rather unexpectedly become the pride and joy of Wallace and Eleanor's ministry, with a budding Christian community that flourished with their attention.

The church of Atrel, about 20 miles away from the growing congregation in Porrier, was led in its early days by a converted Vodou priest named Olifas Geffrard. Olifas' conversion brought with it many new believers, and since he had been their priest once, it felt natural to them that he would lead them still. The hastily constructed arbor from 1949 had quickly grown too small for the rapidly growing congregation, and Olifas turned to Wallace for help. The missionary couple contributed materials and funds, and the people of Atrel built "an extra-long palm thatched hut for a new chapel," Wallace writes in his journals. "It was used for years, eventually becoming Atrel's first school."

In the years to come, Wallace would help Atrel first, then Porrier to build a fine church, and this time he would build it with his own hands. For over a month, Wallace used the Jeep truck to shuttle stone from a nearby mountain. Cement and galvanized roofing were sent by sailboat from Port-au-Prince. To unload the boat, which couldn't dock on shore, the men would wade up to their waists, balancing against the crashing of waves, carrying the heavy cement bags and unwieldy roofing on their heads—a seemingly endless line of human dinghies. "We had to clean the salt spray off of everything," Eleanor recalls. "And I remember watching these men wading in the waves, carrying the heavy supplies and thinking to myself, 'How can anyone do that?' But they did it; it was the only way."

Wallace led the men of the church in mixing the mortar and forming the foundation walls. The galvanized metal structure's hardwood pole frames required 800 hand-drilled holes. The buildings were naturally simple in form, but strong and sturdy, and they would go on to host many services, becoming in some ways the center of the community.

While Wallace laid the foundations for the new church buildings, Eleanor built on that foundation through tangible acts of service, strengthening the church day by day through her tender care of the sick and injured. Using the basic medical training she had received from her mother, Eleanor treated the gaping infections of yaws, cleaned the dirt and pus from injured feet, and ministered to the ailing with tools and supplies that must have seemed, even to her, and even in accordance with the times, inadequate. She had received no formal training— she wasn't a doctor or a nurse—but she was all they had. As she herself had said about the men fighting the waves, "It was the only way."

• • •

With churches and schools in nearly half of Haiti by 1952, Wallace and Eleanor realized that well-educated leaders were "badly needed," he writes. And so, the Summer Bible Institute was born. "We announced that young people chosen by their churches might come to Fermathe the next summer for three months. It was a great time. The first students were all young men, so we had them do manual work a couple of hours each afternoon and hike into the hills on weekends for practice evangelism. They went on to win souls and founded a number of churches."

Wallace and Eleanor had reached a milestone many missionaries only dream of in their ministries. They weren't planting churches, but rather the churches were propagating themselves, a growth led by Haitians, not by foreigners. It was by all accounts an indigenous movement, and Wallace and Eleanor but provided the fuel to keep the engine running.

During their trips to the scattered churches in those early years, Wallace and Eleanor used a Coleman kerosene projector to share Bible story filmstrips. The projector, screen, slides, and other camping materials would have to be carried on the heads of the community members. But if they minded, they never said. Perhaps the spectacle of the film was enough of a welcome and all-too-rare entertainment for what was otherwise an often isolated life.

On one particular night in Porrier, having shown the films and engaging in a short time of question and answer, Wallace and Eleanor used the projector as their only light in the church; it had now grown dark outside. People had gathered from all over the countryside for the special visit.

"I will never forget the thrill of seeing husky farmers from the new groups on La Montagne proud as little boys singing for their parents," Wallace writes. "Each man stepped into the projector's spotlight before the screen, repeated a favorite newly learned passage of scripture and sang a hymn through all verses. Worm medicine, Bible studies, nights scratching fleas, and training our students at Fermathe had paid off."

• • •

While moments like the one at Porrier would be highlights for Wallace and Eleanor, they felt acutely many of the heartaches of their neighbors. When Hurricane Hazel swept through Haiti in 1954, they lived and saw the devastation. "Seventeen inches of rain in forty-eight hours fell with roaring winds that toppled trees and homes alike," Wallace writes in his journal. "We could see that the plain below our mountain was under water."

By now, Wallace and Eleanor had gained the respect of the poor and wealthy alike—Haitians, Americans, and other foreigners—for their relentless forays into some of the nation's most isolated communities. They knew the mountains and her people. And so it was they found themselves transformed temporarily from missionaries to emergency aid workers, a position made official when the Haitian Red Cross, itself shorthanded in the crisis, equipped them as members with the tools and supplies needed to bring relief to some of the hardest hit remote areas.

"I remember riding in the U.S. Navy Marine helicopter working with the Red Cross," my grandmother once told me. "We flew over the mountains, and everywhere were tiny patches of exposed red earth carved in the mountainside. That was how we knew a home had been there once. It had been washed away."

After waiting a few days for the waters to recede, Wallace and Eleanor headed out to check on the people of Bassin Général, where they had a growing congregation of believers. To get there, they'd have to cross the gulley of Rivière Gris, which drains the mountains to the east of them. The gulley, which had once been only thirty-five feet in width, had enlarged to several hundred yards. "Rushing, silt-laden waist-deep water still filled its bed," Wallace recalls. "I stripped to my shorts, put pen and pad in my helmet, and went across and back, bracing myself as the 'passers' I saw taking people across." Wallace found the church and little school still standing and was grateful to learn they had served as a sanctuary for flood victims. "No one had drowned," he reported back to the relieved Red Cross headquarters in Port-au-Prince, "but the people were hungry."

When Catule, one of the members of the Fermathe church, told that a cliff had fallen down a valley called Barrière Roche (Stone Gate) and buried the valley's inhabitants, Wallace and Eleanor set out with the blessings of the Red Cross, a doctor, a sack of bread, and some strips of *siam*—an unbleached cotton cloth—to signal search aircraft.

To reach Barrière Roche, Wallace and Eleanor had to journey by foot across the narrow mountain trails. When they were about halfway into their journey, near the community of Bongar, they met Senat who had a scar across his face and was dressed in what Wallace describes as "medieval European peasant-style" clothing, a not uncommon way of dress for farmers in the more rural mountains. Senat told Wallace and Eleanor that he was from the Berly mountains, the area of the landslide, and he offered to serve as their guide.

Senat had two daughters, eighteen-year-old Carmen and her sister "with no face," as Wallace described her. As was too common in mid-century Haiti, Yaws had infected Carmen's sister and destroyed her eyelids and nose, "making a great, scarred hole, so that she wore a light veil for protection from gnats," Wallace writes. After meeting Wallace and Eleanor on this trip, Carmen brought her sister to them in Fermathe for treatment. Carmen went on to become their laundress and stayed on for most of the rest of her life, doing all the washing and ironing for Wallace and Eleanor, the other missionaries and volunteers, the guest housing, and even the hospital. By the time

I was born, Carmen had a ringer washer, an improvement from the plastic *kivet* or wide basins that required her to do all the laundry by hand. The clothes and linens were hung out on lines to dry. A retaining wall held one of my grandfather's terraces, and the top of the wall was level with the roof of the laundry building, leaving about a one-foot gap that had a single-story drop. My cousins and I would jump the gap from the wall and lie on the warm, flat cement roof. I can still smell the lye of the laundry soap and the dampness of the clothes hanging only a few feet away as Carmen hummed from one load to the other.

While Carmen would eventually become an essential part of the mission family, I imagine that at their first meeting Wallace and Eleanor barely had time to register her, let alone imagine a decades-long working relationship with the young woman. They were on a pressing mission with a horrific scene waiting for them at the other end; the travel itself was difficult and dangerous.

"Storm runoff water had all but obliterated the trail down the volcanic earth slope of Gros Morne which reached to the rushing Rivière Momance," Wallace writes. "I kept my work boots on my sore feet, and passers helped us across the torrent." In a country that has more flooding rivers than bridges, the "passers," as Haitians refer to them, are men who know the river well: where the sure footing lies, where dangerous holes have been carved, where the mud will suck you in. For a fee, they help travelers cross safely, passing their belongings and bundles overhead, safe from the rushing waters.

The journey to Barrière Roche would take Wallace and Eleanor 37 hours, overnighting with Senat and the Red Cross doctor in the hut of a Vodou priest. "He had scavenged hides from drowned cattle washing downstream and had tried to salt down some of the meat, Wallace recalls in his journals. "His wife put clean sheets on their bed, and we slept well near the roaring river, oblivious of the drip from hides overhead."

The next morning, as they set out once more for Barrière Roche, the Vodou priest's neighbors told the travelers that there were no injured survivors of the landslide. So Wallace sent back the Red Cross doctor, who had been filled with anxiety and frustration throughout the journey. "The doctor with his stave flew back up Gros Morne and quickly disappeared," Wallace writes.

Some of the local men and women led Wallace and Eleanor as close as they could to the scene of the disaster. "Trails were entirely obliterated. We skittered, praying, along the steep, muddy mountain's flank, from one tiny bunch of grass to another, finally arriving at a Christian widow's hut," Wallace recalls. "We spent the night on her hut floor, with a thin mat for a bed. A boa chasing after rats went by our heads and disappeared. The next morning, we pressed on over a tiny, dangerous trail that often disappeared, arriving in the stone-filled valley."

The scene that awaited Wallace and Eleanor was gruesome. "People from over the ridges next to the valley told us how they gathered pieces of bodies of relatives and buried them in a corner of the valley. Boulders as big as houses sat where they had stopped in house sites. The searchers found two pairs of feet protruding from under one such monster boulder. Ants were working among the stones."

Area farmers had lost more than 75 family members in the storm. But the landslide hadn't come without warning. In what could just as easily have been a scene out of the Old Testament, Wallace writes, "It rained all day and people were huddled indoors next to little fires. A man in a glowing white dress appeared and spoke to a woman named Peirrezine. He told her that he had tried to marry the people of the valley, but they had refused, so he was going to destroy the valley. He told Pierrezine to warn them."

Using a big banana leaf as an umbrella, Pierrezine went out in the storm to every household and told of the impending disaster. She was met with laughter. She was saved when her daughter who lived over the ridge to the west sent to say that she was in labor. Pierrezine took her young son to help her daughter through the birth.

In the night, amid torrential rains and wind, Pierrezine's prophecy came true. "The cliff of Barrière Roche burst amid lightning and thunder. It roared down the valley below. The ground shook," Wallace writes.

A young girl, about 13 years old at the time, was not to be spared as Pierrezine had been, but she also wasn't to be lost. Named Ti Jeté, Little Throw-Away, the girl's name, while cruel, was prophetic. "In the night, as water ran down the valley floor, it came in through the mud and wattle of her family's hut, running across the little room. Her mother and older sister lay on a mat in a higher corner, as she stood, shivering," Wallace writes. "The next thing that she knew, Ti Jeté was surrounded by a terrible violence. She found herself in the dark, one leg buried in rubble, and lightning flashing. Pulling her leg out of the ground, Ti Jeté scrambled up the hill to the west and safely away from the landslide. She is scarred for life by the hut's wattle that stripped her back." While the skin on her back bore witness to the miracle of her survival, one must wonder if it was not also a constant reminder that she was the only living survivor of the landslide.

In what only could have been a relatively short distance from where Ti Jeté sought refuge, neighbors lay packed together on the floor in the home of one of the area's few Christians. This fragile building had become "an ark of safety," Wallace writes. "As one hut after another collapsed in the hurricane, neighbors fled there. The man of the home had a friend help him hold the door shut against the terrible wind."

In the end, there was little Wallace and Eleanor could do. They found no injured survivors, just as they had been told along the way, with the exception of one old man who hobbled to them from across the rubble. "He had been squatting in his kitchen hut next to a little fire when a rushing bolder hit his bottom and shot him like a billiard ball to safety," Wallace said. Eleanor gave him a penicillin shot to ward off infection from the scrapes and cuts. It was really but a gesture amid what Wallace describes as "scrambled desolation." And yet, their journey wasn't for naught.

"Our caring was a tonic," Wallace writes. From that initial contact amid sorrow of helplessness and the shock of loss, two churches were born, one with "a little meeting house and school on the site where the helicopter once landed to pick us up." By the mid 1990's the area's Christians had so grown in numbers that the churches could no longer hold the congregations.

Having assessed the damage and knowing there was little else they could do, Wallace and Eleanor placed the strips of *siam* fabric on a knoll when they heard a plane circling overhead, but the pilot was flying too high to see them. The next day, they heard the familiar sound of a helicopter and hurried to once again lay down the fabric as the Red Cross had instructed. "In fifteen minutes, we were flown to be received by a waiting group of friends and government and Red Cross dignitaries at the

Port-au-Prince waterfront. It had taken us 37 hours to reach the landslide on foot."

The devastation caused by Hurricane Hazel was perhaps unmatched until the horrific earthquake of 2010. During the hurricane, roads had been washed away, communities were buried, and as many as 6,000 people had been killed—the bodies of people and animals washed out to sea—with over 100,000 left homeless. The hurricane, which later made landfall in the US as a Category 4 hurricane, claimed another 95 lives before hitting Canada as an extratropical storm and killing an additional 81 people. So extensive was the damage and death toll that the name Hazel has been retired from use for North Atlantic hurricanes. In Haiti, the real damage from Hazel would be felt for years to come, as the storm had washed away about 40% of the coffee trees and 50% of the cacao crop. The already fragile livelihoods of the peasant people had been torn apart by the winds and rains of a single storm.

As is often the case in a crisis, Hurricane Hazel proved to be a turning point for Wallace and Eleanor. They soon found themselves at the center of the ongoing relief efforts and were made responsible by the Haitian Red Cross for the international relief in the mountains south of Port-au-Prince, including the devastated area of Barrière Roche.

For their extraordinary efforts in the aftermath of the hurricane, Wallace and Eleanor were later decorated by the Haitian Red Cross and President Magloire "in recognition for exceptional services rendered on the occasion of the operations of Rescue to those Stricken by Hurricane Hazel." For the missionary couple, the decoration wasn't a reward for a job completed, but rather a cue that their work was just beginning.

"We handled hundreds of tons of food and clothing, issuing it to 3,000 people per day for weeks on end," Wallace writes. Early on, it became clear to Wallace and Eleanor that this was accomplishing little more than what a tourniquet might do for a severed artery. They could stop the bleeding, but they weren't fixing the wound.

Wallace saw the food relief as an opportunity not only to relieve the temporary hunger but also to help put back some of the infrastructure that had been lost and even to put in new roads where there had never been any. He had no money to pay workers to build roads, and he couldn't very well ask them to work for free, even if they would ultimately benefit by improving access to their isolated communities. The mountain men had families to feed, and they were hungry themselves. But Wallace also recognized that there was little value in giving temporary relief when hunger would soon set in once more.

In what eventually became dubbed as the "Food for Work" program, Wallace offered men food as compensation for their day's labor of building roads into their own communities. Despite its practicality, the program was initially met with criticism from a variety of sources. The more liberal aid workers felt that Wallace was cheating the men out of wages and forcing them to work for food they desperately needed, while the more conservative missionaries felt that his job was to build churches, not roads. But Wallace persevered. And in truth, the communities themselves responded positively. They could see that at the end of a few weeks they had roads and access to their homes. Their daily tasks would be made easier; going to market would take less time; trucks could now make it into the community with building supplies and other needed materials.

And in the process, the men had received plenty of food to care for them and their families. The investment was one well made.

Wallace's "food for work" experiment would eventually become US international policy in the wake of a visit from another man named Wallace—Henry Wallace, the former US vice president under Franklin D. Roosevelt. "In late 1962, Eleanor told me that a gentleman named Henry Wallace had visited our home in my absence and left a check for $25.00." Eleanor hadn't recognized him as the former vice president, but upon learning who he was, she questioned whether or not they should cash the check or keep it as a memento. Wallace found another option: they cashed the check, but not before making a photocopy for their records.

Even more remarkable than a former vice president showing up on their doorstep was the fact that he returned the next day. "We sat on our little couch and talked," Wallace writes in his journals. It turned out that while in Haiti Henry Wallace had heard tell of a "Pastor Wallace," and he went to investigate out of curiosity, should there by chance be any relation to him. With the question of a pending relation resolved—there was none—Wallace got down to business. "I told him that the worried mountain people pushed and shoved when in a crowd seeking post-catastrophe rations," Wallace writes. "I thought that if legal, all aid should be used as cash, and the people would have double benefit—the lasting work project results and their temporary rations."

"Mr. Wallace was gentle, easy to talk with," Wallace remembers—though many from his own party in DC might recall differently. "He said that he was no longer young, so he'd be leaving politics. But he liked my idea and he still had some friends in DC, particularly in the Department of Agriculture, so he'd see what he could do." The result of their meeting was the creation of plan PL480. For the next 40 years, shiploads of American food aid would be sent to Haiti and used as a bartering payment for constructive projects. "Hundreds of miles of dirt roads now crisscross previously isolated parts of Haiti," Wallace writes. "Many other needy countries south of the Equator also benefitted from PL480, because the Lord sent Henry Wallace to me. I often repeat, 'The Lord sees far ahead.'"

Truth be told, Wallace always had a builder's heart, so it would have taken much less than an act of Congress as encouragement to continue building roads. All in all, he helped build half a dozen roads throughout the island nation, several of which were later expanded and improved by government projects. In fact, the remaining part of the 1950s and all of the 1960s would be filled with building projects from roads to a hospital to churches and schools.

One of the most visible projects would be that of the new Fermathe Church, which Wallace built into a solid, large stone church with a peaked roof and room for a thousand people. The DeMatteis family donated the lumber for the benches, and Cyril Powell donated bench and pew supports for the church, building them in his garage woodshop. Decades later, Wallace would write to Cyril's second cousin, General Colin Powell, admonishing him to have mercy during the deadly embargo, but as the dedication for Fermathe church neared, Wallace could never have imagined the trials and challenges to come in the 1990s.

The Fermathe Church would remain one of Wallace's favorite structures, for not only did it have a simple elegance with a choir loft and a bell tower with purple glass windows in the shape of a cross, but it was also his home church.

The construction, though it inevitably had its challenges, came together well. But when Wallace sought to place a cross at the front of the church, directly behind the pulpit, as a finishing touch, the church association's older pastor—Pastor Rosemond—and several others balked at the idea. They saw it as reflection of the Catholic crucifix or, worse still, the crossroads of life and death, the symbol of the Vodou *lwa* Dambala. Wallace explained that the empty cross was indeed a powerful symbol, for it marked Christ's victory over sin and death, which, through the very nature of grace, is our victory by extension—we need only claim it as our own.

When compared to the cathedrals of Europe or even the mega churches of modern America, the Fermathe church is not an imposing building by any means. Then again, perhaps churches shouldn't ultimately be imposing but rather inviting: its large shaded porch invites people to gather out of the sun; its tall open windows invite the cool mountain breeze into the sanctuary; its proximity to the hospital invites all into God's healing embrace, both physical and spiritual. To this day, the Fermathe church stands prominently in a direct line of sight with the main entrance to the mission headquarters, a simple wooden cross behind the pulpit.

In 1958, Wallace, Eleanor, Granny, and sons gathered with over 1,500 guests, including members of the Fermathe congregation, Haitian pastors, other missionaries, and senior-level dignitaries who came to "return thanks and pay tribute to the work in Haiti of the Rev. Wallace Turnbull and his family," the *Haiti Sun* reported. A church dedication—enormously important and symbolic for Wallace and Eleanor and the Fermathe congregation—wouldn't normally draw such a crowd. Rather, the other guests had all come for something else: Wallace was to be knighted into the Order of Toussaint Louverture, Haiti's revolutionary hero. The Knighthood had been bestowed by the President a few days earlier, but the official ceremony was to be linked to the church dedication, in large part, one would imagine, because Wallace wanted the connection to be unmistakable: This wasn't *his* glory; it was God's. "The citation was read by Mr. Clement Vincent, the Chief of Protocol, who expressed the government's admiration and his personal deep emotion at the tireless efforts and spectral accomplishments of Mr. Wallace and his associates for the spiritual, material and physical welfare of the peasants of Haiti," reported the *Haiti Sun.*

Twelve years had passed since Wallace first sat surrounded by a forest of poles, whittling model joints for a makeshift roof, praying that God would help him build a church. On this day, the voices of 52 young men and women from the Fermathe congregation stood in their black choir robes, singing the lyrics to one of Wallace's favorite hymns—translated by him so they, too, might share in its blessing. His desperate plea had grown into a song of endless praise:

Then sings my soul
My Savior, God, to Thee
How great thou art
How great thou art

EIGHT
Deputation

THEIR RESPONSE TO HURRICANE HAZEL and the knighthood had propelled Wallace and Eleanor's ministry onto the national stage. To move ahead at the pace now demanded of them, they would need a source of solid, reliable funding—and that would be found from churches and individuals spread across the United States.

This time, when Wallace and Eleanor disembarked from the plane in Miami, the steam rising from the asphalt and fogging their glasses, they had three children in tow. David Rodney, their third son, had been born on November 26, 1953.

Sandy's birth had been a difficult one. There had been hemorrhaging and the doctors warned that another pregnancy could put Eleanor's life at risk. Still, by the time Sandy could toddle around the house, David was on his way.

Born with an intellectual disability, David became the center of the Turnbull home. In the Haitian tradition of giving a nickname by repeating two syllables from one's given name, he was affectionately called Da-Da by nearly everyone who knew him. Eleanor and Granny worked on developing his motor skills, teaching him to crawl, to walk, to live as normally as his condition would allow. Though adults never speak of such things to children, as least not in my family, while growing up I always had the sense that an air of guilt clung around the memory of Uncle Da-Da, as a cobweb might cling to a cloth used to wipe it away. It was as if at one level Eleanor blamed herself for his disability, as if it were her fault for not following the doctors' orders. Of course, the doctors had been worried for Eleanor's safety in childbirth, not for her son's development, and it was no more her fault than the hurricane that blew through on her wedding day or the valley that flooded with the rains.

David's life, however challengingly it began, would serve as a blessing to countless people. Whenever she spoke of him in my childhood, which was rarely, Eleanor would say, "Da-Da loved Jesus. And he loved to tell anyone he met about Jesus." In the end, David's story would be a full one, touching on the points of a life well lived: adversity, triumph, joy, sadness, guilt, and, one hopes, forgiveness.

But this day, when the family arrived in Miami, David's story was just beginning, and Wallace and Eleanor were entering a whole new chapter for the ministry.

• • •

The phrase about history repeating itself has earned its place as an over-worn cliché because, like so many other clichés, it holds more than a fair measure of truth.

Wallace had spent many unhappy nights in the homes of strangers while his father and stepmother traveled in the name of ministry, raising funds, sharing the gospel, answering a call—a call that always seemed to take them far away from the children who needed them most. Wallace hated deputation and often spoke against it in his older years. But there's another cliché that rang true for him and his young family in 1961: money makes the world go 'round, and it is even more distastefully true for ministry than it is for business. After all, even Bibles cost money in the paper of their pages and the ink of their words.

And so it went that nearly 25 years after his own father placed him and his younger brother David in the Westervelt home and his older brother Jack at Houghton Academy, Wallace's own boys were spread across three homes for the better part of a year. Wally went to live with Rudy and Bea Kronst in Cincinnati, Ohio, Sandy with Bud and Marynell Lewis in Fairfax, South Carolina, and David went to Elim Christian School in Palos Heights, Illinois. When I asked my father to talk about this year, he didn't have much to say, except that he thought it might have done David some good since the school, which specialized in children with disabilities, was well equipped to help David in his development.

The homes Wally and Sandy found themselves in were admittedly a great deal kinder than that of the Westervelts, but at the end of the day, they weren't home, and how could they be? Absent were the patched and wrinkled mountains, a well-worn blanket of gardens in shades of green and brown. Gone was the morning fog that sometimes rested for days in the folds and crevices of the quilt until one glorious morning the sun would rise warm enough to chase it away. There were no mangoes, yellow, orange, and green freckled with brown spots as if to say, "pick me, I'm just ripe enough" before dripping their sticky juice down the pale arms of brothers. It isn't an easy thing to be a child, to have adults—however loving they may be— claim your destiny, uproot you from all you've ever known, and ask you to sacrifice for the greater good. But then again, no one ever said it was easy to be a missionary child.

Many men and women define themselves by their families— first, they are mothers and fathers, husbands and wives, and only later, after a pause, are they what they *do*: teachers, lawyers, plumbers, secretaries. Not Wallace and Eleanor. They were always first and foremost missionaries, servants to a living God. It isn't that their children and family came last, only that we didn't come first—we couldn't. Eleanor often said, "When one is a missionary, one must give up her children to the ministry, must put them on the altar for God." Wallace and Eleanor's sons would be folded into the mission work, taken along on journeys when possible, left behind when necessary.

This year of deputation was no different. Wallace and Eleanor would be traveling from one end of the United States to the other; they would live hand-to-mouth relying on the grace and hospitality of those they met along the way. They believed that was no life for their three boys, their three beloved sons, and so, they left them behind for a time.

• • •

For as little as they liked deputation, Wallace, and especially Eleanor, were very good at it. Traveling from church to church, they brought the stories of the Haitian people to life. Ringing clear in their voices, which I hear even now as I write, would be the note of joy as they shared about the men and women who had become their extended family: Soimeus and the flourishing Fermathe church. Victor who started the ministry in Nouvelle

Terrain. Nicolas, one of the very first converts. Senat, a gentle man who guided them to the devastating landslide in Barrier Roche, a scar across his face hinting at his own unspoken trials. "The gospel to a Haitian is freedom from fear," Wallace would say. "When they're saved, they're freed from all fear of things being sent upon them."

Wallace's face would light into a smile, and the American church members would almost hear the voices of the farmers in Porrier, singing their favorite hymn as they declared their love for Jesus. The women would gasp and the men would frown as Eleanor shared about the gruesome infections she and her mother treated in clusters of homes so isolated that most city Haitians didn't even know they existed. The congregants would wipe away a tear with their thumbs as they told of the wonders wrought with a few simple doses of worm medicine, a shot of penicillin, and clean bandages. They would see in a distant glow families huddled around a dim fire at night as boys and girls read the scriptures out loud for their mothers and fathers who couldn't. They would taste the sticky mango, the salty dried herring, and feel in their teeth the grit of Haitian cornmeal. They would shiver with the cold air of the mountain night and draw near to one another for warmth. Then, they would know: a nation was turning to Christ one soul at a time. And they would support the call.

The year of deputation, however difficult it might have been for the family, proved to be a turning point in the mission's history. At the prompting of the mission's board members, most of whom were pastors in the Conservative Baptists of America denomination, Wallace and Eleanor visited member churches across the country, gaining financial and moral support for the ministry in Haiti. For the first time in their nearly 15 years in

Haiti, Wallace and Eleanor had a generous, steady stream of financial support for the ministry. For years they had learned to *wash the money and drink the water* as the Haitian proverb says, stretching every bit of cash as far as they could without breaking. Now with a more solid financial base, they wouldn't ease up on their frugality—they would just allow it to take them further.

By the time I was old enough to know of such things, the mission had an annual budget of nearly $2 million a year, a sum I couldn't quite wrap my brain around. It seemed like an awful lot of money. Certainly when compared to the $55 a month Wallace and Eleanor had lived on and put toward ministry when my father was a child. And then, I paused to calculate. With the annual budget, the mission—by now long christened the Baptist Haiti Mission—managed to support a 100 bed hospital, over 350 schools with upwards of 65,000 students, more than 400 congregations scattered across half of Haiti, and set some aside for emergencies and growth. Even now, I don't quite know how they did it.

But in 1961, those days were still a long way off, no more imagined than their great-grandchildren when they looked into the eyes of their three boys, measured their growth, and ruffled their hair before telling them with a gruffness only half-felt to "run along."

• • •

With the mission's work growing steadily, a mission board to back them, and a fairly reliable base of support finally in place, Wallace and Eleanor understood the need to formalize their ministry. The projects were now too large and too many to hold them in their minds, to calculate costs on scraps of paper, to administer alone. And so they set about working to institutionalize what had, until then, been in a way the family business.

Though Wallace had sought missionaries to partner with him from the very beginning, no foreigners seemed to stay the course, except for his wife and mother-in-law. Even his father had long left the work to his young son, perhaps as others might teach a trade to their children or leave them a shop to administer.

Those who have worked alongside Wallace for any length of time would know that it's unfair to place all the blame on the other missionaries. Wallace himself was also part of the problem. My father put it best when he said that if one were to judge my grandfather by his actions alone, one might say, "What a saintly, godly man," and if one were to judge him by his words alone, one might say, "What a cruel person." The truth, as with most of us, lies somewhere in the long stretch of in-between. Wallace would be the first to admit that he's no saint, but it would also be unfair to call him cruel.

While my grandfather has given his life to serving those in need with a compassion that could only come from the Divine, and would do so a thousand times over, he cannot, for the life of him, handle confrontation without lashing out. Time and again, Wallace has spoken words in anger that he later regrets, or worse, that he has no idea were hurtful. Once the moment has passed, he's ready to forgive, to move on, to continue the work—and he often doesn't understand the seeds of bitterness he planted, the pride he wounded, or the feelings he cut. What makes matters even more difficult is that as astounding as Wallace is in his own actions, he is equally demanding of those who serve with him. He has little patience for learning curves or perceived weakness. "If God has called us to serve," he might say, "then we must give Him our all; we must be prepared to sacrifice all—even our families as Abraham was called to do with Isaac."

Having a bit of perspective on his childhood, we may now better understand where this character flaw had its start, even if we don't justify it. But the missionaries who went to Haiti to serve with Wallace had no such benefit of perspective. They often arrived ill-prepared, suffered deep culture shock, and struggled to find their footing. Wallace, while eager to serve with them, to dust them off, to share even the food from his plate, was unable and even less willing to provide any emotional support. Rather, he would be quick to identify their weaknesses (to help them grow, he might say), to chastise their errors (to help them correct their ways) and to push back when they lashed out (to protect the ministry). And yet, with the slightest hint of repentance from his targets, Wallace stands ready to forgive, to start again, to put the past behind him.

Perhaps what makes Wallace's words so utterly devastating for many is the infuriating fact that more often than not, he is right in his judgment of a person. If he weren't so harsh in the delivery, one might say Wallace has a gift for understanding a person's true character. In his letter to the Ephesians, the apostle Paul encourages the early Christians to "speak the truth in love," to help one another grow in faith. Wallace, for all his shortcomings, might say that he is trying to do just that. He speaks the truth because he loves the person, but somehow, time and again, he fails to speak *in love*, to translate the grace of his actions to his speech.

For a young missionary struggling to simply get through the day in an unknown country with an unknown language while living amongst unknown people, learning to see the love in Wallace's actions and ignoring the hurtful words is, perhaps, a step too far to ask someone to travel. The perspective of time has illustrated that many of the earliest missionaries who arrived to serve with Wallace and Eleanor were indeed ill-equipped and naïve, but Wallace's quickness to point it out to them certainly didn't help.

In at least one particular case, enmity from a young missionary couple—Eldon and Joy Ausherman—was very nearly his undoing. The Aushermans had joined the expanding mission and were intending to aid in the growth of the churches. In the end, the Aushermans would prove to be much more dangerous than any preceding missionaries, involving themselves in an attempted takeover of the mission.

NINE

Exile

THE CUBAN MISSILE CRISIS, the Civil Rights movement, and the assassination of John F. Kennedy have taken on auras unto themselves, so deep was their effect on the identity of a nation. But we would be wrong if we thought these events unique to America, for their ripples could be felt the world over, even across the ocean and up the winding mountain paths, through the mud huts, meandering across terraces, and walking straight into the heart of a missionary's home, threatening to tear apart the fragile fabric of a family.

"These are important and crucial days for us here in Haiti and all over Latin America," Eleanor wrote in one of her many collections of notes and thoughts, typed or scribbled on pieces of paper and squirreled away in folders and boxes. In this piece, titled "Thinking Aloud" from the early 1960s, she recognizes the desperation in Haiti, and indeed the entire continent of

Latin America—desperation that made the nation ripe for communism.

"The 98 percent of the masses struggle hopelessly against erosion, lack of roads— and thus no transportation to market for produce—overpopulation, 95 percent malaria and 20 percent TB and no industry to create employment," she writes in a sad catalog of the daily challenges she and Wallace labored to help their neighbors overcome. "One is depressed to see millions struggling against such impossible odds. Two percent live in great wealth while 98 percent earn perhaps $12 a year and have no immediate hope of improvement... Beginning to realize their desperate state, they frantically clutch anything that might promise improvement... They wonder if Castro has the answer. A prominent Haitian leader said recently to us, 'To all Haitian men between the ages of 14-40 years, Fidel Castro is not a man—he is a god.'"

Eleanor is famous for rounding her statistics, but regardless of their exact accuracy, the story she outlines for us is dire indeed. In the 1960s, Wallace and Eleanor began to see their work not just as a calling to build God's kingdom through love and service, but also as a frantic fight against the threat of Communism and the atheism it would bring with it.

"The need of Haiti is Christ," Eleanor writes. "He is the answer, not Castro... If our words and our works are balanced, the Communists will find little occasion to accuse that, 'They come and save the soul and the body goes to hell.'"

Today, Wallace and Eleanor's stance of balancing the needs of soul *and* body is so commonplace in missions that we find it hard to imagine missionaries any other way. But in the 1960s, the widespread belief in missions until that moment had largely been that missionaries were to care for the peoples' souls, doctors to care for the peoples' bodies, and the government to care for the peoples' land and infrastructure. But as Eleanor wrote, "Jesus healed the lame man, He fed the hungry multitude, He gave sight to the blind; we're told many times over that 'He looked upon the multitude with compassion' and that 'He went about doing good.'"

My grandparents' desire to live out the works of Christ's ministry put them at odds with other Protestant missions many times throughout their years in Haiti. They were the target of great criticism for "using God's money to do the government's work," but they also weren't afraid to prescribe a healthy dose of critique to their fellow missionaries, making clear all that was at stake. "I'm wondering if Protestant missions in Haiti have established the witness that our Master would have chosen," Eleanor writes. "I listened heart-heavy as one young American missionary ranted before his mission's leaders, 'My wife is not here to give medicines, I am not interested in your schools, it is not my problem if your children are hungry, don't tell me that your children have no clothes to wear. I did not create this situation for you—I came to your country and found you in this state and my *only* purpose in being here is to preach the GOSPEL and see people turn to CHRIST.' It would seem to me that our fundamental missions have sent out too many men like this and thus opened the gate for the communist accusation against our Christian message..."

Communism wasn't birthed out of the air, Wallace and Eleanor recognized, but out of a dire human need. "The final test of our effectiveness for Christ is spelled out in our having ministered to human need," Eleanor writes. And it was a test they'd stake their lives on passing.

• • •

By 1962, Communism had grown from an existential threat to one planted at their doorstep. A man by the name of Calyxte Delatour had worked as a private secretary to President Estime but had been replaced when General Magloire took power. With few roads open to him in the current political environment, Calyxte grasped the promises of Communism and began to see a way ahead.

Despite Calyxte's political leanings, Wallace saw him as a friend. Worried about the rising tensions between Duvalier's *Tonton Makout* and Haiti's National Police, Wallace remarked to Calyxte that the tension between the forces "was an abscess that needed to be lanced" lest it lead to armed confrontation. Calyxte cautioned Wallace against speaking out so openly under the strict rule of the current regime. "Some day, a jealous man will put you out," Calyxte warned.

François Duvalier had already been in power for 5 years, and he was firmly entrenched as the island nation's leader—if not by the people's choice, then by force. His rule, relying on a carefully controlled military and a ruthless rural militia known as the *Tonton Makout,* would eventually result in the deaths of up to 60,000 Haitians and the exile of countless others. Duvalier was so successful, in part, because he used the one power Haitians most feared and revered—Vodou. Duvalier adopted the identity of Baron Samedi, the Vodou *lwa* of the dead, and one of the most feared. Baron Samedi is traditionally depicted wearing a black top hat, sunglasses, and cotton stuffed into his nostrils, as was the traditional preparation of a Haitian man for burial. Duvalier would wear sunglasses to hide his eyes and speak in the nasal tone attributed to Baron Samedi. His Tonton Makouts (literally translated to "Uncle Feed Sack") were named and dressed in the image of the dreaded Haitian bogeyman, another vestige of Vodou, who was said to kidnap children, stuffing them into his feed sack and later eating them for breakfast. While Duvalier's Tonton Makouts didn't eat any children for breakfast, they were responsible for the horrific deaths and disappearances of countless men, women, and even children.

In many ways, Wallace and Eleanor were fighting a war on three fronts: the spiritual battle for Christ, the growing threat from Communism, and the very real dangers of Duvalier and his administration. When the three came to a head, it was nearly their undoing.

• • •

"My darling, this past month has been a year, as I look back over it. Life is not too normal when each day a fellow wishes it away—wishing *this* day were done," Wallace wrote Eleanor in September of 1962. In an abrupt turn of events, he had been exiled from Haiti, sent away from those he loved, those he had come to see as "the whole Haitian body."

In August, Wallace had received a visitor who came to collect him to report to the national police headquarters. When he arrived, he was questioned by Colonel Fred Arty, a man whom Wallace considered a friend. The Colonel questioned Wallace about a possible enemy who would have him expelled. "I was treated with politeness, given a cot to try to sleep," Wallace writes in his journals. "I heard Eleanor come to talk with the police downstairs. They told her to get a suitcase ready for me. As I had not a cent on me and had not eaten all day, a kind young police recruit brought me a hamburger, and I got a few swallows of water from a faucet."

Wallace had named John and Rhoda as his next of kin and listed their address in Puerto Rico for notification in case of his death. Exile wasn't death, but in Wallace's case, his next of kin were his only option. "The next morning, Eleanor was allowed by kind Captain Pierre to see me sent off on a Pan American plane for Puerto Rico where my folks lived at Cayey in a cabin in the hills," Wallace remembers. "He told her that he had orders to put both of us on the plane, but he was leaving her to make efforts to contact Dr. Duvalier so I could come back."

Pierre's decision to allow Eleanor to stay behind was an act of kindness that would alter the outcome of their lives, though he wouldn't live to see it. Pierre was later shot by Dr. Duvalier, who personally executed a group of officers. "Ambitious politicians denounced intelligent people to remove possible opposition," Wallace writes in his journal. Eleanor wept at the news, crying, "Not *my* Pierre!"

The reason for Wallace's exile would remain a mystery almost until the end—Duvalier's rule was rife with false denouncements, political scheming, and paranoid officials. What was known acutely was the fact that Wallace had been arrested and deported by members of the Duvalier regime. At the time of his arrest, the killings and disappearances that would become the hallmark of the regime were near a peak. "When he was arrested, he wasn't sure he wouldn't be killed," my father told me in a conversation about Wallace's exile. "It's something that even as a family we never really spoke about."

Wallace wasn't killed nor did he disappear. He received the luckier of the options: a one-way ticket out. Wallace spent the first few days of his exile in Puerto Rico with his parents, but when he arrived, they had already sold their house and belongings and were in the process of packing to leave for Beirut. Once John and Rhoda left, Wallace moved to Miami to stay with his friend Paul.

Wallace would write almost daily to Eleanor and implore her time and again to join him in Florida with the children. Each time, Eleanor would either ignore the request or give an excuse to buy herself more time. From his letters, it's clear that Wallace struggled with her decision to stay behind, and it was undoubtedly difficult not to take it personally.

"You say, 'If it goes into years, of course the children and I'll join you.' In how many years are *we* going to start work again? …The way you talk, we may never live together again, for all you care. You are so attached to that pile of stones, mud, lime, boards, glass, and tin roofing that you think that it represents our life's work," Wallace wrote in October, three months into his exile. "Have you never heard of pastors changing pastorates? Honey, it's taking a long time for it to sink in, that we *may* have another field ahead of us. I believe that the Lord would have us at the point where HE places us. (I do not say it will *not* be right back there at Fermathe, and Haiti.) Until *you* are *willing*, we will remain in confusion."

But Eleanor knew that if she left the island, they would likely never discover the reason behind Wallace's exile, and, even worse, they'd probably never be able to return. She likened the experience to a soldier in battle with the loved ones waiting at home. Only, in her comparison, she was the soldier and Wallace the "homebody." The fight, as she would call it, would take its toll on her health, strain her marriage, and pain her children who were separated from their father. In moments, even her life and safety would be at risk. Yet, she was willing to sacrifice everything to her life's calling—to serve the Haitian people, body and soul.

Eleanor's courage took its toll. A friend would report to Wallace that Eleanor was "tired of being brave." In my mind's eye, I can see her clearly: Lying in her bed, unable to sleep, she would pray. She would pray for the Lord's guidance, His peace, for her husband, her three boys, her mother. She would pray for the Haitian church, for the woman in the hospital who had been admitted with hepatitis, for the boy who had come with a compound fracture that was now infected, for the daughter of the witch doctor. The tree frogs would join her with their song, calling back to one another. *Ki-ku. Ki-ku.* The crickets would add their chirping. And the morning fog would roll in from the valley, blocking the sunrise and seeping into the already damp limestone. In the space between night and day, Eleanor would remember fragments of Wallace's instructions, imagining his voice speaking them to her in the quiet. "Please try, for everybody, to rest and look fresh, as best as you can. Like Monfort said—'brave soldier for Jesus.'" "Tell workers not to use word 'communist' in public, for safety." "Pick up washing machine from Firestone (I gave new motor, $10 for parts)." "Have you seen about shipping your car?" "You are my wife, and we've drawn attention, see?" "When shall I expect you?" "You have my prayers—that's all I can do." "I'd hate to take off for Nassau, and you arrive when I'd already gone." "I hope that by this time you're sleeping well. I can't, with only papers for company." "May the Lord be with you. I love you." "I'll tell the folks to pray for you." "I love you." "I love you."

With the dampness of the night air still around her, Eleanor would rise to carry her load and work to complete Wallace's instructions. Always on her mind was the seemingly eternal wait that was her desperate campaign: to reveal the true reasons of her husband's exile and to restore him to his family. The weight of it all would bring her down with an illness that she kept from him. But Granny wrote to Wallace; after all, she might say, he had a right to know. "You should have told me you were ill," Wallace wrote to Eleanor, "but I guess you think I'll say 'I told you so.' I don't need to—that's just you, burning the candle at both ends and breaking it in the middle for good measure. What for? Please take it real easy now, for goodness sake, and as soon as you can, get over here, so you'll not see what there is to be done and try to do it… May the Lord be with you. I love you."

Eleanor wouldn't leave or take it "real easy." "I felt somebody should stay and try to find a crack in the wall of isolation surrounding 'the source' of Wallace's exile," Eleanor told me. But even in her tenacity, she was well aware that her role as Wallace's wife placed her in a delicate position—attention was fixed on her, and even if the authorities didn't seem keen to arrest an American mother with three boys born in Haiti, they had already deported her husband. She lived under scrutiny with an unknown enemy waiting for her to stumble so that they could make their move—whatever that was to be. Wallace feared not so much for their life's work, as Eleanor would call it, but for those who made his life worthwhile.

Eleanor knew the great risk she took, and so she armed herself with a strategy countless other great women have used throughout time. As Wallace put it in one of his early letters to her, "Honey, if you keep sugarin' up the enemy, we'll keep 'em guessin'. Play dumb and despairing and pleading and all your other adjectives, and the Lord keep you, my love, my dove, my too far away."

And so she did. Playing dumb and despairing and pleading, she moved from one official to another, gleaning bits of information along the way that she would weave together. Eleanor had found intermittent access to one of Duvalier's personal doctors and a leader of the Makouts. As she sat in his home, waiting for an audience with him, Eleanor witnessed men entering the home and leaving with guns in hand. Of course, she suspected them to be Tonton Makouts, but no one ever told her; she was wise enough not to ask. As Eleanor pleaded with the doctor for news on her husband's exile, he would tell her, "You're going to have to wait for a little while. There will be people who want to help with this. You just have to give us time." But Eleanor knew they were running out of time—the longer Wallace remained in exile, the harder it would be to have the decision reversed.

While she waited for news from the doctor and others, Eleanor's inquiries and bits of news from Wallace confirmed what they had suspected from the beginning: his exile was only a small piece in a global struggle of ideologies. Wallace and Eleanor may have been living quietly in the rural mountains of a tiny nation, but they were two pawns in a much bigger political game.

• • •

In 1962, the Cuban Revolution was cementing itself on the island while using its success as a springboard to spread the movement throughout Latin America. A failed invasion attempt at the Bay of Pigs in April 1961 had only heightened tensions with the US, and just months after Wallace's expulsion from Haiti, the world would sit at the brink of nuclear war. While Haiti's role in the Cold War is rarely thought of as crucial, one can't help but notice that on a clear day, at the top of the mountains in Haiti's northern peninsula, one can see Cuba. Despite the barriers of language and water, the people share a surprisingly common history bound by sugar cane, coffee, poverty, exploitation, and revolution.

After the Haitian War for Independence, many of the island's French elite escaped to Eastern Cuba where they began again, taking with them the coffee that Cuba would become known for the world around. Decades later, Haitian laborers would go to work in the cane fields of eastern Cuba; many would stay. Indeed, even today Haitian Creole is still spoken by some of the families around Guantanamo and some of the hymns sung in the area's Baptist churches were written in the rural churches of Haiti.

Where revolution once took Haitians to Cuba, Fidel Castro was now ready to take his revolution to Haiti.

• • •

With everything to lose in the Cold War, the United States was well aware that Latin America, marked by widespread destitution, was a low hanging fruit for Communists. If the U.S. were to win the Cold War, she would need allies. The CIA had approached Wallace, asking him to serve as an informant. But he refused on the grounds that he couldn't hope to gain the spiritual trust of a people whose secrets he was betraying. The fact that he refused to serve as a CIA asset, however, didn't mean that he hadn't held onto the contact. On September 28, Wallace shared what was to become the first clue of his exile. "The CIA man said that the movement, (anti-Duvalier radio, etc.) is all from Haitians in CUBA, *not* the DR," Wallace wrote to Eleanor. "Thus you will see why Castro is using the many Haitians there, and training African reds in Creole, and why the reds in Haiti keep up a smoke screen, hollering against the agitators in the DR—to divert attention of non-red anti-Duvalier people from the danger to them and the man they dislike, by hiding the origin of the broadcasts, rumors, etc."

Communist propaganda was being circulated throughout Haiti, and especially in the mountain communities around Fermathe and Kenscoff. The campaign had penetrated the Duvalier regime. Some of the local leaders were secretly communist, working against Duvalier—and anyone else who might stand in their way.

Eleanor would take this knowledge and begin to ask more questions, moving from one person to the next, meeting with one official after another, only to be received with bureaucracy, pat answers, and non-information. But they had met their match in Eleanor. My grandmother is a master at gleaning answers—even from what isn't said.

"Find out just who is giving out the propaganda," Wallace wrote to Eleanor. "Make Micius talk… Impress him that this information may lengthen his own life."

Micius was a lay leader from the Callebasse church, and Communism was flourishing in that area marked by an especially desperate poverty—even by Haitian standards. Eleanor likely did her best to encourage Micius to talk, but if he ever did give useful information, Wallace never mentioned it.

Desperate, Wallace wrote a letter to Duvalier. The letter was given to Atherton Lee "to be handed personally by a friend to the gentleman to whom it is addressed," Wallace wrote to Eleanor, enclosing a photostatic copy of the letter. "I figure I have nothing to lose, and that gentleman has everything to lose, the way things are going, whether or not his 'friends' inform him of what is going on in the country."

In his letter, Wallace detailed the social work of the mission in addition to their efforts to share the Gospel of Christ. "We have consistently led in the battle against illiteracy, aiding the establishment of 40 schools for peasant children. You are aware of the fact that the influence of evangelical missions has been largely responsible for the awakening to this need, and the subsequent growth of literacy from 2% to 10% in the past 15 years."

Wallace also highlighted his leadership in road building, the mission's well-received medical ministry, and the hospital that was currently under construction in Fermathe.

"Not everyone is happy with our efforts, especially the communists who have come to the Fermathe area, but have not been successful..." Wallace wrote. "The whole group are at present employed by your administration and are spreading among other communist propaganda the prophecy that they are going to take over the whole of Haiti's government in the very near future. They tell the peasants that yours is the last administration which will be elected in Haiti.

"Doctor Duvalier, you can ill afford to allow the deportation of those who are unselfishly aiding your people, on some jealous man's pretext, while the group which we Christians oppose are openly using minor positions in your government's offices to plot its overthrow."

To this day, we don't know for sure whether Duvalier received the letter, though I suspect he did not based on what followed only a few days later.

One day, after having sought out nearly every government official she could access, Eleanor stopped for a sandwich on the balcony of the Belle Creole gift store. During the 1960s, the Belle Creole's snack shop, which offered a panoramic view overlooking Port-au-Prince and the bay, was a popular dining spot for Haiti's middle and upper classes. It wasn't unusual to bump into a friend or business contact while dining. And that's how it happened for Eleanor.

Sitting in the glass-enclosed balcony, Eleanor was approached by Aubelin Jolicoeur, a journalist and friend of Wallace. He mentioned that he hadn't seen her husband in a long while and asked where he was. Shocked to learn of Wallace's exile, Jolicoeur asked if Eleanor had spoken to the authorities. She explained that she had seen every minister, but they were afraid to go against the president's decision, for Wallace's exile papers had supposedly been ordered by Duvalier himself. In a single move and at a time when the smallest infraction could cost a man his life, Jolicoeur proved his friendship to the Turnbulls: he told Eleanor that the American doctor who worked with Duvalier had an office in the palace, and he told her how to reach him.

Eleanor would waste no time in contacting the doctor, Elmer Laughlin, who had worked on the World Health Organization's Yaws eradication program with Duvalier and now served as his American advisor. Under pressure from Wallace, she had agreed that if his exile wasn't reversed by October 31, she would join him to begin again in the Bahamas. Time was running out: there were only a handful of days left in the month.

With the information Jolicoeur provided, Eleanor was able to schedule a meeting with Laughlin and through him passed a message to Duvalier.

The president was purportedly "horrified" to learn of Wallace's exile and opened an inquest into the matter. Duvalier "found only praise everywhere we worked," Wallace writes in his notes. The inquest revealed no legitimate reasons for Wallace's exile, and it was soon suspected a bribe had been given to have him expelled. Duvalier ordered Lucien Chauvet, the chief of the secret police, to authorize Wallace's return. Chauvet was also the one whose signature was on Wallace's order for expulsion, and it was suspected he had been bribed to order it in Duvalier's name. Had the bribe been proven, Chauvet would more than likely have been executed—not for his corruption but rather for taking liberties with the President's name.

As if to remove all doubt about Wallace's standing, Duvalier took an extra step in facilitating his return. Not knowing where Wallace was currently residing, the president telegraphed every Haitian consul in the United States, asking them to find Wallace and return him to Haiti.

Laughlin also told Eleanor the good news. She phoned Wallace who got on a plane the very next day, just days after the Cuban missile crisis came to an end. When Wallace disembarked on October 31, 1962, he found Chauvet and Colonel Arty leaning against the low fence separating the terminal from the tarmac.

They asked Wallace for his visa, and Wallace replied simply that Doctor Duvalier had told him to come.

• • •

Upon his return, more facts began to reveal themselves. With the news now out about Duvalier's inquest and the dictator's intervention on Wallace's behalf, government officials and other individuals were more willing to speak. Wallace's suspicions were proving to be true: a friend had denounced him.

"Some day, a jealous man will put you out." Calyxte's earlier warning foretold of the betrayal. Someone close to Wallace had twisted his words about the Tonton Makout and the national police, saying the missionary had called Duvalier an abscess. Strategic bribes sealed Wallace's fate.

While Wallace had been in exile, the Aushermans, who harbored strong jealousy against him, saw their opportunity to take over as the mission's directors. Not only were they guilty of inaction on his behalf, but Wallace and Eleanor would discover the couple had been working to sully Wallace's reputation as a leader and deepen the divisions within the mission board.

Stories that several parties may have colluded with one another, each seeing an advantage to be won by Wallace's ousting, seem plausible, but some details have never been proven and likely never will.

While Wallace's exile marked 1962, and its effects would be felt on him and the family for years to come, the social and gospel outreach of the mission had by no means stopped during his expulsion. The construction workers built roads; Granny treated her patients; pastors preached; teachers taught; and students still gathered by the evening fire to read scripture verses to their parents. Wallace's universe might have been in turmoil, but the world marched on—even the early morning fog and midday sun continued their dance across the mountains.

TEN
A Split

OVER THE COURSE of the previous few years, Wallace and Eleanor had begun construction of the Fermathe Hospital, which opened before his exile. The hospital construction had come at the request of the Haitian pastors who had approached Wallace and Eleanor and asked them to build a rural hospital. "That's what we really want," the pastors told them, so that's what Wallace and Eleanor worked to give them. Several buildings, including an x-ray room built on a cistern and an old schoolhouse, were joined together under one roof along with some new construction to form what is now the highly respected Hôpital de Fermathe.

Help in finishing the project had come from an unexpected source: the crew of the *USS Forrestal*, bringing what the *Haiti Sun* called "a new dimension in Haitian-American co-operation." According to the *Haiti Sun* article, "Eighteen *Forrestal* carpenters, plumbers, and electricians, co-operating with Haitian farmers and the Baptist Mission at Fermathe, contributed their time and skills towards the construction of a 12-bed hospital in this mountain community."

The US sailors donated their services as well as $400 in building materials and "large quantities of food for both Haitian and American workers." At the end of the weekend's 12-hour days of work, in one last act of goodwill, some 45 members of the USS Forrestal donated blood to the mission's tuberculosis sanatorium. The sanatorium had started out of necessity in the struggle to battle the disease that claimed thousands of lives throughout rural Haiti.

While the technicians from the Navy were instrumental in advancing the construction of the hospital, especially with installing the complex wiring and plumbing needed, the Fermathe hospital was the result of the efforts and donations of a wide range of people, including financial contributions from 50 Haitian Baptist churches, donations from individuals, and volunteer labor from Haitians and foreigners. The hospital's first operations were thanks to the First Baptist Church of Windom, Minnesota, which donated all the hospital's operating room and pre-operative room equipment.

In a letter to Messiah Baptist Church, Wallace describes Eleanor as "the force which has built her mother's first aid work here into a hospital with full facilities. I have had the pleasure of building the structure."

Eleanor will be the first to recognize that she didn't do it alone. The support she received from Haiti's medical professionals from the Department of Public Health to the donated time and talent of doctors was unprecedented. The fact that the doctor who was most instrumental in founding the hospital was Haiti's first woman surgeon—and only the second woman doctor in the country—is remarkable in and of itself, but also, perhaps, not so remarkable. For who would better understand the pioneer in Eleanor than another pioneer? The fact that it should be Lucy Paultre and no other, however, was a story more than two centuries in the making.

Mr. Paultre, a Huguenot Christian, left France for the Americas in the 1700s. Eventually settling in St. Marc, he had a small business, married a black woman, and had several bi-racial children who would join the growing mulatto class. When the French betrayed Haiti's revolutionary hero Toussaint Louverture during the war for independence, Jean-Jacques Dessalines, who would become the first leader of an independent Haiti, was enraged. Dessalines ordered that all French on the island were to be killed indiscriminately as retribution. Dessalines' soldiers killed Paultre and his wife, but the servants hid the mulatto children in the hills around St. Marc. Lucy Paultre descended from one of those children, born in a time of tumult and saved by the kindness of the rural people. Throughout her long life and career as a doctor, she would pay back that kindness a hundredfold.

To this day, the Hôpital de Fermathe remains the only rural hospital within a day or two's walk for tens of thousands of people. Over the years it has grown to include 100 beds, two modern operating rooms, an outpatient clinic, a maternity ward, and a pharmacy.

The *Haiti Sun* reports that the foundation of the "non-denominational Baptist Mission hospital" had been laid five years before. Of course, one might argue the foundation of the hospital was laid one bandage at a time from Granny's medical box under a shade tree, or perhaps it began even earlier when Rhoda first treated the injured foot of Jean Baptiste.

But I think the real seed of the hospital was planted in Jerusalem in 1927 when a toddler welcomed his baby brother and grieved the death of his mother. What must Wallace have felt when he entered the hospital he helped to build, when he heard the first cries of an infant safely nestled in her mother's arms?

• • •

The Fermathe hospital didn't open its doors a moment too soon. "Erratic killer hurricane devastates Haiti and Cuba," *Life* magazine reported on October 18, 1963. "The deadliest ever," the article screams in bold headlines. The Haitian government reported 4,000 dead and 100,000 homeless from Hurricane Flora. In the same month, nine years earlier, Hurricane Hazel had wrecked havoc on many of the same areas. Flora was even worse.

Flora was so deadly in part because the storm moved slowly, trapped between winds. The "easterlies fed its strength," *Life* reports, while the westerly winds slowed it down. As devastating as the storm was in Haiti, creating deadly landslides, washing away crops, and destroying villages, Cuba fared even worse. The now infamous winds trapped Flora over Cuba for five days.

"Never in man's memory had a storm behaved so capriciously or so viciously," *Life* reports. "Hurricane Flora moved out of the Caribbean to strike at dictator-ruled countries that already were in such deep economic and political trouble that it seemed the plight of their peoples could hardly get worse. But worsen it did..."

• • •

At the time the hurricane hit, Wallace was in Michigan. In July, the Conservative Baptist Home Missions Society board voted to "withdraw from the field in Haiti as a result of a problem which we had been unsuccessful in resolving." The problem was, in part, Wallace's exacting demands on the CBHMS missionaries and the difficulty they were having in getting along. But it went much deeper. The Ausherman's plan to discredit Wallace and take over the mission had failed, and Wallace's resentment at the lack of intervention and assistance from the CBHMS during his exile was raw. CBHMS had seen its role as a governing board—the Turnbull's work in Haiti now belonged to the mission society. Wallace and Eleanor, however, saw themselves as directing an independent mission. The split was inevitable.

Not long after the CBHMS withdrew its support, Wallace and Eleanor decided to reinforce the board of directors. The mission would be independent from now on, separate from the Conservative Baptist Home Missions Society or any other association.

Under the new organization, Wallace and Eleanor and the board decided to formally incorporate as the "Conservative Baptist Haiti Mission Society." The initials would remain CBHMS, a move that must have been more strategic than coincidental. Eventually, the mission would become widely known as BHM, the "Baptist Haiti Mission" and in Haiti as the *Mission Baptiste Conservatrice d'Haiti.*

By October, Wallace and Eleanor were in Michigan for deputation, visiting a number of supporting churches, strengthening alliances after the break with the Home Missions Society and raising funds for the rapidly growing work.

Hurricane Flora struck Haiti October 2, 1963, one day after Wallace and Eleanor had left the island for deputation. In a letter dated October 6, Wallace wrote to Gerard Philippeau, the Minister of State of Public Health and Population in Haiti. "I have been very distressed upon hearing of the devastation left by hurricane Flora, and have waited for news of you folks down there," Wallace wrote. "Naturally, the people of the United States will want to do what they can to help. I am contacting what influential people I can."

Wallace continues on in the letter to address the option of a formal "Food for Work" program, which he tried with great success on his own after Hurricane Hazel. His idea was simple in approach but potentially profound in results. Roads had been washed out and there was no way to transport badly needed food into isolated areas. Even if the rural people had money to purchase food, which they didn't, there were virtually no supplies to buy. Hence Wallace's remuneration strategy: using the desperately needed food to pay the community members themselves to fix the roads. "Beginning at centers of distribution, roads can be opened very rapidly by contracting pieces of road lengths and drainage to gangs of people in return for fixed wages of food, a means requiring a minimum of controls, as payment is made upon completion of contracts," Wallace writes. The food would be gone in a short while, but the roads would remain, opening up a pathway for men and women to move in and out of their communities to conduct business and trade.

"I believe that after hurricane Hazel, we missed something. We just handed out food to needy people without organizing them to help themselves. This was from a lack of experience," Wallace recognizes in his letter, going on to write, "Yes, the people of Haiti are brave and used to hard work, and we simply handed out uncounted tons of food, neglecting to guide them to the work of reconstruction, leaving them aimless. In the years following, Haiti has suffered from this neglect or lack of foresight.... I am convinced that again Haiti will suffer for years if the work of reconstruction is not attacked from the present. Human dignity will suffer too.... Perhaps you will agree with me that the governments of Haiti and the United States should cooperate in using surplus US food relief to open and to improve Haiti's roads and drainage projects now while that aid is available.... Please discuss this seriously with Dr. Duvalier."

Gerard Philippeau phoned Wallace and urged him to return to Haiti to aid in the relief. Philippeau made Wallace and Eleanor responsible for managing the relief in seven counties, some of which had been the hardest hit by the hurricane. Wallace agreed, again insisting, "we must use every bit of relief aid received as if it were cash." The Food for Work program was formalized, and the results are standing to this day.

In an article written for Church World Service in 1964, Naomi Hunsberger, a close friend to Wallace and Eleanor, reports, "Husbands, wives and able-bodied sons, working as human bulldozers, are carving in the mountain... in southeastern Haiti, a lasting monument to man's dignity and courage. In torrential rains, in slick, sticky clay that adds discomfort and hazard to their every step and move, they are engaged in a labor of love for this two-fold purpose: To earn, in payment for their contribution of time and brawn, desperately needed food and clothing provided by Protestant churches in the U.S. and distributed through Service Chretien d'Haiti."

At Fort Jacques, a Food for Work effort was organized to benefit a maximum number of families. Work groups of approximately 200 laborers were rotated every two weeks, and only one member of any given family would be hired. The first week, the laborers were paid in food, such as 15 pounds of beans, and the second week, they received clothing.

The school was set in motion by Bobbie Childs Sampson, a volunteer with the Friends Committee, sent to Fort Jacques to live among the people. The school was built according to the layout Bobbie drew and would become the Fort Jacques School, which still operates today. Children would walk up to an hour each way to school—and today, their children do the same. "Work having replaced charity, these proud people are able to maintain a certain sense of grace and, at the same time, they are building a more secure future for their children by making an education available to them," Naomi wrote.

The Food for Work program was so successful that members of other more distant communities would travel across mountains and valleys to join one of the work groups, only to be turned down in many cases because there was no temporary housing available for them near the work site, a grim fact that still gnaws at Wallace.

• • •

Eventually, the international aid relief dried up, as it always does—but not the need. Wallace and Eleanor's newfound independence in BHM had come at the cost of significant funding from the mission society. "We turned fathers, old women, and the sick away, having no food or cash to give them for work," Wallace wrote in his notes about the beginning of 1965, following with, "We read that in the USA 3.5 billion dollars annually are spent on pets."

Wallace doesn't comment on the statistic of how highly valued pets are in the US or on its stark contrast to the destitute poverty facing millions of Haitian men and women, especially in the years immediately following Hurricane Flora. I imagine he supposed he didn't have to. The numbers, he might say, speak for themselves.

And yet, the Haitian church continued to "grow in the grace and knowledge of our Lord and Savior Jesus Christ," as encouraged in 2 Peter. A shortage of funding may have been a burden Wallace and Eleanor carried, but it didn't seem to be a hindrance to the Haitian churches. The new believers had already learned to live without: without food, without clothing, without education, without the joy of watching their children live to have their own children. Their whole lives for generations had in many ways been a story of living without. Now, they were writing a new story for themselves, a story of living *with*—with faith, with grace, with love, with God.

Through the example of the new believers, Wallace and Eleanor were also learning to redefine *with* and *without*. As the New Year dawned in 1965, Wallace writes that he shared communion "with 40 Christians in a rented shanty" on Haiti's second-highest mountain and sang:

It is glory just to walk with Him,
Ala bèl glwa, mache ak Jezi

It is glory when the shadows fall.
To know that He is near.
Ala bèl glwa, menm lè li fè nwa
Poum konne li tou pre

It is glory just to walk with Him,
Ala bèl glwa, mache ak Jezi

With Christ. With their Haitian brothers and sisters *in* Christ. Together, *through* Christ. That was the way forward, the way to glory.

ELEVEN
Refuge

IN A COUNTRY LIKE HAITI, there are moments when fear is as palpable as the air that sticks to one's skin. In these moments, Wallace and Eleanor were regularly called upon to serve as a safe haven for those running from the bloodlust of corrupt regimes. Throughout their years of ministry, they provided refuge to any number of men, women, and children who found themselves on the wrong side of a conflict. Some were running from the political leaders, others were running from their victims. In one instance Wallace remembers providing refuge to a policeman who himself had been persecutor until he suddenly found himself being hunted. On several occasions, Wallace and Eleanor provided a hiding place for those running from the President. But perhaps none of their interventions would be as dramatic and risk-filled as that involving the Benoit Affair, an event so heinous that more than 50 years later, the bloodstains still feel fresh.

On the morning of April 26, 1963, an unknown assailant drove by the car taking the Duvalier children to College Bird, where Wallace and Eleanor's own son Sandy was attending school, and fired several shots, killing the three escorts. The children escaped to safety inside the school. Papa Doc's response rang clear: the affront would be paid in blood.

Knowing that the lives of his family were undoubtedly in jeopardy from the forces opposing his regime, Francois Duvalier had long pronounced that any attempt on the lives of his family would result in the absolute obliteration of the assailant's family. As such, when it was suggested to Duvalier that the only one who could have attempted such a difficult shot from a moving vehicle so far away was Lt. Francois Benoit—a star member of the Haitian sharp shooting team—Duvalier sent the Makouts to make the family pay.

"The bloodbath began at the home of... Lieutenant François Benoit, an elite marksman who had been dismissed from the army," the Haitian author Edwidge Danticat wrote in an article for *The Progressive* to commemorate the 50th anniversary of the massacre.

"They were like madmen," Wallace recalls.

"The massacre was led by Captain Max Dominique," Georges "Ti Joe" Edeline wrote in a testimony for *Black Looks*. Ti Joe was only 12 years old at the time of the massacre, and his story, while just beginning, would become forever intertwined with that of Wallace and his family.

In his testimony, Georges goes on to write, "Once Max Dominique cleared the gate, on his way to the waiting vehicle, the Makouts spread fuel on the house and the dead bodies... The remains of the house, in that vacant lot, have not been touched since." Those killed in the Benoit household included

Judge and Mrs. Joseph Benoit, a pregnant visitor mistaken for Jacqueline Edeline—Francois Benoit's wife—two maids, and a young male gardener. Gerry Benoit, who was only 17 months old, was taken from the house and disappeared. It's suspected that he was raised by one of the Tonton Makouts who, in a rare act of mercy, couldn't bring himself to kill a baby. To this day no one knows for sure what happened to the child.

"Hundreds were rounded up or disappeared into the bowels of Fort Dimanche, the notorious dungeon prison where many of Papa Doc's victims lost their lives," Danticat writes. "It was one of the most brutal days of the twenty-nine-year rule of Papa Doc and his son, Jean Claude 'Baby Doc' Duvalier."

Among those imprisoned were Paul Rene, Jacqueline's father. His wife Georgette Edeline, noting a truck of Makouts through the window, called to her husband, yelling for him to escape. "But he replied that he had not done anything wrong and had no reason to run," Georges writes. "So she and the servants took off."

Paul Rene was escorted to the waiting vehicle, never to be seen again.

Georgette jumped the wall in her backyard and escaped through the neighbor's yard. "From her hiding place, blocks away, she managed to gather several of us, from schools and work, and sent us into separate hiding places for the next four months," Georges recalls.

Francois Benoit himself wasn't home and was spared in the initial bloodbath; his wife Jacqueline Edeline was also spared, for she was at work in the US embassy. Word reached Francois before the Makouts found him, and he was able to seek refuge in the Dominican embassy; Jacqueline, who was pregnant, remained safely inside the US embassy.

The bodies of those killed were left behind to rot as a reminder to all who might contemplate rising up against Duvalier.

When Duvalier learned that Francois Benoit had escaped the Makouts and sought refuge in the Dominican Embassy of all places, the already strained relations with the Dominican Republic neared a breaking point. Arguing that the Dominicans were harboring his family's would-be assassin along with other political enemies, Duvalier sent Haitian police armed with rifles into the embassy. The Dominicans were deeply offended by the affront.

"Early the next morning, Saturday, I heard that [President] Bosch said if the Haitians jump on the Dominican Embassy in Port-au-Prince, he intended to bomb Port-au-Prince," John Bartlow Martin, the former US Ambassador to the Dominican Republic, recalls in "The War with Haiti."

In the end, the Dominicans did not bomb Haiti, but the resolution of the crisis was long and complicated, involving, among other diplomatic solutions, the careful intervention of US Ambassador Martin.

As it is with all great conflicts, there are heroes of nearly every kind, some who choose to be heroic and others who are chosen. Wallace and Eleanor were chosen, the lives of the Edeline boys thrust upon them.

Jacqueline's three siblings were taken to the French embassy. French Ambassador Charles Le Genissel and his wife Madeleine said they'd be able to take the sister, Gertha, and 5-year-old Eddy but wouldn't be able to take Georges because they had several daughters and feared it would be improper. Instead, they sent the 12-year-old boy to Wallace and Eleanor.

Wallace had only been home a few months from his exile, and those who had conspired against him could easily have been looking for new ways to bring him down. His smartest choice was to lie low, to keep his head down and focus only on his ministries. But Wallace and Eleanor had never been ones to lie low, and they weren't about to start—not when the lives of innocent children were at stake. A few months earlier, Eleanor had sought the mercy of Papa Doc for her husband, and now her family harbored the child of his most hated enemy, a man whose very existence was driving the country toward war with its neighbor.

Even with the recent drama of Wallace's exile, nobody suspected the couple to be involved, for it was understood that they wouldn't interfere in politics, and the politicians wouldn't interfere with them. Their allegiance as missionaries was to another kingdom altogether. The matter settled, Ti Joe moved in with Wallace, Eleanor, and their sons. Sandy continued going to school, and all pretended life was normal. Except it wasn't normal, and they each knew it couldn't continue forever.

Sandy, only 11 years old at the time, passed notes back and forth between Ti Joe and his older sister who was in hiding at the French Ambassador's residence. Sandy drove the family Jeep—"there was hardly any traffic in those days" Wallace says nonchalantly—and would deliver the notes in person. Being a child, it was supposed that he would draw less suspicion. On one occasion, however, he was greeted at gunpoint by Ambassador Le Genissel who saw the Jeep and feared it was the Tonton Makout coming for his ward.

While the children were temporarily safe, it was clear to all involved that the family could not remain in Haiti, but getting them out of the country would prove just as risky, and it would take time.

Eventually, Francois Benoit was moved to the Ecuadorian Embassy, where he remained in hiding for over a year. When Jacqueline, who by this point had given birth to her son inside the US embassy, was taken to the airport to leave Haiti, her vehicle was met on the tarmac with two rows of armed Tonton Makouts forming a deadly aisle between her and her plane. As long as she remained inside an embassy vehicle, she was protected by international law, but the moment she stepped onto Haitian soil, she and her infant were, so to speak, fair game.

Ambassadors from several nations were called, and each brought the flag of their nation. One by one, they laid the flags on the soil as international stepping stones to freedom. Flag by flag, nation by nation, Jacqueline and her infant walked the gauntlet until they were safely inside the plane.

The only ones who remained now were Ti Joe, Eddie, and Gertha. Their salvation would come through a delayed flight and missing luggage.

• • •

Nearly two years after the Benoit Affair, Wallace began 1965 with only Sandy and Granny at home. By now the Edeline children were living with others in town, though their safety was still precarious. Wally was in boarding school at Wheaton Academy; David was at Elim Christian School in Palos Heights, Illinois undergoing continued intervention for his learning disabilities.

Eleanor also traveled to the US, to spend five months studying the Doman-Delacato theory of brain development through The Institutes for the Achievement of Human Potential

(IAHP) in Philadelphia. The method is based on the belief that for children who have suffered brain damage or other developmental disabilities, the brain can be programmed to learn through patterning. The idea is that the brain builds new pathways through movement. Children are taken through a series of patterned movements that mimic a child's normal developmental stages. Through the movements of crawling, especially, a child's brain is taken back to early development and, in a way, is reset. Typically with this method, the younger the child the more dramatic the difference.

David was nearing adolescence and was significantly older than the ideal age for beginning the therapy. Even so, in just six months of applying the method, David advanced two years in his development. Amazed at the results, Eleanor was later sent by the IAHP throughout the Caribbean to start Doman-Delacato institutes for brain-damaged children to help them learn reading and writing. The method has since been criticized by the American Academy of Pediatrics who believes the IAHP greatly simplifies brain development and places an undue burden on the parents through the therapies prescribed. Eleanor, however, saw the results: while the Doman-Delacato method might not work for every brain injury, trauma, or developmental delay, it worked for David and countless others—and it worked with very few resources, tools, or expensive interventions.

Eleanor had gone to Philadelphia to save her son and in the process saved countless other children, as is often her way.

Her trip was also the salvation of the Edeline children. For on the way from Haiti to Philadelphia via Miami, the baggage for the entire plane of passengers had been lost—rerouted or loaded on the wrong plane or some other occurrence that wasn't altogether rare in those days. While filling out the lost baggage forms, Eleanor took a moment to help a fellow passenger who seemed overwhelmed by the process. In that moment, a man approached her and offered a casual hello. Eleanor, aware that she was a married woman traveling alone, was friendly but wary: She was traveling with a sum of cash along with a wedding ring her dear friends had commissioned from a jeweler in Haiti. Still, Eleanor is hard-pressed to pass up a good conversation, and those who love her often joke that she doesn't know the meaning of the word stranger. Within a few short moments, she had found out that the man was named Jacques Bailhe and he had been in Kenscoff.

"Oh?" she likely asked. "What were you doing there? I'm from Fermathe, just down the road from Kenscoff. My husband and I are missionaries."

Jacques replied that he had been looking for a source of carrots for racehorses. The produce from Kenscoff is legendary in its quality—the cool mountain air, the limestone from the mountains, the long growing seasons all combine to produce beautiful, abundant crops at the hands of a knowledgeable and well-equipped farmer. Still, Eleanor found his response odd. Kenscoff is fairly remote; carrots are universally abundant. Haiti had no racehorse scene—large or small—to speak of. Would he be shipping the carrots to the US? Eleanor puzzled over his answer but said nothing of her doubts. She was nonetheless intrigued.

Jacques also had a way of turning the conversation back to Eleanor—he was, it seemed, equally armed with questions. She had met her match.

In the conversation, Eleanor let it be known that she had a wedding ring to deliver to her dear friends Gary and Gail Boekel who lived in Delray.

"I have a car. I can drive you," Jacques offered.

Eleanor recalled how nervous she felt. "This was a total stranger. And I had money on me for the course I was going to be taking. I was not eager to get in the car with a strange man."

She went anyway.

Through the course of the long drive, Jacques eventually turned the conversation to the political situation in Haiti and asked what she knew about the Tonton Makouts. Eleanor saw an opening and felt a prompting. This man was a stranger, but he had been sent to her. She had a feeling about him, and her instincts were usually good ones.

"I don't know if I should tell you or not," Eleanor began, "but we have this young boy living with us. He's in danger."

The conversation was cut short by their arrival at the home of the Boekels. The visit with them was brief but friendly with Eleanor awkwardly explaining how she had come to show up at their home so late in the evening—by now it was past 10:00 pm—with a strange man. Gary and Gail, however, knew Eleanor well, and this was likely far less surprising to them than she imagined.

On the way back to Miami, Jacques said plainly, "Why don't you bring the boy to the states?"

"He has no passport," Eleanor replied.

"You don't think you could get him out?"

"I could get him out. He has fair skin and could pass as one of my sons. But I can't get him into the US without a passport."

"Well..." Jacques replied in a drawn out way, Eleanor remembers. "So it's getting him into the States that's the problem."

Jacques then steered the conversation to Eleanor's husband and learned that Wallace was still in Haiti.

Still mulling over the previous part of the conversation, Eleanor said, "If I can get him into the States, I'd have to go back to Haiti." She knew the price of this decision. She wouldn't be able to complete her Doman-Delacato course on which she had pinned so many hopes for her youngest son. Yet, she couldn't possibly risk someone else's child, equally beloved, to advance her own. That wasn't Eleanor's way.

"We could write to your husband," Jacques proposed. "I'm going to tell you how to contact your husband. Then, I'm going back to Haiti and I will get the boy. I can get him into the US."

"How?" Eleanor asked.

"That's my problem, not yours."

"A man will come," Eleanor later wrote as instructed. "You must receive him and he will give you instructions."

Eleanor continued to Philadelphia while Wallace awaited his visitor.

• • •

Haiti's crescent shape has created innumerable harbors, big and small, making it at one time among the most desirable lands of the West Indies. Nestled in the void of the mountains are the Caribbean's ocean waters, deep enough for the most regal of liners and calm enough for the humble dugout. From the time of the Arawak, those natural harbors have been a hub of economic activity. One need only think about the capital's name to understand how crucial the shipping industry has been to Haiti's formation: Port-au-Prince. In that natural harbor the French ship *Prince* docked in 1706 and eventually gave its name to the city.

When Jacques returned to Haiti for the Edeline boys, it would be another French ship that would play the leading role.

The liner *SS France*, put into service in 1962, was at the time the longest passenger ship ever built and would hold onto that honor until 2004, when it would be usurped by the RMS *Queen Mary 2*.

In 1965, the *SS France* was docked at the Port International de Port-au-Prince and was, as one can easily imagine, a popular attraction. From mountain lookouts, she would appear long and lean, floating above the secrets in the Caribbean depths, hiding secrets of her own.

Capitalizing on the curiosity surrounding the ship, Wallace followed Jacques' instructions. He invited Sandy and several of his son's friends to board a lighter at the docks to visit the famous *SS France*. There, on the lighter, were a number of children in a range of ages, shades, and family backgrounds. What they each had in common was their enthusiasm for adventure, and what could be more adventurous than the world's longest passenger ship docking right there in their own harbor? Wallace, Jacques, and the children boarded the ship, toured her swimming pools, imagined the feasts of her dining rooms, and peeked behind the doors of her staterooms. When the tour was finished, they all boarded the lighter and returned to shore—all but four of them.

The plan was elegantly simple, based on the principle that people in a busy city have little time to notice the details—only someone *did* notice. Shortly after Wallace returned to shore, the Tonton Makout boarded the *France* asking to take the Edeline children who had been spotted. The captain's answer was unequivocal: "This is French territory. You touch no one on this ship."

Jacques and the Edeline children made their way safely out of Haiti to a new life with relatives in the United States.

• • •

A cursory glance at Wallace's hastily jotted daily notes from this time show that amongst the intrigue and adventure, the ministry marched on at an ever increasing pace. On one day alone, Wallace noted, "We paid 300 people (food & clothing), had 11 weddings, so no time to write details for Esther's newsletter."

Drought was now claiming the villages left behind after the rains of Hurricane Flora, and "whole families of mountain poor" were dying of hunger, Wallace wrote to the US supporting churches. In what seemed to be another cruel twist of the knife, Wallace had seeds to distribute, but even he couldn't summon the rains.

In part because of the drought and in part because of continued public health education efforts, rural men and women began to request help with "family planning." At their prompting, a new branch of ministry sprouted from the hospital. By the beginning of May, the decision had been made to hire a new doctor and initiate a birth control program. Within two weeks, Eleanor had acquired the IUD contraceptives and Wallace had hired a doctor at $150 a month with lodgings. With a drought raging and food supplies dwindling rapidly, family planning wasn't about increasing the *quality* of life; it was about saving lives altogether.

Today, the idea of a rural hospital aiding with family planning is hardly given a second thought—more newsworthy would be the hospital that doesn't offer contraceptives. But in 1965, the birth control pill had only been approved for 5 years, and birth control was still illegal in many countries as well as in eight US states, despite the fact that nearly 6.5 million women were on the pill in the US. In Haiti, a nominally Catholic nation, the debate was no less pronounced. After all, the Catholic

Church prohibited the use of artificial family planning methods. For a small Baptist mission to initiate a rural family planning program was incredibly progressive—and full of risk. And yet, Wallace and Eleanor likely didn't think twice about their choice. The people they served were begging for a way to prevent pregnancy, to preserve the lives of the children they loved.

Eleanor has always been a woman of immense character, but the previous few years must have been a second coming-of-age. How could it have been any different? She had not only weathered the exile of her husband—managing the affairs of home and ministry—but she had also seen him vindicated, refusing to give up until his name was cleared and he was safely back at home. With the smoke of intrigue still swirling around them, she had helped to shelter a child marked for death by a brutal leader, arranging with a CIA operative to smuggle him and his siblings out of the country. Somewhere in the middle of all that, she had been decorated as a Grand Officer of the Department of Public Health, an official recognition of all she had accomplished for the people of Haiti despite having never taken a single medical class. And so, for her, in this moment, perhaps taking on the Catholic Church and all the controversy surrounding contraceptives seemed not so great a task after all—and even if it were, she would do it anyway, for the people she loved had asked it of her.

Eleanor admits today that she didn't know much about contraceptives and felt ill-prepared to begin a formal family planning program. So she turned to another woman for support: Bobbie Childs Sampson. When Eleanor first found Bobbie and Polly, another Friends Committee volunteer, she said to them, "What do you do here?"

"We live here," Bobbie replied.

"What do you teach the people?"

"We use what we have."

But they didn't have much—no equipment, no materials, and limited language skills. So Eleanor found an old sewing machine and some needles and gave the young women direction on what to teach. She also lent them something else that was much appreciated in their sparse living conditions: her shower.

Eleanor realized that these women, despite lacking direction, might be able to contribute in a significant way. "These two girls were more sophisticated in the ways of the world and knew more about birth control than I did," Eleanor says.

The women helped her search out information on family planning and options for contraceptives. After the women's assignment ended, Eleanor and Bobbie kept in close touch with one another. And when Eleanor was in Pennsylvania for her Doman-Delacato training, she reached out to Bobbie: they were ready to begin the family planning program in earnest.

"I can get you the IUDs," Bobbie said, "But you'll need a doctor to put them in."

The first doctors Eleanor approached turned her down. Contraceptives still weren't technically legal in Haiti; they were worried about overstepping their bounds and inviting unwelcome attention. But there was one doctor who gave resounding support to the idea: Dr. Lucy Paultre, Haiti's second woman doctor and the nation's first woman surgeon.

The fact that it should be a woman doctor who would help Eleanor is perhaps of little surprise—for she, more than any man, would understand what was at stake. Armed with a doctor willing to perform the procedure, Eleanor returned to Haiti with 100 IUDs in her handbag. Dr. Jean Claude Bernard, who has served at the Fermathe hospital for over 40 years, was fairly new at the time. But still, he trusted Eleanor and Dr. Paultre and, despite his devout Catholic faith, agreed to help found the program. His conscience, and that of many others, he argued, would be eased if the work could be regulated by several guidelines. Eleanor agreed and worked with Dr. Paultre and Dr. Bernard to draft the guidelines. From a modern perspective, the program's rules might seem overly strict, but when viewed within the cultural context and under the lens of the potential risks they were taking, one might also see them as prudent: To receive an IUD, women must be legally married and already have three living children, with the youngest child at least three years old. That way, no one could accuse the program of "promoting promiscuity" or of trying to "reduce the population of Haiti's black citizens."

The first women to join the program were the wives of the pastors already working with the mission. Wallace and Eleanor knew these men and women were community leaders, able to set an example. They also knew their needs personally and understood that the IUDs would relieve a tremendous burden.

"We could see the wives of pastors having all these children that were mouths to feed with no food to put in," Eleanor said. "Even so, other parents were turning to them for help feeding their children."

Eleanor would later dub this first phase of her program 'Double or Nothing.' Out of 100 women, 98 prevented pregnancy and two had twins!

Eleanor especially remembers the case of Pastor Stephen who went to her with his grievance. "I had a hard time getting my wife to come for this," Pastor Stephen said. "Finally, I told her that if she didn't come, she better not go home. So she came, and now she's pregnant."

Eleanor, of course, felt terribly awkward and also sorry that the IUD hadn't worked in a case when it had caused so much domestic stress. She explained that the IUD is only 98% effective, which means that two out of every 100 women can still get pregnant.

After a moment, Pastor Stephen responded, "Oh, I understand. It's like when you put a fence around your garden and a goat jumps over."

Eleanor delighted in the explanation and has used it ever since to help explain the effectiveness and limitations of the IUD.

The mission's family planning program would undergo much growth and formalization over the course of the next few years. When the Pan American Health Organization (PAHO) started a national family planning program in Haiti, Eleanor was able to use their resources and build off them.

The IUD continued to be favored by Wallace and Eleanor over the pill, in large part because a monthly medication would be nearly impossible for impoverished rural families to maintain: the cost of trips to the pharmacy alone was unfathomable, not to mention the cost of the pills themselves. An IUD by contrast could be inserted once and left for years, significantly reducing the burden to couples. By 1966, Eleanor had written a brochure for the national family planning program, and BHM was collaborating with Haiti's Protestant churches to further the project. The Protestant Committee of Literacy even incorporated family planning education into literacy booklets.

Mr. Benoît and His Wife (*Mésié Benoît ak Madanm Li*) is one such booklet. The booklet tells the story Mr. Benoît and his wife who, shortly after their first year of marriage, are beside themselves with joy to welcome their first child. "We're going to work for him. We will send him to school, and we will give him a good education," Mr. Benoít tells his wife. Three years later, three more children have been born, and Mme. Benoít is expecting a fifth. What was once joy has turned to despair. "I can't send them to school. The children need medicine. Where are we going to find clothes to dress the children?" Mr. Benoít laments. "The children need to eat," his wife reminds him. When Mme. Benoít complains to a neighbor, she's told about the family planning program and is encouraged to go visit the local doctor. The book ends with the Benoít family lined up and smiling, encouraging the readers to seek out an IUD from a clinic supporting family planning. The book also included an insert with a list of clinics providing IUDs.

Mr. Benoít and His Wife serves as more than propaganda for family planning. It shares in a most simplified way the centuries-long struggle of men and women who, with no way to prevent pregnancy, would end up with more children than they could adequately care for, perpetuating a cycle of poverty. The story also illustrates how in Haiti the referral of one woman to the next spread the news of the IUD, eased fears associated with it, and encouraged women to take control of their bodies—not just for their own well-being but also for the health and future of their children.

By mid 1966, Wallace was absolutely convinced that lack of family planning and soil erosion were two of Haiti's main contributors to widespread poverty. Many development experts would agree today that they still are, though significant progress has been made on both fronts.

If IUDs were part of the solution to the birth rate crisis, then terracing was part of the solution to erosion—and Wallace would tackle it with full force.

"Saving souls, he holds, is his primary function but not his only important one," Nancy Anderson wrote of Wallace in "The Modern Missionaries of Haiti," published in *Coronet*. "Saving bodies through saving the *soil* is also his energy-consuming responsibility."

• • •

The name Haiti means in Taino, "the land of mountains," an island pushed up from the seabed in a violent shifting of the earth. The pressure of the plates continues to this day and mountains rise, imperceptibly, year after year, a living, breathing topography. If one were to tell a legend about the mountains, one might tell how the earth and sea fought one day. In the struggle the earth was pushed up and out of the sea, forced apart from what had been her beloved home. To this day, the earth seeks a way back to her ocean bed, racing down the steep sides of the mountains, carving paths into the valleys, and rushing over everything in her path until she can finally seep back into the salty water.

Haiti's story of erosion and landslides is much more real than a legend—and much more deadly. The severe erosion has carried tons of rich topsoil into the ocean, wreaking havoc on marine life, and the landslides have claimed countless lives. In addition to the erosion and landslides, the mountain slopes themselves made for dangerous farm work. In fact, it wasn't unusual to have a farmer taken to the hospital with a broken arm, leg, or cracked skull. When asked what had happened, the doctor would be told, "He fell out of his garden."

The destruction of Haiti's mountains and waters are the result of environmental sin, Wallace argues—and Christians have been no less guilty of this. "Because Christians were continuing to sin against the ecology," Wallace writes in his notes from 1965, "we were going to train young men from every area in planting nourishing crops and in erosion control." Pastors would tell the churches to choose candidates for training.

These young men became known as *agronoms*, or agronomists. Planting trees and controlling erosion were ministry as much as praying with the sick, hosting a Bible study, or sharing the gospel with one's neighbors. After all, what are mountains and trees and dirt and water but elements of God's creation entrusted to men and women for stewardship?

The rural farmers had been hesitant to adopt Wallace's methods of agriculture. They had been farming in their way for generations, and in their minds, the dirt wasn't washing away. "No, Pastor," they would tell Wallace. "Can't you see the rocks are growing? They're having children and multiplying."

Despite their insistence, Wallace knew he had to do something to help the farmers improve their methods. "The people were dying of hunger," Wallace says, remembering the famine that had struck the area.

Inspiration came one day when Wallace was in Fort Jacques and saw a dry stacked wall. Asking who had built it, Wallace was told that a Belgian man named Mouton had taught the men Eloizi and Genera how to build it. Recruiting Eloizi and Genera, Wallace began his terracing program in earnest.

As a demonstration of the power of these miniature plateaus, Wallace first established several wide, beautiful terraces at the mission in Fermathe. He used them to grow fruit trees, vegetables, and flowers; he even constructed buildings on several of the largest terraces.

Using the Food for Work concept to broaden the program, Wallace searched out dry beans from Arlin Hunsberger, a friend from Goshen, Indiana, who was directing the Mennonite Central Committee mission and new hospital in Grande Riviere du Nord. With great admiration for their work ethic, commitment to scripture, and compassion for the Haitian people, Wallace and Eleanor would become good friends over the years with the Mennonite missionaries in general and with Arlin and his wife Naomie in particular. On a number of occasions, "Arlin was able to direct food from Mennonite farmers to us, to help our area's people who were starving from bad farm practices and hurricanes," Wallace writes in his notes. This occasion was no exception.

Seeds in hand, Wallace sent word out across the mountain. He told the people of each habitation to come to the church in Fermathe and, once gathered, he addressed them.

"You're all going to die like your neighbors if you don't listen to me," Wallace said in his usual frank way. "I'll show you how to get the maximum result from the plot God has given you." Wallace then took one member of each household knowing that the food received as payment would be enough to sustain the family.

Eloizi and Genera taught the people how to cut the foundation for the terrace, dig the rocks, and stack them to build a dry wall without cement. Next, they would layer in rubble behind and fill it in with the dirt. Terracing is incredibly effective against erosion and creates much safer spaces to farm than the steep slopes of the mountains—it didn't take long for the farmers to see that. But it's also hard work. A terrace isn't just built. It must be carved with hand tools from the mountain, set into the steep sides, and filled in with the dirt that's been moved, creating a level plateau. And it must be done again and again and again, all the way down the mountainside, for as much area as one wishes to claim.

Wallace also taught composting to the rural farmers and encouraged them to stop burning all their trash so they could rebuild the soil that had washed away. "Throw the debris into a hollow and let it decay, then add a handful to each hole for planting seeds," Wallace told them.

The crop yields of the farmers who chose to terrace and compost increased dramatically. They not only had enough food for their families, but they also had enough to sell. Within a few short years, the fertility of the soil, the deep beds formed by terracing, and the naturally cool weather turned the region into a nationally acclaimed center for vegetable production. For many, "Kenscoff vegetables" is as much a promise of quality as a description of origin.

The program for terracing met significant resistance in the beginning, but today the terraces in southern Haiti could no more be disentangled from the landscape than the ridges and valleys themselves. Layer by layer, garden by garden, the rolling patchwork greens and browns have been stitched together with seams of limestone, like quilting on a favorite blanket.

As a child surrounded by these miniature plateaus, I never thought of them as having been built; I never imagined the shovels of dirt, the stones held together by yet more stones, or the men laboring under the sun. They simply *were*—strong, unmoving, as much a part of the landscape as the mountains themselves.

Of course, the terraces hadn't always existed. They had been constructed, one shovelful at a time, stone upon stone, reshaping the mountain that had stood for millennia, forming a pact with her: they would hold in the rain and she would hold up the homes, the gardens, the churches and schools.

• • •

The terracing and composting methods had just started to gain ground when Hurricane Inez struck on September 29, 1966. With news that the hurricane was arriving, Eleanor sent runners to the surrounding mountain communities, urging residents to move themselves and their animals to a downwind shelter. Eleanor also oversaw the hurricane preparation at the mission, weighting down the roof and stocking up on water. The damage was less than that from Hurricane Flora, but still, "trees fell, banana and coffee crops were stripped, roofs flew," Wallace writes in his journal. "A messenger made his way up from the city by the road that had trees felled across it. He brought news that the government asked us to be responsible as in the last post-hurricane efforts for the same seven counties!" Once again, the mission would find itself at the center of relief efforts.

Granny, who was still actively working in the ministry, helped oversee the immediate sending of supplies and began writing to supporters asking for their help with hurricane relief. Hurricane Inez had claimed another 1,000 lives across Haiti and the Dominican Republic.

The relief dried up quickly as all the large agencies ran out of food to disperse to partners like BHM. In his notes from October, Wallace writes, "We were relieved that, a month after the hurricane, tomorrow we are to receive through Gerard Philippeaux, our friend the Minister of Health responsible for all relief, 500 pounds of bean seed and nine cases of vegetable seeds. Unfortunately, the hurricane hit at the normal time of planting." Without seeds for the farmers to replant, Wallace knew the immediate hunger following the hurricane could rapidly escalate to famine yet again.

What is remarkable about Wallace's leadership during the relief efforts isn't his ability to stay calm during the crisis or even his ingenuity in stretching limited resources, but rather his foresight. He had learned to look past the immediate need, to silence in his mind the pleading, and even to harden his heart against the temporary suffering in order to prevent even greater hardship in the future. He was sorry, of course, when food aid was insufficient during the crisis, but he was even more grateful for the seeds: one bean cooked wouldn't feed even an infant, but if allowed to grow, one bean could feed an entire family.

In his notes and conversations, Wallace doesn't talk about how he learned to think of the future while the world was washed away around him, and in some ways I'm not sure he's even made the connection—"it's sensible," he might say, or "it's wasteful to do otherwise," or perhaps even, "people need to keep their dignity." That which outsiders might see as remarkable is simply logical to Wallace, and it would remain that way from one crisis to the next, earning him the respect and admiration of rural farmers, government ministers, ambassadors, and even presidents.

• • •

In spite of the seeds given in the wake of Hurricane Inez, hunger did set in across much of Haiti. The relief provided had been a help, but it was insufficient: late rains in the following year made the hunger even worse. By the fall of 1967, severe hunger was spreading across the island. "This year, rains have been very late and very light. At our altitude, we've had a late season, but with night dews things haven't scorched off as in other areas," Wallace wrote in a letter to supporters, dated September 28, 1967. "Last week, we sent a bit of cash for seed for three especially hungry congregations who had eaten up their aging grain seed in desperation. Weevils and rats would have finished it off if they hadn't. The ordained moderator of the area will buy and distribute seed corn and millet. In a few months we trust it will give a bit of temporary relief."

In an effort to draw attention to the vast physical need, Wallace and Eleanor had put together a small brochure earlier in the year: "This is Easter in Haiti." The brochure paints a picture of dire need. "The night before Easter few homes will have the advantage of cheering rays from a single lamp to pierce the weird darkness. The dark, mysterious mountains rise all around, and only the monotonous beat of the drums and dancing rahrah bands are heard," the brochure says. For Wallace and Eleanor, the ultimate cause of Haiti's misery is clear: the absence of Christ. The poverty isn't a punishment of God, but rather a direct result of "inhuman wickedness." "They lie down haunted by life's most horrid harassments: hunger, disease, over-population, skimpy harvest, desperate poverty, and spiritual darkness," one sentence reads. In the minds of Wallace and Eleanor, spiritual darkness was as much a misery— or more— as hunger or disease, for the soul cannot live without God, and the body cannot live without a soul.

"On Easter day, 2,000 people will die. Typhoid and malaria fever, tuberculosis, and a starvation diet all contribute to this daily harvest. Little is done to stop it."

Wallace and Eleanor knew that this scene was indeed the daily life for millions—but not for everyone. Even in the midst of "life's most horrid harassments," as the brochure reads, Christians would awake on Easter morning. "From the highest mountains through the river plains… there are those who have heard of that empty tomb and join to sing the songs of victory." The transformation, Wallace and Eleanor would say time and again, wasn't from their work, but rather from "men and women scattered in little groups throughout Haiti… The life of the risen Lord in His people makes them as a city set on a hill."

• • •

While Wallace continued to fight the long fight against hunger with erosion control and improved farming practices, Eleanor developed a weapon of her own: Project Apron.

The project was born at the request of a group of parents and young women who wanted an alternative to the dangers that often plagued the young girls in the crowded city markets. The young women would go to the market to sell produce from the family garden or look for work as a helper to one of the wealthier merchants, but too often they would fall prey to sexual exploitation. "It is often necessary for the mountain girls to spend days and weeks in unbelievable filth and immorality of the crowded city market, sleeping on sidewalks and battling with small benefits to earn a penny's profit," a brochure for the project reads. "Christian parents often come to the mission brokenhearted when their daughters return home from weeks of 'commerce'... having fallen victim to some man's offer of rice, beans or a headkerchief."

Eleanor began to work with a small group of women, teaching them to sew and embroider. They would make aprons, which Eleanor and Granny would buy from them to sell to visitors. The project was a hit. "Eleanor just figured out that last month one young lady named Jacqueline made $9 clear profit making aprons, three quarters of the annual cash income of the ordinary mountain breadwinner," Wallace writes. In 1967, $9 was no large sum of money, but for a woman to make in one month three quarters of the household's typical annual income was unheard of. Project Apron was more than needle pulling thread to make souvenirs for tourists—it was a subversive act of empowerment, making women the key providers for their families.

Decades later, research would back what Eleanor had stumbled upon: in international development, dollar for dollar, the best investment is made in women. "Investing in women is recognized not only as the right thing to do but also the smart thing to do," reads a 2016 article from the website of the International Center for Research on Women. "Mounting evidence demonstrates that increases in women's income lead to improvements in children's health, nutrition and education."

Eleanor may have started Project Apron, but it received a huge push from May Raynolds. May was in Haiti with her husband Dave who was serving at the US Consulate. Eleanor soon learned that May and Dave "were different—their values and goals were more missionary than that of the U.S. State Department," as she writes in her book *Those Who Passed By*. When May visited Eleanor one day, her presence in and of itself wasn't remarkable—Wallace and Eleanor were daily receiving visitors of all levels of prominence, from the most impoverished young man seeking work to the wives of Haiti's most elite businessmen to State Department dignitaries like Dave and May. What was special about May's visit was her contagious zeal for Project Apron.

"I showed her from my wooden trunk a few simple aprons and coarse cotton tea napkins made by some mountain women we were helping to begin the self-help project," Eleanor writes. "The items were obviously the work of beginners, but May showed a genuine interest in the project and appreciated them. She purchased several… she wanted to help."

May would eagerly bring other women and visitors to Wallace and Eleanor's living room, where Eleanor would pull out the aprons, tea napkins, and other simple items. Whenever she came by, the women in the project quickly learned they would make enough money that day to buy their basic supplies: a bit of food, maybe an item of clothing, some oil for cooking.

As the years passed, Project Apron grew into a larger, broader scoped Self Help Project with approximately 1,400 artisans contributing.

Tying in to the same philosophy that propelled Wallace to create the Food for Work program, the Self Help Project was Wallace and Eleanor's bold answer to abject poverty. Long-term charity isn't just inefficient, but in many ways it's cruel, trapping the supposed beneficiaries in an ugly cycle: all available resources are used to provide the charity, so little to nothing is left over to address the root cause of the poverty. With the institutional and social obstacles still in place, men and women find themselves unable to meet even their most basic needs, and so they must accept the charity, which uses all the resources.

Wallace and Eleanor believed that if their neighbors could not only learn a trade or craft but also have a place to sell their wares, then they would have an honest chance at providing for themselves and their children. May again proved instrumental, taking on the role of voluntary creative director, helping to identify which embroidery designs would sell better and what additional crafts could be added. She also aided in establishing a quality control of sorts, ensuring that the products purchased would indeed be able to sell and generate income to purchase even more crafts.

Eleanor began saving all profits from Project Apron in a fund designated to construct a storefront on the now busy road to Kenscoff for the Mountain Maid Self Help Project. Through the help of Dave and May Raynolds, the mission received a substantial USAID grant to construct the building. That, along with a generous personal check from the Raynolds and the money Eleanor had saved from the sales of aprons and napkins, was enough for the building to be completed.

The architect for the project was Albert Mangonez, who sculpted Haiti's iconic *Nèg Maron* statue. He played on the setting and the name, creating a cement roof made from three peaks that mirror the mountains around them. The peaks also help to funnel water into the cistern, which is essential since all water used at the mission has to be collected during the rainy season. While there was considerable help from the architect and other building professionals, Wallace himself oversaw the finishing touches of construction, using his team of masons who had by this point helped to build dozens of churches and schools.

The Mountain Maid outlet was built on a terrace. As part of the store, Wallace built a large fireplace with stones of different shapes and colors that he had collected from across the country. The fireplace would chase away the damp cold that often settles over the mountains, inviting people to sit in warmth and conversation. Once the outlet opened, Granny and Eleanor began serving lemongrass tea and sandwiches one day a week to the shoppers who had taken a 4:00 a.m. plane from the U.S. Naval base in Guantanamo, Cuba for a little rest and relaxation in Haiti. The ritual was an extension of when they would serve tea to those who came to Eleanor's living room to shop from the wooden trunk. Eventually, Wally would add a Tea Terrace to the store, creating a covered, open air, dining area that's cantilevered out from the building and sits suspended, as if floating across the valley.

Shortly after the Mountain Maid outlet was completed, Wally, who had by this time graduated college, married, and received his Masters of Fine Arts in Photography, returned to Haiti to help at Mountain Maid for "a couple of years." Wally and his wife Betty arrived in Haiti in 1972, and they would stay not for 2 or 3 years as they originally intended, but for 30 years, raising my two brothers and me.

Mountain Maid became a second home to all of us. As children, my brothers and I would play hide and seek in the dusty storage depots, count inventory, help on the sales floor, and generally get underfoot, but nobody complained. We were, in some ways, the children of all who worked at Mountain Maid. And when we'd do something we knew wasn't allowed, we might be scolded by one of the employees, but more often than not, they'd smile, wink, and send us on our way.

The Mountain Maid Self Help Project would use the model of cottage industry, allowing men and women to produce their crafts at home, minimizing costly transportation and allowing women without childcare options to participate, earning vital income for their families. With the income earned from the sales of their crafts, families weren't just able to meet their basic needs; they were also able to send their children to school, buy medicine when needed, and even save to build stronger homes. More than 1,500 families, or about 6,000 men, women, and children, benefitted from the Self Help Project at its peak. All told, Eleanor's wooden trunk Apron Project eventually went on to help tens of thousands of artisans, each of whom chose to learn a craft, buy materials, travel miles over winding mountain trails to sell their items, and then turn around to do it all over again, week after week. Wallace and Eleanor and then Wally and Betty provided the infrastructure that had been lacking to support local artisans, but it was the men and women of the Kenscoff mountains who chose to do the hard work, to offer a future of possibility to their children.

Women like Lucienne. As a patient in the tuberculosis clinic, Lucienne was facing a fragile existence. Her condition meant that she could no longer carry heavy loads. Going to market, the main source of income for a rural woman, was no longer a possibility. She also needed ongoing medication to stay healthy, and even with the hospital supplementing the cost, it was expensive. Wallace and Eleanor recognized that if Lucienne was to become more than a statistic, she would need to find a new way to make a living.

Eleanor took Lucienne under her wing and helped her learn how to make tiny "popcorn flowers" out of scraps of cloth. These flowers were then stitched together in rows and columns. At the very end, Lucienne would add a lining to back what had become a beautiful children's quilt. "She made a decent living with that," Betty recalls. Lucienne was eventually able to cover her own medical expenses and even tithe to the church. But most importantly to Lucienne, with a few stitches of thread and scraps of fabric, she had gone from being a charge to being a contributor, productive and healthy, no longer defined by her condition.

Giving and contributing would be important also to Dieudonne—whose name means "God gives." She was the only daughter of Victor Felix, one of the early Christians and evangelists in the Fermathe church. She grew up in a simple house of two rooms along a winding mountain foot trail; she was better off than most in that regard. And she had a loving father who married her mother—a rare occurrence at the time, for rural men had often prided themselves on how many families they could maintain, never marrying but rather "keeping" the women and children with no legal obligation. Victor, having given his life to Christ, wanted more. He wanted a home and family with deep roots, with commitment.

Victor saw to it that his daughter learned at least the very basic skills of reading and writing. Though her nuclear family was unusually small for the time, her extended family was "ever enlarging," Eleanor recalls. They would crowd together in the home for bits of food, attention, camaraderie. She grew up poor but loved. Singing was one of her greatest joys, and she and her mother would lift their voices together, singing out the words of local Christian songs. "Learn something you can teach the many others of the family," Dieudonne's mother told her.

When Dieudonne had the opportunity to learn embroidery, she jumped at the chance. And, as it turned out, she was quite good at it. She went on to teach nearly a dozen other women plus cousins and neighbors to pull threads, hem stitch, decipher the different shapes in the designs of leaves, flowers, petals.

Together, when fatigue would begin to set in, they might sit, pulling needle and thread, singing out the songs from a beloved hymn to renew their spirits.

Mwen te vi-n jwin
Jézi byen fatigè
Jézi ban mwen repo
I came to Jesus
So very tired
Jesus gave me rest

Dieudonne eventually married and had four children of her own—each of whom she put through school with the money she earned from her craft. Dieudonne. God gives. She gave back.

Decades later, Marie Francoise, a mother and widow, would join the Mountain Maid family. Known to all as Mme. Jeanty, she appeared at my home one day. Her husband, Jeanty, had been a volunteer *agronom*, working with my father Wally in the reforestation project. Her husband had died unexpectedly, and his loss was felt throughout the community. Mme. Jeanty was left with two young daughters to care for and no income. She turned to Wally and Betty for help. She didn't want charity; she needed a job.

My parents employed her to sweep, something Wally undoubtedly learned from his father. At any given moment, up to a dozen sweepers could be found on the mission grounds and at our home. It was a job easily invented out of thin air, a skill every mountain person learned in childhood. If Mme. Jeanty suspected the ruse, she never said. She showed up on the appointed day and the days that followed. She swept.

Around the same time, handmade soaps were becoming very popular in the US, and Wally and Betty saw an opportunity to add a new item to the Mountain Maid outlet. They taught the craft to Mme. Jeanty, who had shown herself to be a faithful, hardworking woman of integrity. She began working at Mountain Maid making glycerin soaps with essential oils. Earning more than enough to support herself and her children, Mme. Jeanty put her girls through school. They eventually graduated with high school diplomas—a feat accomplished by only about 20% of Haiti's youth.

When Eleanor folded the first aprons into her wooden trunk, when Wallace helped lay the first stones for Mountain Maid, they couldn't possibly have imagined the impact it would have. But for women like Lucienne, Dieudonne, and Mme. Jeanty, Mountain Maid was the difference between a life of need and one of enough.

• • •

Encouraged by the early success of Mountain Maid and the agriculture projects, Wallace and Eleanor wanted to do more for the Self Help Project. By the mid-1970s, Wallace had built the vocational school, a large multi-story building on the far side of the Fermathe property. The vocational school was built in layers carved into the mountainside, with its own well for water and a separate shed for the mechanics training.

The heavy equipment for the automotive, metalworking, electrical, and woodworking programs was generously donated by Lowell Yoder, a friend to Wallace and Eleanor. Acquiring the equipment had been Wallace's first challenge, but moving it into the building would be the greater of the feats. The first floor of the building was a ledge dug into the rock. It was the only floor with the structural strength to hold the weight of the equipment. "Using a heister, which was slowly driven up the mountain instead of being brought on a truck, we lifted the equipment into the building and used pipes on the floor to roll pieces to the end," Wallace remembers. "They'll be there 'til doomsday because they weigh a ton apiece."

With several programs sharing the first floor for the major equipment, Wallace and Eleanor took the second floor for classrooms and additional workshops.

Wallace and Eleanor both believed that charity was an ineffective bandage approach to the hemorrhaging wound of poverty. The incredibly limited resources available to them must be leveraged to teach so that people could do for themselves. "We want to put ourselves out of business," Wallace and Eleanor would often joke with visitors. But for my grandparents, it is no laughing matter—it is their calling.

Named the Hope Center, the vocational school would teach area residents to learn a trade since options for secondary school, called *college* in Haiti, were even more limited than employment opportunities. The center gave certificates for trades such as electrical, plumbing, woodworking, mechanics, baking, and sewing.

Wallace helped found and build the Hope Center, but eventually its direction would be turned over to his son Sandy, who had returned to serve in Haiti with his wife, Mary. Sandy became the director of the mission's now expansive education ministry, and Mary ran the rapidly growing child sponsorship program.

The late 1960s and early 1970s had been a time of explosive growth for the mission, but as the mission grew up, so, too, did Wallace and Eleanor's sons. Wally, Sandy, and David would each leave home and go to college: Wally on a full scholarship to Rockford College in Illinois, Sandy to Asbury College in Kentucky, and David to Liberty Baptist College in Virginia.

I can imagine the sadness in the parting, the distance even greater then than it is now, for there was no instant communication—no text messaging, no video sessions, not even a telephone call except for the rare occasion, and even then the call would be punctuated by the clicks and static of a bad line, passing a hurried message from a long-distance phone booth in Port-au-Prince as the minutes—and the cost—ticked up. Letters, written in long, scrawling script or punched out character by character on a typewriter would fill the absence of the boys' chatter at the dinner table; advice in longhand, admonishing the boys to "be good," to "study hard," to "mind their manners," to "keep Christ first," would be a poor substitute for the daily presence and contact, however thin that might have been during the hectic days of ministry. It is no secret that my grandparents were never ones to coddle their children, to kiss the boo-boos, or to wrap their boys in a hug so tight it would take the breath out of them. But I do not doubt for a moment that Wallace and Eleanor have always loved each of their children deeply and fiercely, in their own way. And so I can imagine the void that was felt when the sons went off to find their way, and the great joy that would accompany their homecoming. There would also be relief, for Wallace and Eleanor needed help: they needed leaders to move the ministries ahead, to train new leaders, to put in place a system that would carry on long after they were gone.

Even with their sons and daughters-in-law managing the burgeoning, nationwide ministries, Wallace and Eleanor both stayed heavily involved in all aspects of the mission work: Wallace with his hands-on, get-it-done builder's approach, and Eleanor with her detailed attention to programming and people, having developed an extraordinary understanding of her neighbors and the skills needed to train them in trades that would provide sound livelihoods.

By the time the vocational school was underway, Wallace and Eleanor and the family had earned an international reputation for their Self Help program, so much so that they once received a letter addressed to "Mission Help Yourself," a moniker that has been the source of endless delight at dinner parties.

TWELVE
The Miraculous and the Mundane

BY THE 1970'S, THE MISSION WORK was firmly established and well-respected across the nation. Wallace found himself director of more than 50 employees, which included drivers, carpenters, and welders, not to mention his additional responsibilities of forming ASEBACH—the Association of Conservative Baptist Churches of Haiti—which by then had more than 200 member churches. Simply managing the projects would have been daunting, but Wallace and Eleanor both had to juggle endless visitors from places such as the US, Canada, Europe, and even Israel, not to mention their friends and contacts from around the country.

So Wallace wasn't surprised when one morning in 1970, a man knocked on his office door and introduced himself as Leandre Page, a professor from the University of Montreal. "He said that he had asked people in Port-au-Prince for advice and they had told him to come to me," Wallace writes in his notes.

Leandre had rented a house across the road from the mission entrance and came to Wallace because he had theological questions to ask him. "I was stunned," Wallace writes, "and replied that I am not a theologian, but just a simple Christian. I said I'd answer what I thought, and I'd lend him any of my books pertaining to his questions."

Leandre went on to explain that he had come to Haiti with his wife and two little children. Immediately, Wallace's thoughts went to the wellbeing of Leandre and his family. "I knew that the house he had rented with several dark bedroom chambers of concrete was hidden among a grove of big trees," he recalls. "I told him I feared for the health of his children in the winter damp, so I lent him two electric heaters. In those day we had fairly regular electric current."

With the formalities out of the way and Wallace already extending a hand of hospitality, Leandre proceeded to ask his first question. In that moment, Wallace had no idea of what would follow, but today he recognizes, "This man is one of the biggest miracles of my life."

Leandre explained to Wallace that he had been "reared as a Huguenot in France, but that he had been shocked by experiences in a Nazi concentration camp and had not opened a Bible in twenty years. He asked why a God of love would permit such horrors," Wallace tells. "I replied again that I'm not a theologian but I'd say it's because He is a God of love. He does not force anyone to make decisions, and those men made bad ones. He agreed."

Leandre's visits with Wallace extended over the course of six months, covering a total of fourteen theological questions. "I regret that I made no written record of our conversations, and I remember no more answers," Wallace writes. But what Wallace has never been able to forget is what followed.

"Toward the end of our contacts, on Sunday, February 14, 1971, Leandre appeared again," and this time it was Wallace who had a request for him. "I told him that I had a problem. E. Stanley Jones, a very famous missionary to India, 92 years old, had spoken that morning in the Methodist church of Port-au-Prince. He was to speak in the evening service of the Baptist Church... We were also invited to a reception that afternoon in Pétionville for the new president of Goshen College and his wife. But, the elderly doctor and his wife who directed our hospital also wanted to hear Dr. Jones, and they would feel out of place in the Pétionville reception, speaking no English." Wallace hoped that Leandre would accompany the doctor and his wife to hear Dr. Jones, freeing Wallace and Eleanor to attend the reception and join their friends later at the church. Leandre, by now a close friend to Wallace, was happy to oblige.

Dr. Jones preached, with Pastor Reuben Marc interpreting in French. "He said, 'Jesus is God's Yes to all of man's questions,' repeating it after each of the fourteen questions Page had asked me and giving the exact same replies that I had given over the preceding six months. Both Page and I were stunned." At the closing of the service, Page went forward with tears streaming down his face, taking Jones' hand and saying, "Oui!" Then, he took Wallace's hand, winked, and exclaimed the same. "Oui!"

Soon, Leandre returned the borrowed heaters and said goodbye, writing only one brief letter from New Orleans.

"After he left, our neighbor Andre St. Lot asked me if I knew who my friend Page was," Wallace recalls. "I said only that he was a Frenchman, a professor from the University of Montreal. Andre proceeded to say that Page was a genius dying of cancer.

He had during his stay in Haiti been the mysterious 'Professeur X' who answered any question posed to him by a student, eight hours a day on a phone-in radio program."

"I have seen many miracles," Wallace reflects, "but this is the most intricate, intimate, and humbling that God has put together to show me His hand in our lives."

• • •

In the days preceding and following Leandre's friendship, Wallace's days were varied from administrative tasks—which he has never cared for—to intervening for friends and fellow missionaries, to organizing the latest lumber shipment in the storage depot. No task has ever been too menial for Wallace, whose attention to detail has been called maddening by more than a few. Neither has a task seemed too great to tackle, for if God has called one to serve, God will equip, Wallace believes.

"We rejoiced at many saved, baptized, or married, but we must pray much for leaders who are as human as all, that they'll not fall," Wallace wrote on February 24, 1970. A few days later his rejoicing would have to give way, temporarily at least, to battling an antiquated French law. The law mandated that people who suffered the loss of home and possessions in a fire must be held in prison five days for the shock to pass, so they'd not commit suicide. A Christian couple, Mr. and Mrs. Augustin Louissaint and their five children from Boucan across the valley, had traveled to ask Wallace for his help after a fire claimed their home. "The local policeman had asked five dollars fine, a fortune to cashless peasants," Wallace writes in his notes. "I wrote to Major Leveille in Petionville, area police chief, asking a dispensation for the couple. I asked that the couple who worked for us be allowed to live with us until we could help them to rebuild, and that as they were broke, they be freed from menace."

Not long after the incident with the Louissaints, Wallace found himself intervening on behalf of Reverend Robert Steinhauer from the West Indies Mission. One of the mission's principals, Anthonio Louis-Jean, had been kidnapped in retribution for reporting one of his fellow teachers as corrupt to the Department of Education. "I wrote letters sent to Papa Doc, Col. Fred Arty, and others, asking for help," Wallace writes on April 8.

But of all the projects that have claimed Wallace's attention, none has been dearer to his heart than training the next generation of preachers and leaders. The Summer Bible Institute, which Wallace founded near the very beginning of his ministry, has always been a source of great joy, albeit tremendous work. During the six weeks of the program, as many as 200 young active church leaders, including some from other missions, would join in lessons and conversations about a world many had only imagined. Even into his nineties, Wallace would continue teaching at the Summer Bible Institute, finding immense pleasure in his lessons on geography and astronomy. "God's creation is marvelous," Wallace has said. "And the students are awed by all He has made."

The Summer Bible Institute was one of the first programs Wallace and Eleanor implemented after their marriage. Eleanor, in fact, was the one who gave most of the classes in the very beginning. But as the program grew, Wallace's involvement increased, eventually making it one of his favorite parts of the ministry. Both men and women were invited to the Summer Bible Institute, and more than a few marriages sprung out of the weeks-long program. With over 60 years of summers, the classes have been handed down from one generation to another.

"We taught, and our students won souls and created churches. They taught disciples who created more churches, and so it continues," Wallace wrote years after he had stopped teaching regularly. "One day when I said I wished that I could help teach, a pastor said, 'Don't worry, Pasteur Wallace; we're doing what you taught us.' It was a great consolation, but I'd still enjoy teaching the young folks."

As the students' level of education increased, Wallace worked with the STEP seminary in Port-au-Prince and *Seminaire Theologique Baptiste d'Haiti* (Haitian Baptist Theological Seminary) in Limbe to enroll them for more formal education and training as pastors. In 1993, the seminary in Limbe became a full-fledged Christian university under the name *Universite Chretienne du Nord d'Haiti*, allowing students to earn a college degree at a fraction of the cost of the universities in Port-au-Prince.

The greatest teaching moments, however, wouldn't come in the classroom with chalk dust and theology papers but rather in the quiet moments of his office. Wallace's daily notes are filled with bits of news from visiting pastors. "Pastor Lange brought a good report of his young people; Pastor Senat told of various places doing well, and Kenscoff had no end of sorcerers and big servants of demons delivered," Wallace wrote on April 13, 1970.

On a given day, pastors from any of Haiti's departments would settle into one of Wallace's large leather chairs by his desk and lean in as he spoke with them. They would share the triumphs of their children, the hardships of their marriages, the joyful stories of the newly converted. They would pray together, asking for God's continued guidance. The pastors were more than Wallace's greatest ministry: they were his friends; his brothers in Christ; and on more than one occasion, his counselors. Pastor Lange from Port-de-Paix was one of Wallace's long-time traveling partners. He and Wallace would travel together for a week at a time to visit rural churches in the area surrounding Port-de-Paix. By Jeep, by horse, and on foot, they would make inroads to the nascent churches, building them up through teaching and encouragement. Wallace speaks admiringly of Lange as "a faithful fellow" to his friends and, more importantly, to Christ.

Perhaps one of the sources of their bonds was that neither Wallace nor Lange was particularly well suited on paper for the job at hand. Wallace, who came from a deeply flawed, unstable, and abusive home, was not by earthly standards to be expected to dedicate his life to compassionate service. For his part, Lange had a speech impediment that made him stutter, which, one might argue, isn't an asset for a teacher and preacher. And yet, Lange did teach, helping the fledgling churches to grow into strong, stable congregations. Like Wallace's wife, Lange's wife, known by all as "Mme. Lange" or sometimes "Mme. Pasteur," left her mark on the community by caring for the sick who couldn't pay for the hospital in Port-de-Paix. "When she died," Wallace told me, "hundreds showed at her funeral to honor her memory and give thanks for the care she had shown them," and, no doubt, to offer their support to Lange, who was, above all things, faithful in word and deed. I can't help but wonder if Lange was so effective not in spite of his impediment, but because of it, for surely it must have taught him perseverance, courage, and compassion.

As Wallace would point out time and again, Pastors like Lange were men of God, yes, but they were also human.

Wallace's fervent prayer was that God would keep the men from temptation, that they might bear witness to the light of the gospel. While the vast majority of the ASEBACH pastors have been good and honest ministers throughout the mission's history, there have been a handful of "scoundrels," as Wallace calls them.

Handling a crooked pastor takes more than a little finesse, for if handled poorly, the scandal could cause far more damage than the pastor's corruption. In one example a pastor in Gonaives was funneling ministry funds to build his own home. A sum of $2,000 US had been sent to make a cistern to collect the rainwater from the church roof. When Wallace took a visitor—who happened to be a police investigator from the donor church—to see the country church with its new cistern, he was dismayed to find only a small water tank with a new, beautiful parsonage nearby. That same pastor also claimed to have a school with the church and sought support for the school, but he would never present the attendance records, which was commonly accepted as the proof of enrollment, and to this day, Wallace doubts there ever was a school. Wallace recognized early on that the pastor would need to be stopped, for if he wasn't, he could ruin the gospel witness in the community for years to come. But without hard evidence, it would be impossible to fire the pastor or bring criminal charges. So instead, Wallace presented the case to the leaders of ASEBACH, the association of Baptist pastors. Soon after, they announced the pastor's retirement and eventually named a new pastor for the church, who, Wallace says, is to this day "the most competent pastor we have in Haiti."

• • •

Wallace and Eleanor were by this time entering the public eye, taking on a bit of a celebrity status in the missionary world, a status that would continue to grow throughout their lives. With Haiti's proximity to the US, the country has often been in and out of American headlines.

As one of the early missionaries to begin both religious and social work across the island, Wallace became a natural source of information for reporters. Journalists from each of the major US television networks have visited him or sought him as a source at one time or another.

Wallace would become known for treating all people—no matter how famous—as ordinary human beings. Wallace and Eleanor were often invited to diplomatic affairs, a circle not always open to missionaries, but one they happily entered, for they knew that powerful people when put to the right task could make a powerful difference—and, Wallace might add when he's feeling especially wry, if peasants need the Gospel, diplomats need a double dose. While the majority of their invitations were to US Embassy events, in 1973, Wallace and Eleanor were invited to the Liberian Embassy at a reception in honor of The President of Liberia, William R. Tolbert, Jr.—once a Baptist pastor himself and the first African to serve as president of the Baptist World Alliance. President Tolbert had traveled to Haiti with his wife Victoria on a state visit. Wallace was to be the representative for Haiti's Baptist churches, offering a welcome and a prayer for the visiting president.

But perhaps no embassy event was more colorful than one in the summer of 1996 when US Ambassador William Lacy Swing held a Fourth of July celebration at his home. In honor of the Summer Olympics in Atlanta, he asked that all guests come dressed as an Olympian. Costume parties are rare in Haiti, as dressing in costume is often associated with Vodou and is simply not done in the upper circles of society. But Wallace was all too happy to oblige. I remember this event well, for it was my first embassy party. Perhaps I was finally old enough to leave the children's table, or perhaps the costumes made my grandparents believe they could break with formality and bring one of their grandchildren—I don't really know—but that night, we went to the Ambassador's home. The house was glowing as the sun set over the perfectly manicured lawn. Hors d'ouevres were served by suited waiters to the guests in the garden. It was as if we had walked onto a movie set. There were the women in gowns, the men in suits (remember, many of Haiti's elites simply don't do costumes—not even for the Ambassador), and the Americans dressed as athletes. Most wore tracksuits. I don't remember what I wore, but it was likely a horseback-riding outfit, as my childhood dream was to be an Olympic equestrian, perhaps because that was the only sport for which I ever showed any promise. Likewise, I don't remember what my grandmother wore. I doubt anybody else remembers either. But I imagine that nobody in attendance that evening has forgotten what Wallace Turnbull wore.

Sliding behind a bush, he removed his shirt and pants to reveal a 1930s swimsuit that reached from his shoulders to the top of his knees. His white legs practically glowed in the twilight, anchored by his black socks and black shoes. Once in proper uniform, Wallace joined the receiving line, greeted the Ambassador, and shook the hand of Prime Minister Marc Bazin. As my grandfather turned, Ambassador Swing noticed the number 1925 pinned on the back of the swimsuit and asked what it meant. Wallace responded nonchalantly, "Why, that's the year I started swimming in the amniotic fluid."

While Wallace might have been the star of the 1996 Summer Olympics party, Eleanor is the most infamous of the couple when it comes to adding a dose of color to formal social engagements. One of the boldest of her exchanges came when Eleanor and Wallace were invited to attend the 1980 marriage of President Jean Claude Duvalier and Michele Bennet. This was not the type of invitation one could turn down, nor would they have wanted to give up the opportunity to share with—and witness to—the most elite members of Haiti's social and political realms. The lavish $2 million ceremony, broadcast on national television, took place in the Cathedral of Our Lady of Assumption in Port-au-Prince, which was later destroyed in the 2010 earthquake.

Michele was described by one of the news anchors as splendid and radiant; her Parisian couture headpiece resembled a halo from a Catholic icon, symbolism that was unlikely to be lost on the woman who would prove herself to be the most calculating and dangerous of Haiti's first ladies.

After the ceremony, the guests filed one by one past the bride and groom, undoubtedly repeating the expected and welcomed congratulatory remarks. We can only wonder if Eleanor's words were equally welcomed. Approaching the couple, Eleanor grasped Michele's hand and shook her finger in the first lady's face, imploring, "I know you have a good church upbringing, and you must be a good woman now. You are the first lady. You must be a good woman and help this country."

"She probably remembers that to this day," Wallace laughs, recounting the incident.

• • •

While speaking with the press, shaking hands with diplomats, and playing tour guide for visitors were important ways to spread the word about the ministry—and, just as importantly, to raise money for the work—Wallace and Eleanor's primary focus remained on the projects themselves.

By the 1970s, erosion in Haiti had reached critical levels. Drought, landslides, and decreasing yields were wreaking havoc on already poor farmers. Wallace was determined to move ahead with expanding the agricultural ministry, and he turned to his son Wally for help. Under Wally's leadership, the agricultural ministry would be wrapped under the larger "self-help" umbrella of Mountain Maid and expand beyond terracing to encompass a substantial greenhouse project that grew ornamental plants and specialty vegetables. These would serve to introduce new crops to the mountains for small scale, sustainable farming. The sale of the plants and vegetables was also a way to raise money for reforestation seedlings. At its peak, the reforestation project sent more than half a million seedlings twice a year across the mountains for planting.

• • •

In a seemingly constant cycle of drought, famine, and brief reprieve, I often wonder if Wallace and Eleanor didn't stumble into the temptation to find their work futile. How could they make a dent when even the forces of nature seemed to be against them? Their ultimate goal was eternal, yes, but surely the present must have weighed heavily on their backs.

In 1977, famine had once again hit—this time it was claiming lives in Atrel, one of the earliest and most beloved congregations they had helped to disciple. In Atrel, as in nearby Porier, Wallace helped build the church with his own hands and then watched as new believers stood at the front of the dimly lit church and sang hymns of praise. It was in Atrel that for the first time every family in the village had turned to Christ, so I can only imagine the hope Wallace must have felt when a young man appeared at his home and introduced himself as Doug Achilles.

"Thinking of Doug brings a comfortable warmth," Wallace writes. "He was a gentle, caring brother who might get impatient and frustrated like any of us, but he held no bitterness."

Doug had been sent by none other than Jerry Falwell to "find counsel for involvement in church development," Wallace remembers. Through the budding partnership with Jerry Falwell, Wallace and Eleanor received help for a number of projects, but the greatest by far was for the congregation of Atrel.

"A third year of drought had killed sprouting crops in Northwest Haiti. People died of starvation before we could find help," Wallace mourns. "I remember giving a happy little naked boy a five-gallon can of crackers and the people's assurance that he could carry it home. The next trip, he had been buried, starved."

Falwell believed he could make a difference in the famine, so he sent Doug and two others to document the need as part of a fundraising effort. In the end, he offered over a million dollars to put toward Atrel.

"I told Jerry I wouldn't know what to do with a million dollars. So I asked him to send it in monthly installments instead, so that we could manage the funds better. He sent $10,000 a month," Wallace remembers.

Ninety-two people of the Atrel church died before the help arrived, buried in what has come to be known as Atrel's "Hunger Cemetery."

But the money from Jerry Falwell saved thousands of lives in the end. And the partnership would continue throughout Jerry Falwell's life with him financing a number of other projects.

Doug remained a close friend to Wallace and Eleanor until his death in 2003. And while the impetus for Doug's visits was always one of grave importance, it didn't stop Wallace from having a bit of fun with him.

"Coming home on an abandoned 'highway' at midnight, Doug and I were blinded by the lights of a vehicle tailing us," Wallace recalls. "If I slowed almost to a stop, the driver did, too, or if I sped up, he did, too. I asked Doug if he had a mirror in his suitcase. He did and dug it out." Wallace directed Doug to use the mirror to reflect the offending light back into the driver's eyes. The result, as Wallace put it in his own colorful way was, "the fastest disappearing *on-ahead* of another vehicle that I have ever seen. In the years to come we had hearty laughs over the incident."

"We have always loved Doug's family," Wallace says. "Our visits in Lynchburg with Doug found him bedridden but always the same gentle Christian as he slowly died, cancer killing his body but not his spirit. He lives on in his special family who mirror his person and his faith."

• • •

With the ministry continuing to expand, so, too, was the family. As the 1980s approached, Wallace had three beautiful grandchildren—his namesake Wallace Rutherford Turnbull III (Rhet) and Andrew Roy Turnbull, born to Wally and Betty, as well as Ariadne Marie Turnbull, born to Sandy and Mary. Life, for a brief moment, must have felt incredibly full and complete.

But three family deaths in as many years would threaten to upend it all.

THIRTEEN
The Death of a Son

WHEN A MAN LIVES past 90 years old, he will have seen more death than most of us care to. Wallace is no exception. What is exceptional, perhaps, is the way Wallace views death, especially the death of fellow Christians: for him death is a homecoming.

"We grieve," I've heard my grandfather say at any number of funerals, "not for them, but for ourselves." Upon hearing of the death of Pastor Edner Jeanty, a Haitian pastor with Crossworld and a close friend to the family, Wallace wrote to his son: "We regret to learn that your dad has preceded us to Glory, but we rejoice for him."

Wallace has also become famous within the family and tight circle of friends for his matter-of-fact approach to his own mortality. He regularly updates his funeral program, reminds us of the coffin stored in the rafters of Antoine's depot, and expresses his readiness to go "home" and visit once again with the many loved ones who have been made whole. To a friend who had been confined to a wheelchair by his old age and failing body, my grandfather, hunched over by his own deforming back pain, once said with a broad smile, "When we both get to heaven, I'll race you."

But in looking back at a time when death hit too close to home year after year, I wonder if Wallace was always so accepting about our inevitable end. He doesn't talk about those years except to say, "Those were hard years. We had about one death a year, you know."

One Sunday afternoon in 1978, Wallace and Eleanor awoke from a nap to find his father dead. Since the death of Wallace's mother so many years before, John had already buried two more wives—Rhoda at sea in 1953 and Carrie in Beirut in 1966. Now, it was Wallace's job to bury his father. John had been ailing for a while, which was why he'd moved to Haiti to spend his last year in the care of his son and daughter-in-law. His death at 88 years old may not have been tragic, and he may not have been the model father, but is one ever ready to say goodbye to someone who gave them life, who is half the cause of their existence?

Following a funeral service held in the packed Fermathe church, John was laid to rest in the family tomb—the first of the family to be buried there.

Barely a year later, in that same tomb, Eleanor would bury her mother, the woman who had become "Granny" to thousands across the island nation. Granny had been in the US on deputation when, at 90 years old, she became ill with pneumonia. When Granny was taken to the hospital in Fort Worth, Texas, Eleanor rushed to her side from Haiti. Granny drifted in and out of consciousness for almost two weeks. Eleanor was with her throughout, and Ross, her son, also spent several days with her. Granny succumbed to her illness in Fort

Worth on February 15, 1979, and was buried in the family tomb in Fermathe just a few days later.

As one might expect, Eleanor took her mother's death hard. Thousands of families shared the burden of grief, but sorrow is a bit like love—we can share it with endless people and never reduce our own portion. Only time and the grace of God provide any respite.

For Wallace and Eleanor that respite would be long in coming, for as one grief would begin to trickle away, another, greater sorrow loomed on the horizon.

• • •

When David earned his degree at Liberty Baptist College, he accomplished what nearly everyone had said would be impossible. The Doman-Delacato therapy, begun when he was entering adolescence, had him learning to crawl all over again. The simple acts of reading and writing had been tremendous breakthroughs for him; living in a dormitory across the ocean and far from home, attending classes, and studying on his own—all of these went beyond expectation.

A master diesel mechanic, David had always been adored for his happy help, especially by drivers stranded near the mission. Puzzled by sudden problems with their vehicles, they were grateful for David's jovial stops by the side of the road and expertise in getting them on their way.

David's kind heart, his ebullient love of Jesus, and his tremendous desire to share the gospel with others made him quick to love and to be loved. So, when David returned to Haiti to work alongside his parents, college degree in hand, one can barely imagine the gratitude and joy they must have felt.

Only four days after his return home, David went to the beach at Montrois with a family friend. David and a friend decided to go scuba diving and were separated. Assuming David had returned to shore, his friend also returned, only to discover that David was missing at sea. A thorough search up and down the coast began. In an airplane, Wallace directed searchers using the tide charts and Eleanor rode in a helicopter scanning the coast. David was found two days later on the seafloor at a depth of 115 feet, his arms crossed peacefully over his chest. The cause of death could never be declared with certainty, but David appeared to have had a heart attack.

"It is natural to bury one's parents," I once heard my grandmother say. "We are sad, and we grieve because we miss them, but it's the way the Lord intends. There is nothing natural in burying a child."

David's death was felt across the lives of all who knew him. Condolences poured in from across the country and overseas. But none was more touching than the taxi drivers who mourned the loss of "Coconut Tree," their nickname for their friend who, like a coconut, was stubborn and hard to crack, and who, like its tree, stood tall, gave generously, and bent into the hurricane of life, weathering the winds and storms.

Wallace and Eleanor were shaken by grief, and to this day the loss of their son weighs on their hearts. But even in sorrow, they looked to share the hope of an eternal life in Christ. At their son's funeral, Wallace spoke to the multitude who had gathered to grieve.

"He couldn't keep his voice steady at all times, but he spoke positively of David's death," Mary, Sandy's wife, wrote to the board of directors. "He explained how at a young age they took their brain-damaged child to a specialist. He told them to do the child a favor—'Don't push him, just put him away where he'll be cared for.' As you know, they didn't listen to this advice... When he arrived last week he was mature physically, emotionally, and spiritually. We don't know why God chose to take him at this point. Wallace went on to say that he had come to believe, through the years, that life is a school preparing us for eternity. Dave was ready to graduate!"

Wallace concluded his remarks at his son's funeral by thanking God for the gift of David, sharing a verse from James to describe his life: " But someone will say, 'You have faith; I have deeds.' Show me your faith without deeds, and I will show you my faith by my deeds."

The fact that Wallace had any presence of mind whatsoever during his son's funeral is made even more remarkable when one understands what he'd faced just hours earlier. On the morning of the funeral, when David was to be placed in the casket, Wallace discovered to his horror that his son would not fit. The casket was too small. That day in the fog of unbearable loss, Wallace had to have another coffin made so he could bury his youngest child.

Carrying the weight of this terrible cruelty, Wallace made a pledge to himself: he would be prepared. Shortly after burying David, Wallace had his measurements taken and his own coffin built, to spare his family the trouble in a time of sorrow. To this day, that coffin sits in the rafters of a storage depot, waiting alongside an assortment of coffins in a range of sizes, the tiniest being always the heaviest burdens to carry.

• • •

Faced with so much death and piercing heartache, it must have been impossible for Wallace to ignore his own mortality.

If his beloved son could be wrenched away just as he began to fully live into his potential, how much more could Wallace, with his aging joints and graying hair, be taken? And if he were to die, what would become of the thousands of men and women and boys and girls who, in one way or another, relied on him, even if they did not know of him?

These are the questions I imagine Wallace asked himself, though he's never told me in quite so many words. He had always been the doer, the builder, the problem solver. Wallace was the man who would swing a hammer to re-roof a church after the hurricane, the one who would drive the Jeep across the river, who would say the prayer by the graveside, who would carry the marriage license up the serpentine trail. Now prudence, coming in the form of his remaining sons, required that he take a longer view, that he lay down the hammer.

• • •

The idea that the children of a family business or ministry look to steer the organization in a direction of growth and expansion isn't new. Nor is the resistance of the parents that inevitably follows.

When Wally began pushing to implement ministry-wide policies and protocols, Wallace and Eleanor both resisted: Wallace because his formation of pastors would now require a less hands-on approach, and Eleanor because her intimate knowledge of individuals could be replaced by seemingly cold calculations. Of course, anyone who has ever met Wallace and Eleanor might laugh at their fears: no system would ever be strong enough to confine them.

Eventually, with Wally and Sandy forming a united front, and with the pain of mortality fresh in their memories, Wallace and Eleanor resigned themselves: They would move to a more formal approach in the ministry. The ensuing years were ones of putting in place systems that would last well beyond a lifetime. What had started as a family ministry was now solidifying its place as a national institution.

Even with the growing prominence and development of the mission, what Wallace remembers most from this time period are the building projects, in part because they speak to his nature.

"I believe being made in the image of God also means we are meant to be Creators," Wallace says. So, in spite of the evolving policies now guiding the work, Wallace stayed closely tied to building, overseeing the workshops at the mission. On any given morning, Wallace could be found walking his rounds: his signature straw hat shading his face, a small notebook in his shirt pocket listing his tasks, his whistle around his neck lest he need to summon the workmen. As he passed from one station to the next, he was met by reminders of all that was at stake: Here were children shrieking with laughter on school benches—benches cut on the table saw that even now screamed its labor across the yard. Here were the children's marks carved into the desks' varnish—varnish that had been painted by hand on the other side of the yard. And here was the blinding light of the welder's torch, both itself and a beacon—testifying to the shining light of the gospel in a rural mountain community.

Under Wallace's system, an entire school could be sent by truck in pieces to be assembled on site. The church that received the building would provide the blocks, the cement, stone, gravel, and the sand for the construction. Next, the team of builders from BHM would arrive. Carpenters would work to set up the pole barn structure and tie in the roof trusses. Members of the community could be found nearby mixing the cement and sand to secure the blocks masons used to build the walls. Often, this building might be the only strong structure in the area, serving as school, church, meeting center, and hurricane shelter. In the same space, couples would be married and their children would learn to read and write.

Wallace also continued to work closely with Haitian leaders in the Church, helping them to realize their plans for their communities and congregations. In some ways, to Wallace this wasn't all that different from laying blocks—it was just another form of building.

His desire to help Haitian community leaders execute their own plans and not those of a foreign mission board or international development agenda has been arguably been one of Wallace's greatest distinguishing traits. The pastors would discuss, make a list of requests, and Wallace would act. While this may in all honesty be an oversimplification, the premise is accurate. His practice of working closely with pastors and lay leaders to realize their plans has been undoubtedly empowering and was, indeed, remarkably progressive for the time. Nevertheless, even the best intentioned of men and women create faulty plans from time to time: a school lunch program might falter because a consistent supply chain hadn't yet been established or a housing project might be started without sufficient accountability on who should and shouldn't qualify for the home. Even so, Wallace argues that the learning curve, while steep, is one well worth climbing.

• • •

Wallace's vision was always, and remains, singular: To share the gospel. Sometimes that meant building a school; in other moments it meant training pastors. However, nearly any missionary will tell you the most critical opportunities to share the love of Christ come not through formal ministry but rather through moments of crisis, through being present in a time of need. So was the case one night in the mid 1980s when a night sky turned black by cloud cover and a road made slick by rain led to a terrible car accident.

The "Route Kenscoff"—Route 101—remains the only main road joining the 16 miles between Kenscoff and Port-au-Prince. The road, cut into a mountainside, offers travelers a limestone wall on one side and a steep drop to the valley below on the other. Seeing the edge of the road can be difficult on a good night and impossible on a bad one. And so it was on this particular night. The window of a Peugeot-station-wagon-turned-taxi had been broken out, rain was falling heavily, and any glimmer of starlight had been erased by the clouds. The driver, struggling to see the road, made a fatal miscalculation and went over the steepest edge of the mountainside near Fermathe.

When news traveled via emergency messenger to Wallace and Eleanor, Wallace set out to search for survivors and Eleanor to alert the doctor and hospital. By flashlight, Wallace wove his way down the trail and arrived at a scene of carnage. The car had flown through the air and was flattened when it hit the ground with tremendous force. Passengers and driver were scattered and killed on the way down. Among the passengers that evening were Edouard—a cabinetmaker and the choir director for the Fermathe church—and Prosper—a blacksmith and welder. The two had recently formed a partnership to produce furniture with wrought iron hardware.

News that Edouard might have been gravely injured in the car crash or even killed was a strong blow indeed to the family.

When Wallace located Edouard, who had been thrown from the car, he breathed a sigh of relief. But when Edouard told Wallace that Prosper had been in the car, too, Wallace's concern once again heightened. Prosper hadn't reported alive, and he couldn't be found among the dead. He was missing.

Noting that the flattened car was empty, Wallace took it as a glimmer of hope and began to search. When his flashlight went out, Wallace continued the search with the dim starlight that flickered through a break in the clouds. Standing at the creek bed in the valley, way off to the right of the accident, up a small slope, he saw a figure draped over a boulder. Making his way there, he found a man moaning. Wallace searched for a way to identify him as Prosper, but he looked nothing like the man he knew and Wallace concluded that it must be someone else.

Because of the severe swelling of the man's face, it was impossible for anyone to identify him, but Wallace knew that whoever he was, he wouldn't survive long without proper medical care. Removing his jacket and getting a companion to remove his as well, Wallace stuffed branches through the sleeves to create a short makeshift stretcher. Traveling downstream along the creek bed for hours, Wallace and others carried the man through the boulders and stones until they found a rough Jeep track that was more passable than the slippery, steep trail at the accident site.

Prosper had still not shown up among the bodies and was suspected to be among the dead who were so badly mangled they could not be identified. For two days his family and friends mourned his loss, chief among them the Turnbull family.

Prosper's father Guerisma was among the first and most faithful converts of the Fermathe area. And Prosper's older brother Dieufort was a stonemason who had helped build most of the buildings at the mission along with the surrounding schools.

Prosper himself was a close childhood friend of Wally's. The two had roamed the mountains together, seeking adventures at every turn. When Prosper and Edouard wanted to open their own workshop, Wally stepped forward to help them purchase the necessary equipment and crawled on his belly to run the wiring in the attic of the old building that was to be their shop.

When Prosper's parents went to claim his body from the morgue at the Port-au-Prince General Hospital, he could not be found. With only the smallest glimmer of hope, an orderly took them to look at the sole remaining unidentified victim who was lying in a coma. His face was still badly cut and swollen.

Using the one shoe that had come with him as her proof, Prosper's mother insisted it must be her son. She might have been grasping at loose grains of hope, but as the swelling receded in the ensuing days, she was proven correct. The unidentified survivor was indeed Prosper. The path ahead was long and difficult—Prosper remained unconscious for 6 weeks—but he eventually did recover and went on to live a full life as a faithful friend and loved one, continuing his work as a blacksmith for years to come.

Imagining the carnage of the wreck, some might see answering a gruesome accident as a burden or a trauma, but Wallace recognizes that on that night he received the gift of presence. The community took note and people talked about the accident long after the fact, telling others how they saw firsthand that this man known as Pasteur Wallace had worked and cared about someone close to them. "He carried them to safety," they would say. "He worked hard to save that man."

"It doesn't do the gospel any harm," Wallace says about the retelling. And that, for him, might be the greatest motivation of all.

FOURTEEN
"Without Hope"

WHEN INFLATION SKYROCKETED in the early 1980s, Haiti's most vulnerable citizens found themselves unable to pay for even their meager subsistence living standard. The cycle of hunger and abject poverty seemed to grow worse, and decades of political oppression added to the burden. Thousands of men and women felt they were suffocating: they needed out. Between them and the promised land of Florida lay a deep blue ocean, one they would attempt to cross on practically anything that would float.

While the "boat people" crisis gained increasing international attention, Wallace was quick to point out in a letter to Florida Governor Robert Graham, dated October 10, 1981, "The thousands of Haitians accepted legally each year who immigrate by plane have never raised anyone's questions." But his stance on "the scandal of the boat people" was harsh, arguing that the boat crisis was really being perpetuated by a "racket" of people looking to profit off the lives of "adventurers, seeking to be re-born rich," citing that American lawyers would make a profit of $1,000 per refugee they represented, and the "contraband ship owners" would also received $1,000 per refugee.

While Wallace's perspective that those fleeing Haiti in boats were "not even really economic refugees" is a great overgeneralization, his criticism of those profiting from the life-threatening and all too often deadly journey is well placed. And his disdain for the exodus of the "boat people," as they were dubbed, came as much from a place of concern about Haiti's welfare as a nation as it did about his fears for their safety.

"Last night," Wallace wrote to Governor Graham, "I read in our daily paper how schools here in Haiti are CLOSING because the teachers are not to be found. They are 'boat people.' We are constantly replacing teachers in our own mission schools. Haiti needs production in Haiti, not acceptance of the Haitian penchant for gambling."

The only way to stop the deadly flow of boat people, Wallace strongly believed, was for the United States to refuse them entry, to deny them the refugee status they sought.

Governor Graham must not have altogether disagreed with Wallace, for the governor asked Wallace to write to President Ronald Reagan. In his letter dated November 14, 1981, Wallace tells the President of his then 35 years of experience in Haiti and his "great love for the Haitian people." "But," he went on to write, "I am in accord with many people who feel that the illegal Haitian immigrants, the 'boat people,' are not refugees."

Wallace blamed, in great part, poor family planning and vast deforestation for the deep poverty that was leading to the crisis. As part of his argument to increase access to family planning and to widen reforestation efforts, Wallace wrote, "Our mission was the first group to organize a family planning program, and fewer 'boat people' are from our area, with its lower birth rate and greater per capita peasant production than from other parts of Haiti."

"We believe that Haiti must face the facts and stop producing so many children, begin planting trees in earnest, and seek to produce instead of make requests. Haiti needs help to understand these things," he added.

Wallace concluded his letter, stating boldly, "We are solidly against acceptance of boat people from Haiti. The cost to immigrate legally to the United States is no greater than by contraband ship, and legal immigrants are screened, protecting the reputation of Haiti and the receiving American community."

While decidedly harsh, Wallace's stance in the boat crisis was consistent with his deep-seated belief that each one of us— whether we be American or Haitian or Dutch or Chinese— must learn to produce and provide for ourselves, that we must seek out the road of working hard, increasing our knowledge, and building up our neighbors.

"You read about the boat people, the drownings, etc. in your newspapers. While you read about it we live with it! The plight of these people haunts us. They are our neighbors and our friends," Wallace and Eleanor wrote to mission supporters on December 9, 1981, not even a month after the stern letter to President Reagan. They went on to tell the story of 19-year-old Joineus whose words so aptly captured the sentiment of those fleeing in boats. "I'm exploding with desire and energy to know how I will live tomorrow," Joineus had told them. "I must have hope—I can't live with the empty belly, the sickness, and ignorance of my father." As they listened to his desperate cry, they remembered the words of King Solomon, "Hope deferred maketh the heart sick."

In that same letter, they go on to tell of Lismene, who "trudged over some of Haiti's steepest mountain trails from Zoulien to get to the mission. Her patched, rubber sandals were tied on her feet and her simple, worn dress hung on her thin, straight body. Like so many she had a basic understanding of the Gospel but wanted to learn something. Lisemene knew there was something more—something 'out there.' She wanted to know and to be a part of it." When Eleanor had to tell Lismene that there was nothing she could do for her at the moment, Lismene's response was one of "determined dignity." Lismene looked at Eleanor and said, "Mme. Wallace, God wants me to be somebody. I will not return until I know something. If you don't make me somebody, who will make me somebody?"

"Wow!" Wallace and Eleanor went on to write, "That's so much better than drowning off the coast of Florida or becoming a welfare charge to another society!!"

The modern reader might rightly see Wallace's strict view of the boat person as lacking in compassion and nuance, but as his granddaughter, I'd like to believe that his iron fist approach came, at the very least, from a place of great concern for Haiti and her people, of wanting to see the poor prosper on the island instead of perish at sea.

In fact, a harsh word of judgment followed by a compassionate response has been, more often than not, Wallace's response to just about any controversial crisis. I have learned through the years that this reaction isn't born out of unkindness, though it certainly feels so in the moment, but rather out of a grave conviction that one must act quickly and the belief that the harsher the words, the more urgent the reaction.

I am reminded once more of my father's analysis of his own father. If we are to listen only to Wallace's words, we might say, "What a cruel man!" and if we are to see only his actions, we might say, "What a saintly man!" Of course, Wallace is neither cruel nor saintly—he is merely human, cracked and flawed in his own ways, like each one of us, and it's in that humanity that the grace of God shines brightest.

• • •

Wallace and Eleanor realized they needed a break. They both loved to travel, to meet new people, and to soak in new cultures. So they decided to take what they'd come to call their "Around the World" trip. Wallace and Eleanor took three months to travel in 1983, beginning in France then heading east to Russia and down to India.

The trip was financed in part by buying a Peugeot, Wallace recalls. "In Haiti, a Peugeot cost $5,000. But the French government subsidized tourism by helping the manufacturer to sell one for $2,000 to a tourist. So our trip began in France. We shipped the car to Haiti after touring Europe and kept going."

"We flew from Brussels, Belgium via Warsaw to Russia, then over the mountains to Delhi, India's capital," Wallace remembers. "We also flew to China, Indonesia, Ceylon—now Sri Lanka—and on to Rangoon—now Yangoon—the capital of Burma—now Myanmar. We visited many places in Burma, including Mandalay, a big contraband river port full of marvelous artisans and on across to where the British Tigers flew over the hump to help the Chinese fight the Japanese."

For ninety days, Wallace and Eleanor would float down rivers, bounce across bumpy roads, and fly from one country to another. They would visit with pastors and their families, meet other missionaries, and make new friends, some of whom Wallace would correspond with for the rest of his life. Having learned years before not to be choosy, Wallace and Eleanor are adventurous eaters and enjoyed trying the foods served to them, including flying fish, jackfruit, and coconut curry. Most of the hosts along the way "tried to feed us 'western foods,' so we had little chance to try some of the local foods," Wallace remembers, undoubtedly with some remorse, though likely none for India, where he adds, "the food in the hotels was too fiery, and we fasted!"

In what would surely be some of Eleanor's favorite memories from the journey, the couple would lose themselves for hours in the outdoor markets, meandering between the stalls, driving the hardest of bargains, and laughing with the vendors. The souvenirs they collected would adorn the shelves of their glass curio cabinet and the wall in their hallway for the rest of their years in Haiti, providing endless fodder for stories to inquisitive grandchildren and visitors alike.

"We bought little animals from each country," Wallace recalls. "We got several elephants in several countries and now we can't tell them apart! Too late we learned to put a sticker on a souvenir."

No souvenir was more prized or feared, by their grandchildren at least, than the wooden monkey mask they purchased in Bali. The mask comes from the Chinese opera, *The Monkey King*. "The opera is sung everywhere Chinese culture touched," Wallace explains. But it wasn't the story of a regal monkey born from stone and endowed with magical powers that so affected the grandchildren—rather it was Eleanor who would don the mask and chase us down the hall as we screamed with horror and delight. Later, when we grew a little braver, we'd treat visitors to the same terror, taking turns to wear the mask.

No moment of their travel would leave a greater imprint on Wallace than the days he and Eleanor spent in Gujarat. The state of Gujarat, affectionately referred to as "The Jewel of Western India," is a coastal state, and as such has a long history with the rest of the world. Lothal, which is a part of the ancient Indus Valley Civilization, is believed to be one of the world's first seaports. Like much of India, Gujarat is steeped in history and culture. In the decades following the death of Christ, there is a story of a merchant landing in Gujarat with the Apostle Thomas. Centuries later, the Chinese philosopher and traveler Xuanzang would visit along the Silk Road. And more than a thousand years after Thomas, the ancient state would undergo a number of Islamic Conquests. In many ways, Gujarat is a symbol of the interplay and exchange of cultures, beliefs, and goods that eventually touch each of us in one form or another.

In the early 1920s, this jewel of a city attracted John R. Turnbull and his family. They helped establish a Christian church in Mehmedabad, Gujarat. There, John and his wife Maud conceived their second child, a son, who would be born Wallace Turnbull in Hollywood, CA. "I was conceived in India—in Gujarat, you know!" Wallace proudly declares to this day to any unsuspecting Indian man or woman he meets, looking to make a connection or looking to shock or, most likely, looking for a little of both.

While they never returned to live in Gujarat as a family, the place had worked its way into the folklore of Wallace's existence. John even taught him the words to a beloved local hymn.

With his wife Eleanor beside him, in the home of missionaries in nearby Ahmedabad, Wallace met a 92-year-old man who had served with his father. Together, they lifted their voices in song, completing a circle that had begun 58 years before:

Oh, what joy is mine!

Oh what joy is mine!

That joy you too may know.

For through the blood of Jesus,

my sins are made white as snow

• • •

When they returned to Haiti, Wallace and Eleanor would find their adopted homeland reeling from Asian Swine Fever. The outbreak had begun in 1978 in the Dominican Republic, and the Inter-American Institute For Cooperation on Agriculture (IICA) called for the eradication of all the pigs on the island, even though Swine Fever had yet to reach Haiti.

For a country whose poor already have limited access to protein, the slaughter of pigs proved devastating. The controversy surrounding Haiti's swine fever outbreak has led to untold rumors and conspiracy theories throughout the country and its community of NGOs. Stories range from a CIA plot to destabilize the government to corporate greed looking for an excuse to ship hundreds of thousands of US-bred pigs to the island nation.

Scholarly reports about the outbreak show a consensus in the scientific community that eliminating a population of pigs is the only effective way to kill the tick-born virus, and especially, to prevent the virus from becoming a permanent danger. But what the scholarly reports don't necessarily do a great job of depicting is the devastating hardship the IICA eradication and repopulation program brought to the already struggling rural families.

"Over 95% of Haiti's swine owners were small peasant producers who, though they comprise 80% of the population, had always suffered severe neglect," writes Phillip Gaertner in "Whether Pigs Have Wings: African Swine Fever Eradication and Pig Repopulation in Haiti."

By 1983, Haiti's razorback Creole pig population was reported extinct. IICA had offered a compensation of $40 per pig, which at the time amounted to about 80 percent of a rural farmer's annual income. But in a story that's nearly as old as Haiti itself, many of the rural farmers received only a fraction of the compensation, having been taken advantage of by their own compatriots.

"Haitian 'operators' went to work fleecing farmers by spreading rumors that IICA was only paying forty gourdes per animal instead of forty dollars, then buying the pigs and later selling them to the project at great profit to themselves," Gaertner writes. This meant a profit of 500% for the "operators" and the destruction of a family's main source of protein and income.

"Every Haitian country family was shocked by it as the pig is their only savings account for emergencies," Wallace says. "I witnessed that some hid pigs for months in dugouts," hoping to escape the slaughter.

To allow sufficient time for the Swine Fever to be completely eradicated, and, one can imagine, because bureaucracy moves at an infuriatingly slow pace, pigs weren't reintroduced to Haiti until 1985. And even then, there would be great debate about how many pigs had been culled. IICA's records showed 300,000 pigs had been eradicated, while numbers from Haiti showed a loss of more than 1 million animals. But neither figure takes into account the offspring that were never produced in the gap between when the pigs were eliminated and the new animals were introduced. "The loss of all the Haitian pigs in 1983 created the type of catastrophe that lack of rain or failed crops creates," reported the December 1985 issue of the BHM "Haiti Goodnewsletter."

To help farmers afford to restock the pigs, Wallace's son Wally helped organize a program where each farmer would pay a token price for the pig and then give back one piglet from each of the first two litters to help other families. As the Haitian proverb goes, "It's the fat from the pig that cooks the pig." And in this case, it was the pigs themselves that helped grow the pig project.

"We worked hard with people working to reintroduce pigs, buying piglets from reintroduction projects of foreigners," Wallace recounts. "I built a series of pens and Wally bought and produced and distributed over 2,000 piglets for breeding stock in our area."

In the December 1985 "Haiti Goodnewsletter," a photograph of a "happy farmer with one of the pigs" shows a Haitian farmer with a pink US-bred pig, not one of the long-snouted, black haired Creole pigs that were now extinct. IICA received heavy criticism for the Yorkshire, Hampshire, and Duroc pigs it introduced to Haiti; critics argued that these "Iowa pigs," as they referred to them disparagingly, weren't suited to the tropical climate and were far more expensive to raise. The criticism was one strongly promoted.

"That's nonsense," Wallace says. "The farmers noticed right away how these pigs grew bigger, faster, and produced far more offspring in each litter." While the initial burden of having to feed and care for up to 5 times the number of piglets was a difficult adjustment, many farmers "were grateful for the increased productivity," Wallace recalls.

The research Gaertner cites would seem to support Wallace and Wally's experience. "When indigenous pigs and 'Iowa' hogs are fed the same amount of feed, the 'Iowa' hogs gain more weight, producing a maximum amount of meat from a minimum amount of feed..." Gaertner writes. "The improved breed's single most important virtue is its efficiency in converting feed into meat." Even though the now-extinct Creole pigs had the ability to survive on less food and water than the newer imported breeds, they were so much less efficient in converting that nutrition to meat that they ultimately cost farmers more in lost productivity, researchers argued.

In his notes, Wallace writes, "A peasant keeps a pig or several as a savings account. He will invest $150 over many months to get $100 at sale time, to have the large amount of cash in one sum for a project such as putting several children in school..."

Wallace and Wally both understood that, for rural subsistence farmers, the breed of pig mattered far less than profit. Once more, farmers could raise pigs to feed their families and put their children through school.

• • •

The early '80s had been far from easy on Haiti. In fact, the situation was so dire that in 1982, the United Nations declared Haiti as one of three countries "without hope." "We do not believe that—do we?" Eleanor wrote to mission friends and supporters the morning after she and Wallace had learned of the declaration. "We know that the Gospel is the 'power of God,' and it does make a difference for *time* as well as for God's 'Forever.' Sometimes I think that some of these dear, suffering

Haitian people have more insight than the high people of the U.S. who make these reports."

Indeed, Wallace and Eleanor had many reasons to respond to Haiti's ongoing crises with hope. The ministry was continuing to grow and develop, not just on a project by project basis, but systematically and with plans for longevity built into the programs, thanks to the growing input of their sons and daughters-in-law.

The Fermathe High School, one of the finest buildings Wallace ever helped build, and the country's first rural high school, had opened in 1980 with 100 students; Sandy served as the director. In 1982, the UN saw Haiti "without hope," but Wallace saw a new generation of young Haitian men and women preparing to graduate with a high school diploma, the same men and women whose parents couldn't read or write.

Wallace and Eleanor were beginning to see the fruits of their early years of toil. The progress might not have been visible to the UN, but to Wallace and Eleanor, hope was made not of GDP or failed governments or NGOs; no, hope was found because of Christ in the faces and lives of those who claimed Him as their own, the lives of those like Ti l'Etat.

"It was in 1963, a few days after a hurricane smashed the bits of coffee bushes and avocado trees left by previous storms, and leveled huts," Wallace began a letter to friends on September 13, 1982. "A young woman and a small child, children of people who had died of privation and exposure, appeared at our door."

The woman went on to explain that the small boy was her brother, and she needed someone to care for him. She could fend for herself, she said, but he needed help. The boy stood at stiff attention and gave short, banty answers that earned him the nickname Ti L'Etat, "Little Authority."

"At the time, we kept some 50 starvation victims in various states of distress," Wallace writes. "Little toddlers mostly, they were skinny as spiders, or bloated all over, like balloon caricatures of children.... Lack of protein had caused their kidneys almost to cease to function. Treatment rapidly turned the little spiders into healthy-looking children, laughing and playing."

Wallace and Eleanor have always resisted the idea of orphanages, seeing them as poor substitutes for families. As the book of James instructs, "Religion that God our Father accepts as pure and faultless is this: to look after orphans and widows in their distress and to keep oneself from being polluted by the world." According to the Gospel, it is the responsibility of the church to look after one another, to give homes to the orphans. So Wallace and Eleanor would look for foster families for children who had been abandoned, orphaned, or who were otherwise in need of a safe home.

Ti l'Etat went to one such home, living with Catule Saintime, a deacon of the Fermathe church. Wallace describes Frere Catule, as he was widely known, as "a spark plug—a starter" for the Gospel, but he had once been an outsider himself. "His parents died when he was small, his mother when he was a little over three months old," Wallace writes in his notes. Catule was sent into the care his father's brother who was a Vodou priest. He helped his uncle with his Vodou practice until he had his own hut.

When Catule married, he and his wife suffered a great deal of heartache, burying each of their six young children as each one took ill and died. "When the Gospel began to penetrate the area, Madame Catule said that if she'd have a child that would live, they must be converted," Wallace recalls. In 1954, "they came to live at the mission for prenatal care, until the child was born, a boy they named Reynold. Insisting that only the Gospel would keep Reynold from dying, they bought a tiny site on the Kenscoff Road near the mission to build two little rooms."

"Reynold grew strong, went to school, and accompanied his father at times, reading aloud passages that Catule would remember to tell him of," Wallace writes.

And when Ti l'Etat needed a home, Catule, an orphan himself, and now a grateful father, had only one response: "Yes."

In many ways, Ti l'Etat's daily life was fairly unremarkable, resembling that of any other child in his community. "He kept Catule's goats, went to school, brought water to Madame Catule to wash his clothes," Wallace writes.

Several years later, when Ti l'Etat was a teenager, his sister visited him and the Saintime family. "Chatting, she and Catule discovered that they were cousins! Years ago, their grandfather had been sent back in the mountains as the area policeman, and he had a family there," Wallace explains. Ti l'Etat's sister brought another revelation along with her during the visit. The boy who had arrived dying of hunger a few years before, the one whose cocky answers and bright eyes had captured the hearts of the Fermathe community, was really named Innocent.

After his sister's visit, Ti l'Etat, now known as Innocent to all, continued with his schooling. Granny taught him English in addition to his mother tongue of Creole and the French he'd learned in school. When he graduated, Innocent was hired to work with the mission's rapidly growing child sponsorship project, assisting with tens of thousands of cases. "He has bought a house site, learned to drive and do errands, has come a long way," Wallace reflects in his 1982 letter. "We are happiest though when we realize that he knows the love of the Lord who chose him before the foundation of the world."

FIFTEEN
An Overthrow and a Massacre

WALLACE AND ELEANOR WOULD MARK 40 years of ministry in Haiti in 1986, the same year the Duvalier rule would come to an end. The compounded economic hardships of Swine Fever added to the often-brutal tactics of the Tonton Makout, and the unbridled greed of the regime led to the now legendary ousting of Jean Claude and Michele. While exiled in France, the Duvalier's marriage would fall apart and Jean Claude would fall on hard times. It is admittedly difficult to sympathize with a toppled dictator and impossible to justify his crimes, yet to this day Wallace feels a bit of a soft spot for the man—if not the tyrant—who was Jean Claude. "Poor soul," you might hear him say.

Wallace first met Jean Claude when he was only three years old, toddling into the mission, boots untied, with a military bodyguard following close behind. Worried that he might trip on his laces, Wallace invited the boy into the house and helped him tie his shoes. As Jean Claude went on his way, Wallace muttered, "Poor boy. I feel sorry for him."

Hearing Wallace's comment, the bodyguard said, "Don't you know? That's the president's son."

"I know," Wallace replied.

After that first visit, Jean Claude would stop in from time to time and join Wally, Sandy, and David in play. What an odd picture that must have been: Haiti's darling child, the son of the most powerful man in the land, carrying a makeshift fishing pole alongside three pale missionary boys who lived, at times, hand to mouth.

Jean Claude later went to College Bird and was a schoolmate with Wally. Wally tells how Jean Claude wasn't much interested in books, how he seemed lonely, how he was rejected and feared by the other children who were afraid of offending him lest their families pay a heavy price. Wallace's boys tried always to be kind to Jean Claude; they had seen him away from the noise and gossip, and in those brief moments he was just a boy, like them, trying to find his way in a land that could be as harsh as it was beautiful.

Even today, when Wallace talks of the regime, I don't think he pictures Jean Claude Duvalier the president, but rather Jean Claude the chubby toddler whose shoelaces were untied. "What kind of life is that," Wallace asks, "growing up in a palace surrounded by soldiers? Poor soul."

There was also the fact that Jean Claude didn't even want the job of "President for Life," asking that his sister Marie-Denise be named the successor. He didn't get his wish.

Wallace insists that Jean Claude had no stomach for the violence required in maintaining a totalitarian grip on a country, but he also felt trapped by his father's system of fear. In speaking to Wallace about the brutality of those in his regime, he once said, "When fixing a house, you can't take all the poles out at once." Whether Jean Claude Duvalier would have eventually removed all the poles is a question lost to history, for he was ousted before major reforms could take hold.

Some would argue that in spite of his obvious flaws, Jean Claude did his bit of good; others would argue that no amount of good could wash away the crimes against humanity committed in his name; others still would simply wish him forgotten. But Wallace had seen in Jean Claude an aborning light, had glimpsed the promise of the man he could have been if only he would "look up."

Years later, when Jean Claude was considering moving back to Haiti, he reached out to my father, the loneliness heavy in his voice. Wally offered what wisdom he could: Jean Claude should seek counsel, and he should pray. When Jean Claude did return to Haiti, nearly 25 years after his ousting, he arrived in a country shaken to its core by a deadly earthquake.

Under the government of René Preval, Jean Claude was indicted with charges of corruption, but never the threatened charges of crimes against humanity. Either way, his trial would remain unfinished.

Living with a loose form of house arrest, Jean Claude basked in a relative lap of luxury. Enemies and friends alike swarmed around him, abuzz with rumors and intentions good and bad. Jean Claude also reached out to Wallace, asking that he come visit. Wallace was happy to oblige, offering a word of prayer, sharing a copy of *Our Daily Bread*, and, I imagine, seeking to help a fallen man find the crumbs of innocence he had glimpsed nearly 60 years before.

Long-rumored to have been ailing, Jean Claude Duvalier died of a heart attack on October 4, 2014. Whether or not he ever chose to "look up" is a question to which only God knows the answer.

Wallace's unlikely friendship with Jean Claude Duvalier was far from the only odd relationship he'd have with Haiti's powerful. But Wallace's intentions weren't to aggrandize himself or to manipulate the leaders for personal gain. In fact, apart from Jean Claude, Wallace would only speak off the record of the leaders he's prayed with, of those he still visits, of the ones to whom he regularly sends a copy of *Our Daily Bread*. "I can't say that I prayed with this person or that person," he says. "People will think I'm bragging to seem special, and it would hurt my credibility."

Wallace's goal in approaching these awkward bedfellows has always been singular: "Wouldn't it be something if they were converted!" he exclaims with a twinkle in his eye, as if sharing a secret delight.

And then, with a sigh, he adds, "But I'm no evangelist. My father, he once had a flight attendant leaning over the passenger seat, praying to be saved. He was like that—but not me. I only know to share the Gospel by living it. And that's what I do when I pray with these folks. I talk to them, like people, and I pray for them. But wouldn't it be *something* if they were converted."

• • •

While Wallace had a desire to see Haiti's powerful turn to the Lord, his heart would always hurt the most for the vulnerable. He would work time and again to see justice done on their behalf where others were too afraid or, worse yet, too uninterested. Even when working with the most corrupt of politicians, Wallace had an uncanny ability to seek protection of basic human rights while avoiding political conflict—even when it was the politicians themselves who were violating those rights.

After Duvalier's exile, the seams of Haiti's already tattered political fabric began to tear, leading to widespread unrest and rising violence. It wasn't that Duvalier had been a great pacifist by any means, but rather that his targets were clear and the perpetrators known. In the years following his overthrow, the battle lines weren't yet clearly drawn—nearly anyone, it would seem, could become a victim or a perpetrator or, in many cases, both.

In the area around Jean Rabel, which sits in the Northwest corner of the island, tensions came to a bloody head when members of the country's leftist party set their sites on rural farmers and their land. Going door-to-door, political recruiters would destroy the homes and chase away—or kill—the families of anyone who refused to join the party. When the politics merged with religious rivalries, the stage was set for a terrible massacre.

One evening, Wallace recounts, supporters of the political party "assembled in a great crowd at Cabaret where they were given a drugged drink and sent up onto La Montagne some miles away to take over a fertile area." The residents "saw the top of the ridge suddenly black with people, and wondered if they were friendly." What followed was a bloodbath ultimately resulting in more than two thousand deaths.

"The attackers burned homes and killed people who didn't flee in time," Wallace writes in his notes. "The local policeman emptied his revolver at them, hurting no one, and fled. A little boy thrown into a burning house ran out the other side. I met an old man who fell on a tomb, was slashed across his back with a machete, and had a hand chopped off, but lived."

As the drug wore off, the butchery slowed—but the respite wasn't to last. "Big kettles of food had been prepared for them in a hollow," Wallace writes. The plan was to dose the attackers once more through the food.

Having received a tip that a plot might be afoot, the rural policemen knew to be alert. As the attackers were gathering in the hollow, the watchmen signaled on the conch shell horns, a tradition dating back to Haiti's runaway slaves and forever memorialized in the famous *Nèg Maron* statue. The signal sent, the peasants of the Northwest gathered. "The police told all of the men to remove their shirts for identification and to go deliver their fellow farmers."

"They surrounded the stupefied attackers eating in the hollow and slaughtered them with *machettes*," Wallace recounts. "Some fled, falling to their death over a cliff at the bottom of the hollow. Others were killed as they ran for home miles away. The limestone flank of La Montagne has many mysterious deep holes called *pis-pis*, surrounded by bushes. Dashing into the bushes, men fell in the holes, some groaning for days."

The massacre hit especially close to home for Wallace in the area of Gros Sable near the sea. "At La Montagne's base, men armed with *machettes* were making sharp-ended clubs," Wallace writes. The church members knew that if they refused to fight, they and their family members would surely be killed. More gruesome, however, was being forced to kill innocent men, women, and children.

In the gospel of Matthew, Jesus tells his disciples, "I am sending you out like sheep among wolves. Therefore be as shrewd as snakes and as innocent as doves." On the night of the Jean Rabel Massacre, the Christians of Gros Sable were both.

With not only their lives at stake but also those of their loved ones, they knew they had but one choice: kill or be killed. And yet, the light inside them would not let them be murderers of innocents. They could not do it; this much they knew. Neither could they refuse and watch their beloved slaughtered. Knowing what lay ahead, one of the men shouted, "Everyone from Gros Sable follow me!"—indicating to their captors that they were splitting to go around and attack from another side. Instead, they ran behind a knoll and fled home. In the confusion of the violence, they were forgotten, lost to the night.

Over 200 miles away in Fermathe, Wallace knew nothing of the attack at the time. But when word reached him of the bloodbath, he couldn't keep silent. This was a clear affront to human rights, a massacre of political, and perhaps even religious, motives. Skirting the issue of specific politics as delicately as Wallace does anything, he spoke out against the violation of human rights, against the killings, against the burning of homes and crops. He listened to the powerless; he spoke to the powerful. He reprimanded the actions, carefully sidestepping public accusation of individuals—dancing a dangerous two-step as he had done countless times before. So effective was his strategy that the perpetrators of the Jean Rabel massacre decided to eliminate the threat by destroying Wallace's greatest asset: his character.

Wallace was publicly accused of having incited the massacre himself. His motive? A power struggle with the Catholic Church.

Wallace's disdain for the institution of the Catholic Church and its historic abuse of power was no secret. But neither was the fact that he worked closely with many Catholic priests, monks, and nuns. The men and women from the church were to the institution as a child to the crimes of her parents: sullied perhaps, but not guilty.

An article in the October 27, 1981, issue of *Haïti Progrès*, a left-leaning newspaper published out of Brooklyn, New York, implicates Wallace, speaking of "the control of Pastor Wallace Turnbull on the conservative Baptist churches in the Northwest, that permitted him to... accomplish the massacre in Jan Rabèl." The story of a prominent Protestant leader promoting the destruction of rival Catholics is one as old as the reformation itself.

The accusation would reach a dramatic climax during a television interview in which one of the priests from the Northwest accused Wallace of having organized and incited the massacre. Also taking part in the interview was one of the local farmers, a victim of the violence. When asked if he knew who was behind the massacre, the man answered plainly, pointing in the direction of the priest, "Yes. He did it."

The interview was never aired again, and the subject was dropped. The accusations against Wallace didn't stick. What did leave an indelible mark was his tenacious campaign to help the people of Jean Rabel rebuild their homes and again piece together the shards of their fragile existence. In the months following the massacre, Wallace helped 38 families rebuild and advocated for peace in the area. The scars, however, remained.

To this day, it is repeated, "*La Montagne* made many widows."

SIXTEEN
The Embargo

WE CANNOT STOP A HURRICANE from blowing or force the rains to fall or will the ground not to shake. These are hardships that must be borne on an island nation, however costly. Perhaps it is the inevitability of these "acts of God" as they're called that makes the "acts of men" all the more painful to bear.

One such act would be forever known simply as "The Embargo," two words that hold a world of meaning: painful indignities inflicted on an already wounded people.

In 1990, Jean-Bertrand Aristide, a former Catholic priest, became Haiti's first popularly elected president. Red and blue adorned polling centers, and voters carried small Haitian flags, dancing and singing in the streets. The music of ra-ra bands with their trumpets, drums, and songs filled the air as the promise of a new era brought renewed hope. Within months, however, the red and blue flags would be replaced with the black smoke of burning tires, their stench seeping once more into homes and schools.

The election quickly led to discord with the country's powerful elite. What had been a spirit of hope and change only a few months earlier began to deteriorate rapidly. Wallace handled the latest wave of tumult as he did all things political: he denounced violence and injustice while avoiding criticism of officials. There was no reason to cause offense, for that could only hurt the gospel message.

But not all leaders would take such a peaceful approach. In fact, within eight months of the presidential inauguration, many believed the country was on the brink of a civil war, so great was the divide between political factions. A coup led by army leaders and the national police ousted Aristide. The President found a safe haven first in Venezuela and then in the United States as he campaigned for international support.

Following the coup, the political discord continued. One faction in particular honed in on the President's supporters, forming the Front for the Advancement and Progress of Haiti. Known as FRAPH, they would go on to hunt down and kill many of the people associated with the President. What had been a glimmering hope of democracy rapidly unraveled into a tangle of blood and vengeance.

While FRAPH cracked down in Haiti, the military junta governing the country felt the full weight of international pressure. Within months President George H.W. Bush successfully lobbied the Organization of American States to impose a trade embargo against Haiti on all goods except food and medicine. This meant the decimation of Haiti's already fragile clothing industry. It also meant the end of the decades-long sewing and embroidery project at Mountain Maid. At its peak, the project offered a livelihood to 600 women and their families, but with no way to import fabric and thread and no way to export the clothing, tablecloths, or napkins, the embroidery work was effectively shut down. It never fully recovered, much to the heartache of Wallace and Eleanor, who had founded the project, as well as Wally and Betty who had nurtured and helped it grow.

The impact of the embargo was felt much further than those who lost their jobs. "It was said that each employee in a factory fed thirty people," Wallace says. "With the embargo, thousands were cut off. Children were dying in towns all over."

Wallace remembers one man in particular who came to his office, hat in hand. "Pastor Wallace, can you give me work?" the man asked. His request wasn't unusual; what followed is what marked the interaction so poignantly. "I've spent all my money supporting my employees. First their children died; now they're dying. I had to get away. I can't watch. And now I'm struggling just to feed my family."

Wallace and Eleanor had received aid in the form of "cash for work" from the United States in what some might see as an ironic attempt to ease the suffering of the embargo. "During the embargo, with people dying in the city, they gave me cash to employ people," Wallace recalls. "They also gave me a bunch of tools: picks, rakes, hoes."

Armed with tools and cash, Wallace decided to build a road. It had worked to ease the suffering after a natural disaster—perhaps it could ease the suffering after a man-made one as well. Moved by the plight of the factory owner and compelled by his commitment to the people he'd employed, Wallace hired the man to oversee the building of the road.

"Men came from Port-au-Prince on foot every day to get to the top of that mountain for about $2 a day," Wallace recalls. "They wanted that work, and they were very good employees."

The cash for work program lasted for a few months, but the road, which runs from Kenscoff for miles along the Massif de la Selle mountain range and down to Chauffard, remains. "The work we did is still being used," Wallace says with a satisfied smile. "Some of the people even gathered gravel for parts of it."

The embargo also came with sanctions against the import of oil, thus shutting down transportation across the country. "In a country where driving bumper-to-bumper for 18 hours a day, seven days a week was a way of life, the number of cars now seen moving in any 10-mile stretch can be counted on two hands and less than a foot, and most of them are trying to coast on a shut-down engine," the *Los Angeles Times* reported on November 17, 1991.

The oil sanctions had far-reaching consequences, threatening even hospitals. For, while medicines were technically exempt from the embargo, there was no way to move them on the island. Strict regulations in the US further complicated the situation, making it nearly impossible for hospitals like the Fermathe Hospital to keep the necessary stock of medication and supplies. Helpless, Wallace, Eleanor, and the hospital staff were forced to watch patients suffer without the antibiotics or even basic saline solutions that could save their lives.

In another odd twist, Wallace would find himself in what some might see as a privileged position, and what he would call a space of great responsibility. Because of the hospital, the mission was able to receive a fuel to maintain its humanitarian operations. There might be a shortage of even the most basic supplies, but electricity wouldn't be one of them. While much of the country was living with as little as four hours of electricity a week, the mission had sufficient fuel to run the generator during the hospital's main hours of business. The doctors might not have saline solution to rehydrate a patient, but they could quite literally keep the lights on. There was also enough fuel for vehicles to search out badly needed supplies and keep the core ministries moving forward, an asset Wallace would use to its fullest potential.

Wallace used ingenuity to stretch the fuel as far as possible and make the most of each trip. "Building trucks would go out to the Northwest loaded. On the return, we'd add bags of salt from the salt flats to weigh down the truck beds. That way the trucks wouldn't bounce and be damaged by the rough terrain," Wallace recalls. "That stuff was gold for us. Way out there, at the source, it was so much cheaper than in town. We'd use it in food for the hospital, and the cooks would take some, too." Of course, Wallace knew he could hardly stand by and watch his neighbors suffer. And so, when there was a surplus of fuel—and there was almost always a small surplus, because if Wallace and Eleanor had learned nothing else in nearly 50 years of ministry it was how to ration—Wallace would discreetly fill the fuel cans and gas tanks of trusted friends and ministry partners. He would refuse any money offered, for the fuel wasn't to sell, but he rejoiced that he was able to ease some suffering, however small the impact.

This wasn't the first time he bent the rules to help those in need, and—he likely thought with a twinge of forbidden delight— it wouldn't be the last.

• • •

When the initial OAS sanctions didn't lead to the reinstatement of Aristide, international pressure mounted. In 1993, President Bill Clinton "appointed Lawrence Pezzullo as special envoy for Haiti, and as promised in his campaign, worked to increase economic and diplomatic pressure on the junta," the Office of the Historian for the US State Department reported.

Part of the added pressure would come in the form of the United Nations Security Council Resolution 875. Adopted unanimously on October 16, 1993, the resolution ushered in heightened sanctions and a naval blockade, effectively barring any ships from entering or leaving the island nation. What had been a humanitarian crisis for several years now bordered on catastrophe.

Within a year, the UN adopted Resolution 940, dubbed Operation Uphold Democracy. If the military junta wouldn't transfer power peaceably, then perhaps they would do it through force. Across the country, families gathered around televisions and radios to follow an invasion in progress. A US assault force had launched from Fort Bragg, North Carolina, and was in transit across the Atlantic. Under the immense pressure of imminent invasion, General Raoul Cedras, the junta leader, capitulated to the terms set forth by former President Jimmy Carter, US Senator Sam Nunn, and retired Chairman of the Joint Chiefs of Staff General Colin Powell. The invasion became an "intervention" for "peace-keeping" and "nation-building."

Wallace would once again find himself caught in the middle.

• • •

Among both friends and foes, Wallace is known for having more than a few faults, but a lack of conviction is not one them. And yet, if ever in his lifetime he were to feel ambivalent, I wonder if it wasn't during the time of the occupation. Wallace, many will tell, is as Haitian as any foreigner could be. Some have even said tongue-in-cheek, "He is more Haitian than many Haitians!" For, while millions of men and women would be born into their homeland, Wallace chose it. He adopted the island's joys and sorrows as his own, raised his children and grandchildren in the folds of her mountains. He who had been marked as a "transient" so many years before had grown roots deep and strong, his many branches of ministry forming a canopy that stretched across much of the country.

But none of this adopted identity could erase the fact that Wallace had been born in the United States, that he had chosen his American citizenship, that his children and grandchildren— the very ones who would grow up with the sticky juice of mango running down their chins, who would speak Kreyòl among their first words, who would run barefoot down the mountainside—they, too, carried an American passport. As he watched American soldiers crawling on their bellies across the tarmac of the airport in Port-au-Prince, Wallace surely couldn't ignore that his eldest grandson would soon graduate from the United States Air Force Academy.

Surely, if Wallace ever struggled with ambivalence, it was then, in that moment, however brief.

Decades of living under dictators and military regimes had taught Wallace the important skill of compartmentalizing. He could separate politics from people, policy from individuals. The soldiers were there, and they weren't leaving for a long while—but in the end it wasn't their fault. They hadn't asked to invade Haiti; they didn't choose to live in hot and muggy tents, baking under the tropical sun. As he had done for countless other passersby, Wallace welcomed the soldiers as men and women in need and prayed for the Gospel to shine.

But Wallace and Eleanor wouldn't be able to stay above the fray forever. Soon the political factions found themselves at the gate of the mission.

Exactly why, no one knows, but one night a mob headed out toward Fermathe. Angry shouts of "burn it down!" broke through the lyrical chirping of the crickets and the *ki-kou ki-kou* of the tree frogs. Violence had found its way to their doorstep.

Hearing the shouts of the mob and fearing for the safety of all who resided at the mission, the residents of Fermathe formed a human barricade along the road. To "burn it down," the mob would have to get through them, they shouted back. Seeing the local resistance, the mob decided to turn away. Wallace, Eleanor, and the other missionaries had been saved by the very men and women they served.

To this day, nobody knows for sure what instigated the mob, but it was evident that they had been angered by divisive rhetoric, seeking a scapegoat for their poverty, for their suffering. Following the incident, Wallace realized that the mission was no longer immune to the violence around it. He arranged for a rotation of Special Forces teams to live in the dormitories built for the Summer Bible Institute.

The Special Forces provided security not only for the mission but also for the surrounding community. At the end of each rotation, the missionaries would gather for a pizza party and a moment of prayer before sending off the soldiers. The cool mountain air, the food that echoed of home, the encouragement spoken in English—these must have been a great balm for the soldiers. These earthly comforts were also, Wallace might argue, a living example for the Church.

While some might have worried that such treatment of an invading force would bring about criticism from Haitians, Wallace knew that he had no choice: "Love your enemy and pray for those who persecute you" doesn't come with an asterisk or a footnote. Neither does "love your neighbor as yourself."

SEVENTEEN
Half a Century

WITH THE NATION JUST BEGINNING to heal from the devastating effects of the embargo, Wallace and Eleanor ushered in their fiftieth anniversary of ministry in 1996, marking half a century on the island. Wallace, the once transient boy, had by this time spent twice as many years in Haiti as he had in the United States.

To celebrate the occasion, Wallace and Eleanor's daughter-in-law Betty, the family's unofficial planner, worked to organize a celebration hosted at the newly minted Kinam II hotel in Petion-Ville.

Friends and family from across Haiti and abroad gathered to commemorate what Eleanor dubbed "the Year of Jubilee," referencing the Biblical mandate in Leviticus. "The fiftieth year shall be a jubilee for you... and is to be holy for you." Of course, she made no reference to the passage in between, which says, "do not sow and do not reap…" for Wallace and Eleanor would not stop their sowing, not even once every 50 years.

The fiftieth anniversary of ministry marked a milestone and was a truly joyous occasion, bringing together people from all areas of the couple's lives and giving cause to remember how far they had come. Photographs once locked in a trunk were dusted off, scanned, and shared in a parade of "Before" and "After." The thatched roof church carved into the mountainside (before). The big stone sanctuary with a purple cross capping the bell tower (after). The rickety shelter built from sticks to shade Granny's medical box (before). The doctors huddled over a patient in one of two operating rooms (after). The clapboard single-room school building (before). The multi-story high school with a yard of laughing students (after).

Amongst the memories shared and stories recounted was also the very real reminder that Wallace and Eleanor were fifty years older. Now in their early seventies, they were well passed the age of typical retirement—a concept they never would accept for themselves. Their spirits might be eternal, but their bodies were beginning to reveal their mortality.

Just months after the celebration of the mission's fiftieth anniversary, Wallace very nearly lost his beloved Eleanor. Perpetually active, Eleanor rarely slowed down enough to eat a full meal or drink a glass of water. She has always seemed to revel in pushing her body to its limit, "burning the candle at both ends and breaking it in the middle for good measure," as Wallace has often described with an admonishment. For a woman who has dedicated her life to healthcare, it is impossible to fathom how absolutely out of touch with her own body Eleanor can be. She mastered the art of mind over body, but it's an art that very nearly killed her.

One day after having had supper with her son Wally and his family, she let drop that her thigh had been "a little swollen for a few days." Upon her daughter-in-law Betty's insistence, Eleanor raised the hem of her dress to reveal her thigh, which was more than twice its normal size. To ease her family's distress, she finally agreed to let Dr. Bernard have a look. He diagnosed her with deep vein thrombosis: the massive blood clot stretched from her knee to her naval. Eleanor was immediately placed on bed rest. Even the slightest movement could dislodge the clot and lead to instant death.

Just hours before, Eleanor had been moving boxes in the storage depots and cleaning out the medical supplies. How the clot had managed to stay in place is one of the many Eleanor Mysteries her family has credited to miracle.

She was prescribed a daily dose of blood thinner, which she must take to this day, and sentenced—as she put it—to six months of absolute bed rest while the clot dissolved. She lasted three. And this only because Betty spent hours a day with her, directing a parade of housemaids, mission employees, and visitors through Eleanor's room to keep her distracted and to report back any infraction. "The cure is worse than the illness," Eleanor bemoaned time and again.

During his wife's ordeal, Wallace, too, was facing his own health battle—quietly so as not to cause alarm. After months of extreme fatigue, Wallace was eventually diagnosed with a heart condition in 1997. The diagnosis came just days before the wedding of his eldest grandson Rhet to Sarah Weiford. When Wallace arrived for the wedding, which he would be officiating, he mentioned casually to the family, "My heart isn't working. I need a pacemaker." And then he went on about his business as he had every day before.

He performed the ceremony for his grandson as he had for his sons, as he would for other grandchildren, as he had for thousands of strangers. After the celebration, he returned to Michigan, where he'd met with the heart specialist only days before, and received his pacemaker with the best of prognoses. It has brought Wallace great delight to know that he's now outlived two of the devices.

While his heart was given new life with the pacemaker, Wallace's back continued to deteriorate. A chronic problem with his sciatic nerve meant that Wallace had been living in near constant pain for decades. Back braces, inversion tables, and regular doses of ibuprofen have helped throughout the years, but apart from a miracle, there is no cure for the condition. Year after year the deformation has grown more noticeable. At first, he'd place his hand on his lower back and push himself up straight to walk. Standing at 6' 2", with broad shoulders at the peak of his youth, age and pain have bent Wallace inch by inch, year by year. He now walks folded almost in half. Though he can still reach his toes—and any speck on the floor—with great ease, he can't lift himself much past his waist. When Wallace and Eleanor first began to imagine a life away from the mission, this stage of deformity was likely absent from their considerations. But the symptoms were already advancing, and Wallace must have known that he couldn't carry on with the physicality of his work forever.

• • •

As their bodies began to betray Wallace and Eleanor, the dawn of a new century inched closer. The discussion of transition and succession grew. By now, Sandy and his family had settled in the United States and seemed unlikely to return to full-time ministry. Wally also announced that he and Betty had stayed far beyond their anticipated two years of service and would leave in 2002, having completed 30 years of ministry. None of the grandchildren seemed called to full-time service in Haiti.

What had once been a family dynasty of sorts seemed to be crumbling around Wallace and Eleanor. Help would have to come from the outside, and it would have to come relatively soon, for the couple who were living with a cruel dissonance: as their capacity declined with age, the mission's reach and needs continued to grow. The shift was so gradual that none of us saw it coming, and so it felt rather sudden—it was as if their entire reason for being was ripped out from under them, though in truth it had been shifting imperceptibly for years.

In early 2002, Wallace and Eleanor announced publicly that they would be transitioning the leadership of the Baptist Haiti Mission to a new director. To their innermost circle of family and friends, they made it clear that they weren't happy about the transition, even if they saw the necessity of it.

Before Haiti, Wallace had been a man without a home, a man without roots, without a safety net. Half a century later, he had built a life on the island nation—he claimed Haiti as his own, but just as importantly her people had claimed him. He belonged. And now, as he faced the inevitable indignities of aging, he felt he was being asked to give it all up. He must turn his back on everything he loved in order to ensure its future.

Knowing the process to be exceedingly painful for both Wallace and Eleanor, the family circled around them, seeking to make the transition of leadership not a parting of ways but a celebration of God's continued faithfulness to the ministry.

Our efforts would be only marginally successful, for it seemed nothing could soothe the wounds of a pending goodbye.

With a new leader and ministry partner ready to be announced, Betty organized a celebration on October 19, 2002, which would bring together prominent leaders, missionaries, pastors, friends, and loved ones. As news spread that Wallace and Eleanor would be leaving the mission, letters and recorded testimonies began pouring in. More than 600 people attended the celebration, each eager to pay tribute to "the pastor and his wife."

"By sharing God's teachings with your congregation, you have enriched the lives of countless individuals and served as an inspiration to the community. I commend you for sharing your wisdom, guidance, and faith with others," wrote President George W. Bush.

The US Ambassador to Haiti, Brian Dean Curran, recognized the depth and longevity of Wallace and Eleanor's ministry, writing, "seldom have I seen a couple who has achieved so much and who have devoted themselves so deeply for so long."

Jerry Falwell Sr., while a controversial figure throughout his lifetime, had been a faithful supporter of Wallace and Eleanor during some of their most trying moments. In his tribute, he likened them to some of God's Giants: B.R. Lakin, W.A. Criswell, Vance Havner, Billy Graham, "and in that long list of heroes and great champions, I have Wallace and Eleanor Turnbull listed."

One of the more touching tributes came from Wes Stafford, the former president and CEO of Compassion International, and a faithful supporter of the mission. He remembered when he started as a young field worker in Haiti and was disheartened to learn just how difficult it was to work in the country. Learning about the Turnbulls, he said, "I determined that I needed at least to talk to these people…. Wallace and Eleanor invited me into their home up on the mountain and in that evening explained to me what it takes to survive and even to thrive in Haiti…. I heard their words, but I also saw it in them. They talked about faith; they talked about hope; they talked about a sense of humor. They talked about strength; they talked about tenacity and courage. They talked about intellect and about vision and about warmth, and ultimately about love. These are the words I heard that evening, but in the four years that I lived in Haiti, I had the chance to see that those were not just words…."

Of all the tributes they were to receive, none would mean more to Wallace and Eleanor than those spoken by the Haitians they had worked with over their lifetime. For it was these men and women who truly knew Wallace and Eleanor, who had cried with them, laughed with them, sought refuge, offered friendship. These were the people who had endured the business of living.

Dr. Louis Roy had worked with Wallace and Eleanor in the response to hurricane Hazel, now 48 years past. "He was a young boy then, and I barely knew him," he said. "However, it didn't take long for a solid friendship to develop, first between the two of us, then between his family and mine. I don't think it's necessary to tell you of Wallace's unrelenting devotion to stricken populations, crossing the country on foot, by horse, and by boat. Never tired, Wallace participated in all the expeditions of the Haitian Red Cross in the most remote areas of Haiti."

Most of the accolades they received from friends and leaders spoke about Wallace and Eleanor's dedication to the ministry and praised their accomplishments. But one man who shared that evening understood their heart. Gary Lissade, who had been the highly respected Minister of Justice under Aristide, had also been friends with Wallace and Eleanor for more than 30 years. Gary knew that even though Wallace and Eleanor were ceding leadership to someone else, they would never truly be able to leave. "Their heart will stay in this country that they love so much. It will stay among the people of Haiti," he said "… Haiti became their land."

• • •

Against the backdrop of tributes and accolades, the transition quickly began to unravel. For two years, Wallace and Eleanor had worked with what they believed to be an extensive international agency, the Evangelical Baptist Mission Society (EBM), to find a French-speaking experienced missionary who would take over the directorship of the Baptist Haiti Mission. Instead, Wallace writes in a letter to Jerry Falwell, they received "an Indiana businessman… in place of an experienced missionary. With mental reservations, we accepted a six month overlap."

When they dug a little deeper, Wallace and Eleanor discovered that EBM was more of "an umbrella organization for individuals sent out by individual churches" and thus had "no idea of the complexity of the Haiti field director's job and of the many things that a new person must learn," Wallace explains in his letter.

Shortly before the transition celebration, Wallace was informed by the director of EBM that he, not Wallace, would be anointing the new field director before the 600 guests as an official marking of the transition. Wallace balked at the idea, saying, "I must make any presentation." His concern was that the friends in attendance would resent a stranger introducing Wallace's replacement, as if he was already irrelevant. The strained relationship reached its breaking point. "He told our mission board that if I was not out of Haiti never to return by December 15, he was recalling the people he had sent," Wallace writes. "The man had no residence visa, no language, no idea of the complex legalities of our work.... We paid for their exit visas, glad to be delivered, but with our faces red for having been taken."

EBM closed its doors a few months later due to administrative and financial irregularities, leaving hundreds of missionaries stranded around the world.

With the carefully planned transition now in shambles, the BHM board began a new search for a field director "and this time there will not be the rush for us to leave! ...But we definitely are working toward it, feeling tired at 77," Wallace concludes.

Truth be told, more than a small part of Wallace and Eleanor was grateful for the extended time in Haiti. They hadn't particularly wanted to leave, and for years would complain that they had felt "pushed out." Yet, when pressed on the issue of succession and their own mortality, they would concede that yes, fresh, younger blood was needed.

One needn't look very far to understand their conflict. Haiti was their entire world. They were married because of Haiti; they had purpose because of Haiti; they had children and grandchildren because of Haiti. What could they possibly be outside of it?

Over the years, I've heard hundreds of people acclaim the incredible faith of Wallace and Eleanor Turnbull. "They must have such strong faith to live so long in a difficult land, to serve the way they do." Yet, staying in Haiti had never been particularly hard for them. She might be a difficult land to many, but to them she was home. Their crisis came in being forced to leave the land they knew. What, they asked over and over, was waiting for them in the US? The country of their citizenship had ceased to be home generations ago—yet, in their most vulnerable years they were being asked to return, to settle into a rhythm more suitable to an elderly American couple, a rhythm they had no idea how to follow. They were, in the end, being told they must live outside their carefully constructed identities. Wallace and Eleanor could hardly be blamed for shaking a fist or two at all who made such an absurd request of them. Leaving Haiti—not living there—would be the hardest thing they'd ever do.

• • •

Not long after the original transition plan fell apart, the BHM board would appoint a new director: Rob Baker. He and his wife Patti would move to Haiti in mid 2003 to begin their ministry.

From the very beginning, Wallace expressed his concerns over Rob's role as director—not because he had anything against the man personally, but because Rob wasn't technically a Baptist. Wallace was criticized by the board for being overly sectarian. While Baptist in name and teaching, BHM had always been open to missionaries and supporters from a range of denominational backgrounds. Wallace countered that his concerns weren't because he doubted Rob's faith but rather because each denomination has an inherent leadership culture. He argued that Rob's background and approach to church leadership would create "misunderstandings" with the pastors and others at the Baptist Haiti Mission.

Added to the question of denomination was the fundamental difference between how Wallace and his family versus the BHM board viewed the work of missionaries. Rob, who had served in the US military, desired a clear-cut job description, something in writing that would detail his specific duties—duties he was more than happy to execute with faithfulness and integrity. Wallace, on the other hand, believes that missionaries fulfill a role, not a job description. The service of a missionary is to be present as needed, not to execute a list of tasks, Wallace would argue. Furthermore, as a Baptist, Wallace believes firmly in the sovereignty of each individual church. The pastors, he argues, must be empowered to lead their congregations, to serve alongside, not under, foreign missionaries.

As the day drew closer for Rob and Patti to arrive on the field, Wallace and Eleanor grew increasingly anxious. What should have been a transition filled with hope for the future of the ministry had turned itself inside out into a process of reluctant resignation.

In a symbolic gesture to cement the transition of roles, Wallace and Eleanor surrendered their beloved home to Rob and Patti, moving into a small cottage on the back side of the mission, which had once belonged to the Wesleyan church. The stone cottage was small and charming; it was more than enough space for an elderly couple retired from full-time service. But it wasn't home. And they would never have the opportunity to make it such.

Wallace and Eleanor both were predisposed to dislike the situation, but their concerns about the new Field Director weren't entirely unfounded. Language barriers and cultural barriers appeared at nearly every turn.

Wallace and Eleanor were to overlap with Rob and Patti for six months to a year, depending on who is doing the telling. Wallace saw this as a limited time to gorge on training, to stuff into the new director as much information as possible. Rob, perhaps, saw it as a time to drink in the new one sip at a time, letting it roll across his tongue as he adjusted to the strange and unfamiliar flavors of his new home.

When Wallace and Eleanor finally left for their new home in Lynchburg, Virginia, in 2004, they did so with great reservation and with plans to return as soon as possible. While they were technically living in the US, they would make frequent trips back to Haiti, staying for weeks and even months at a time.

Before long, Rob and Patti made it clear that they wished to work independently, without the involvement of Wallace and Eleanor. They also, one might imagine, sought to be out from under the long shadow cast by their predecessors. But Wallace would have none of it. He could be useful. He should be useful. He must be useful. The more he insisted to be included, the more the Bakers withdrew. The cycle quickly grew confrontational.

• • •

Within a few years, the Baker's annoyance and their concern that his involvement would undercut the authority of the new leaders led to the drastic action of the board asking to prevent or limit Wallace and Eleanor's visits to the mission. This involved Wallace and Eleanor no longer living in the cottage that had been assigned to them.

One might as well have told the couple that they were to live in a dark hole with no sky or to cross a desert without water—for these were no less cruel fates than being asked to live without the mountains to rise up and greet them each morning, to breathe without the cool, damp air to fill their lungs.

Of course, while the request was hurtful, it was completely unenforceable. Wallace and Eleanor had as much right to enter and leave Haiti as anyone; they knew it and they declared it loudly. If the communists in the sixties hadn't been able to exile Wallace, a new missionary certainly didn't stand a chance.

In the end, the greatest loss was felt not by Wallace and Eleanor nor by Rob and Patti, but by the pastors, school teachers, and ministry partners. The couples would eventually make their peace. Wallace and Eleanor would live in an apartment on the edge of the mission. The Bakers remained steadfast in serving the churches through difficult days of political turmoil and the aftermath of the devastating earthquake in 2010.

The early divisions, however, meant that the new director and his wife lost the opportunity to learn from some of the most experienced and well-respected missionaries the nation had ever known. Wallace and Eleanor lost, too. They lost—for a time—their joy, their sense of purpose, their calling.

What was never lost, what can never be lost, is the promise of the Scriptures: *For we are his workmanship, created in Christ Jesus for good works...*

EIGHTEEN
TLC for Rural Churches

As THEIR TIME TO LEAVE Haiti approached and the transition grew increasingly difficult, it became clear to their family that Wallace and Eleanor would need a new purpose, a new mission, one that would be the culmination of all their work yet remain manageable for them as they aged.

When the first of the Baptist churches had sprung up generations before, nearly entire congregations were illiterate. The leaders were chosen almost by default from the select few who could read and write. Later, the qualifications expanded to those who had a primary school certificate, then to those who had a high school diploma. By the early 2000's, it was clear to Wallace and Eleanor that the churches needed more: as the level of education had risen across the congregations, the leaders hadn't been able to keep up. The churches were growing rapidly, but there was a dearth of well-educated Christian leaders—men and women who could make a serious impact at the highest levels of the country. So Wallace and Eleanor made a decision: they would create a scholarship foundation to send members of the Haitian churches to college in the US. In return for a college education, the students would agree to return to Haiti upon graduation and actively participate in their local church. In their honor, a trust was created by Turnbull family members and friends to provide advanced education for young leaders in the Haitian church. They named it the Turnbull Leadership Corp, or TLC.

According to its charter, the mission of TLC "is to provide opportunities for leadership training, professional skills development, and higher education for Haiti's Christian youth, through economic and logistical support, to facilitate young leaders to build up their local churches and communities, advancing the spiritual and economic development of the Haitian people." While the scholarship committee would offer guidance to the students, there would be no strict rules about what the students must select as a major or what career they must pursue. The goal was simple: build up Haiti's human capital with highly educated Christians.

Like Wallace and Eleanor's first forays into education, their newest venture appeared straightforward—and to them it was—but it was also disruptive to the status quo. They wanted Christian leaders in Haiti not only to elevate the church but also to elevate the country; to one day bring in godly men and women to the highest levels of industry, government service, and healthcare; and in so doing to close the circle of change they'd helped ignite decades ago when rural peasants read their first words from Bibles gleaming in the firelight.

With their new mission identified, Wallace and Eleanor recognized the necessity of a ministry partner. The scholarship's pockets weren't deep enough to cover 100% of the costs for more than a single student at a time, which would barely scratch the surface of need. They turned once more to their friend Jerry Falwell, Sr., and Liberty University. Once, the university had given a chance to their son David and had even named a dormitory in his honor after he died. Perhaps now Jerry, as they called him, would extend that opportunity to godly men and women from some of Haiti's most rural areas.

Wallace and Eleanor's request was met with an enthusiastic "yes" from Liberty University, who agreed to cover the tuition, room, and board for two students a year. That meant that eventually up to eight students could attend at the same time. The foundation would cover the cost of travel, books, insurance, and a small stipend for each student to account for basic needs such as dorm room essentials, personal hygiene, and winter coats.

In the end, Wallace and Eleanor's greatest challenge with the scholarship foundation would be not financing but rather finding enough students who met the requirements. Their deepest desire was to work with young people from the rural churches, people who would have no other opportunity to pursue a higher education except through TLC. The problem was that the vast majority of these students couldn't pass the Test of English as a Foreign Language, or TOEFL, that Liberty University and nearly every other college in the US requires for foreign students. Even so, Wallace and Eleanor were able to find their first candidate, deciding to do a pilot year with a single student: Abdias Cesaire. He'd been nominated by the Fermathe church and was able to meet all the requirements: a passing TOEFL score, a US student visa, a high recommendation from his pastor. He was also the son of the woman who had been nanny to three of their grandchildren. Comer, as she was called, came from the remote northwest corner of Haiti; she'd had little opportunity for education herself. But she'd been determined that each of her children would earn their high school diplomas and, if the Lord permitted, go on to college.

Since the program began, more than 30 men and women have graduated with university degrees through the TLC scholarship. Some have even gone on to earn their Master's and doctorate degrees. Not every one of them has honored the commitment to return to Haiti, but most have. Some have become nurses; others accountants; still others engineers and teachers.

For those who chose not to return, Wallace hopes that their education will one day return their thoughts and efforts to Haiti. One such student stayed and enlisted in the US military and married. He still lives in the US with his American wife and children, but he now has business in Haiti and gives back to the Haitian church through building projects. Though the man's decision to stay in the US was initially a great blow to the program, Wallace now sees the Lord's hand at work. From a broken promise has come a life dedicated to serving God and country.

One of the brightest stars to rise from the TLC students might be Daniel Jean Louis who was born in Gonaives, a small city at the bottom of Haiti's northern peninsula and the capital of the Artibonite Department. Gonaives is a city that lives on the brink, threatening to succumb at any moment to the storms, floods, and political turmoil that sweep over Haiti. It is, perhaps, one of Haiti's most vulnerable cities; it's also the crown of the nation's breadbasket. But to Daniel, it was simply *home*.

When he received the TLC scholarship in 2005, Daniel decided to major in Business Administration. Throughout his years at Liberty University, Daniel spent considerable time with Wallace and Eleanor who were living in Lynchburg. On his days off from school, they would visit historical landmarks together or enjoy a home cooked Haitian meal.

"I was learning. It was a tremendous opportunity for me to learn how to become a successful Christian in Haiti," Daniel says of his time with them. "I had no idea the importance of those lessons at the time, but they are the foundation of my professional life in Haiti and beyond."

Daniel returned to Haiti and worked for several years as the country manager for Partners Worldwide, an international aid organization with the mission to end poverty through enterprise. During his tenure with Partners Worldwide, he was instrumental in launching the 100K Jobs initiative, equipping NGOs and Haitian businesses to partner with one another. Since its inception, the project has created over 15,000 jobs with the goal of creating 100,000 new jobs by 2020. Daniel continues to serve on the project's board and train Partners Worldwide's business coaches. At the same time, he runs his own businesses: Trinity Lodge, which provides short-term housing in Port-au-Prince, and Bridge Capital, a private investment firm that helps local businesses finance projects and compete for contracts. On top of all that, Daniel is a professor of business at Quisquéya University and the Haitian State University. Somehow, in his daily life and work, Daniel found time to write. He has been making waves in the international development community with his book *From Aid to Trade—How Aid Organizations, Businesses, and Governments Can Work Together: Lessons Learned From Haiti*, which he co-authored with Jacqueline

Klamer. In May 2017, Daniel was bestowed an honorary doctorate of Business from his alma mater for his work in Haiti.

In many ways, Daniel epitomizes everything Wallace and Eleanor had hoped for when they founded TLC. His experience in Gonaives and his insight as a Haitian who has worked his way up the social and educational ladders are invaluable: he can see what others never could. More importantly, he is giving voice to the change that must happen while working with his own hands to bring about that change.

"Haiti today needs Christian leaders like Daniel—men and women who are highly educated and have a heart to lift up their neighbors as they succeed," Wallace says. "It's an encouragement to us old folks to see young people like him active and serving God."

While Wallace and Eleanor remain active in the scholarship program, Sandy is now leading the foundation, working with the candidates and ensuring the longevity of the scholarship. Under his guidance, the scholarship has grown from an experimental idea to a full-fledged program with increasingly competent and deserving candidates.

"I do feel like we are, at TLC, the last mile of their journey toward leadership training and development," Daniel says.

It's a journey, Wallace and Eleanor believe, that he and dozens of other men and women are walking with grace and integrity.

NINETEEN
Thy Will Be Done

ONE OF THE GREAT GRACES of growing old is that as people age, others tend to become more forgiving of their failings. We make allowances for their shortness of temper, the unkind word followed by regret, the impatience that has plagued them all their lives. These shortcomings are swept under the vast rug of all that has been forgotten.

We choose to remember, instead, the kindness shown to a stranger on their doorstep, the meal shared with a grieving father, the injured child cradled in strong arms. This ever-expanding amnesia of fault is one of God's kindest gifts to his aged servants and to those who abide with them. In this way, we are blessed with the ability to see His light shine through even the darkest corner of sin, infusing it with only His resplendent mercy.

And so it has gone with Wallace and Eleanor both. Those who once called them rivals now call them friends. Those who felt wounded by the stab of an unsheathed truth now praise their frankness.

If the transition of leadership had been harsh to them in many ways, it had one particular kindness: it afforded Wallace and Eleanor the distance required to reflect, to hear as an echo across a vast valley the hymns sung by the children's children of their first students. And in this distance, across this valley, they could each think of what might yet come from their countless journeys through the mountains. They could pray with more earnestness than ever: *Thy kingdom come. Thy will be done.*

Never ones to keep quiet—especially with the added allowance of old age—Wallace and Eleanor are eager to share their vision for the future of the Baptist Haiti Mission. When asked—and sometimes even when not asked—Wallace says, "I pray there will be a Haitian field director." "And that foreign missionaries be present only at the special request of the Haitian churches," Eleanor is often quick to add. With a Haitian yet even to serve on the BHM board of directors, many might say it's unlikely that a Haitian will be appointed field director in the near future. But many also said it was unlikely that a lanky American man of 21 would last any length of time in Haiti. Or that a conservative Baptist Bible teacher would traffic IUDs in her purse. Or that with one hand the couple would tie the shoelaces of a dictator's son while smuggling out his political targets with the other. Almost nothing that Wallace and Eleanor have accomplished has been likely, and even less has been expected.

They left a nation of Jim Crow to live among and serve the citizens of the first black republic. Even more radically, they sought to be accepted by those citizens as their own brother and sister in Christ. They surrendered, in a sense, their citizenship on earth and pledged allegiance to the kingdom of God—a kingdom where "there is neither Jew nor Gentile, neither slave nor free, nor is there male and female."

More upsetting to Wallace than the absence of a Haitian director is the fact that the question must be debated at all. Wallace has bemoaned time and again that for centuries the white Christian missionary had gone out to be the savior of black people—a white Messiah of sorts. "But we already have a Messiah," he groans. The future of missions, he argues, isn't in foreign missionaries but in the indigenous church. Missionaries are to go where there are no believers, and once there is a strong community of indigenous believers, then those missionaries should render themselves redundant.

Though this is his consistent message today, in moments of self-reflection, Wallace must recognize that he, like many before him, is a product of his time. To this day, his language is decidedly blunt and often insensitive. He paints a picture of a people with a broad brush and doesn't remember to share the detailed strokes that he sees in the individuals. But unlike too many of his contemporaries, Wallace has allowed himself to be taught by the very people he went to teach. And he has asked with word and deed to be adopted as one of them. Time and again, the answer from those he loved most—the field peasant, the local pastor, the widow—is simply, "You already are one of us."

In 2014, the hard-earned love of countless individuals reached the national stage. With a ceremony at the National Palace, President Michel Martelly decorated Wallace with the National Order of Honor and Merit, grade *Commandeur*. The National Order of Honor and Merit is the highest honor that the President of Haiti can bestow.

"We want to tell Pastor Wallace thank you. Because when people like him do the work the state should be doing…, you make the state say, if Pastor Wallace is doing this, so must we. You push the state to do more for its people," President Martelly said during his speech.

Perhaps unknowingly, President Martelly answered in a single moment one of the greatest criticisms Wallace had received throughout his ministry. Instead of building roads and infrastructure, instead of looking to public health programs, instead of collaborating with the government, Wallace should, they insisted, concentrate his efforts and limited resources on spreading the gospel and building churches. Of course, he did that, too. By the time he was decorated with the National Order of Honor and Merit, Wallace had helped to build more than 400 churches across the island for congregations affiliated with BHM, and nearly 68,000 children were in schools sponsored by these churches.

"Besides the fact that he has greatly contributed to strengthen the faith of many of our compatriots, he also saved countless lives through healthcare and medication he has made available to the poorest families, not to mention the many jobs he created. For all this and more, I want to say thank you," declared President Martelly. "How many children, how many elderly, how many generations were touched—how many survived—because of the work the Pastor has done?"

• • •

The Haitian Government hasn't been the only one to honor the couple's legacy in Haiti. Wallace and Eleanor were each bestowed an honorary doctorate in March 2004 from Université Jean-Price Mars. Eleanor was decorated as a Doctor of Humanities and Wallace a Doctor of Theology. In May 2017, they would again receive honorary doctorates, this time from Liberty University in Lynchburg, Virginia.

The nation's churches have also wanted to give their own recognition. To commemorate the two-hundredth anniversary of the first Protestant missionaries arriving in Haiti, the Federation Protestante d'Haiti (Protestant Federation of Haiti) hosted a celebration in the city of Les Cayes, near where the Protestants had landed on the south coast. The first missionaries were received warmly by the president of Haiti. "He had them speak on the palace lawn to the public and welcomed them to Haiti," Wallace says. "He said famously '…but don't mix in politics!'"

For the commemoration in July 2016, Wallace was driven to Les Cayes as a special guest of the federation and later on to Parc Larco, a multidisciplinary sports center recently built on the outskirts of the city, where the ceremony was to take place.

Navigating the "huge ball field complex" would prove challenging for Wallace, who by now was 91 years old. Finding his way across the field to the stage, he walked bent over, with his back nearly parallel to the ground. To move steadily, he ordinarily favors his large walking stick made from a gnarled branch of thick wood. But for longer expeditions, such as this ceremony in Les Cayes, Wallace relies on the help of a walker, much to his dismay.

The Protestant Federation wanted to honor Wallace's contributions to the evangelical church of Haiti. He had now served in the country the better part of a century—nearly 70 years to be more exact. So while he wasn't the *first* evangelical missionary in Haiti, he had been active in the country for nearly half the history of Protestants on the island nation.

"I got my padded seat walker up onto a high platform," Wallace recalls. "I was asked to briefly address the crowd. I thanked them and told them time did not permit telling of the great things that God has permitted."

After his remarks, Wallace was presented with a plaque from the Protestant Federation: "Honor and Merit to the infatigable Pastor Wallace Turnbull for his dedication, his sense of philanthropy, and his ministry in Haiti."

• • •

The honors and accolades have been bittersweet for Wallace and Eleanor. They are grateful, of course, for the living testimony this provides. They are eager for others to say, "if Pastor Wallace is doing this, so must we." They are also human and at no small level they must feel gratified that a lifetime of effort has been recognized. We each seek success in our lives, whatever that might look like. For Wallace and Eleanor, success is measured in the narrative of lives saved, of families bettered, of souls repentant. Someday their prayer, they'll tell you, is to hear the words, "Well done, good and faithful servant." Until then, medals and certificates are but an earthly echo of heavenly approval.

With each accolade received, Wallace steps forward while Eleanor stands behind. This has been in part her doing. She takes joy in seeing him recognized—and she's also a pragmatist. In Haiti, she is not Eleanor—she is Mme. Wallace. His wife. His partner. His helper. This is right and good, she says. But as age has crept up on her, it's only natural for her to wonder from time to time, "and me, what have I done?"

Wallace is the first to answer. "Eleanor is half of me. Without her, there would be none of this. These awards are as much hers

as they are mine. I wish they would put her name on them, too."
Yet one does not tell the President to make an addendum to the
highest award in the nation. Wallace and Eleanor know this. In
the bright light of day, they don't give it a second thought. But I
know, as their granddaughter, that the voices of the night can be
cruel and filled with doubt. In those moments, they hold tight
to one another, for they are each half of the other.

• • •

While the nation of Haiti seems to find it easy to get along
with Wallace in his eighties and nineties, the missionaries and
leaders of the very organization he founded have continued to
stumble in their relationship with him and he with them.

Part of the friction with the missionaries on the field lies
with Wallace's insistence that he stay involved in day-to-
day activities. What he sees as helpful—replacing a broken
telephone pole for example or ordering a cage cleaned in the
miniature zoo or offering to teach a class in the Summer Bible
Institute he founded—others see as interference.

"Wallace is working outside his jurisdiction again," they
might say. Or "Wallace is getting after us." Or "Wallace doesn't
trust us to do the work." On each occasion, they are right.

Wallace will counter, "The job needed doing." Or "I told
him three times to fix it and he didn't." Or "I was only trying
to be helpful." He, too, is right. "Like good soldiers, we want to
go with our boots on," Wallace and Eleanor have said countless
times. They both want to be useful to the very end.

Today, a new board of directors and new field leadership
are going out of their way to soothe the hurts of the past. They
seek a balance where Wallace and Eleanor's expertise can be
harnessed while maintaining a healthy distance in the day-to-

day activities. It isn't always easy, but I know that Wallace sees and appreciates it.

The consistent outreach from those with different degrees of power in Haiti's government and public life has also served to validate Wallace and Eleanor in recent years and give them a new sense of purpose. They are to many the face of Haiti's Protestant churches, a reminder of how far the Church has come in only a few generations. As a result, they're invited to one distinguished event or reception after another. In some ways, the invitations aren't new, but perhaps the time and desire to attend are. For, at these gatherings Wallace and Eleanor are able to regale a new audience with the stories of God's great work in Haiti, to share with new leaders the hope of the Gospel. Not in spite of but because of their age, they are able to boldly proclaim truth to those who most need to hear it. Wallace and Eleanor's presence at official functions might be intended as a ceremonial gesture, but for them, they are merely extending the reach of their message from the poor in body to the poor in spirit.

• • •

Even as they've found a new way to serve outside the mission, Wallace and Eleanor continue to find their position uncomfortable. "Where do we belong now?" they have asked again and again, a conflict symbolized in the struggle for their home. Wallace has asked for years to move back into the house he built for his family. And for years he's been denied: "It's the director's house, and you aren't the director." Wallace's response has often been less than gracious, filled with anger, yes, but mostly hurt.

Their request denied, Wallace and Eleanor have remained in an apartment off to the side of the mission, the dust of the now busy Kenscoff Road lining the bookcases and the tabletop. It isn't the conditions they mind, they'll both be quick to say; after all, they still have the beautiful view of their mountains, and neither is a stranger to the ascetic. What bothers them, they claim, is the fact that the small apartment is so ill-suited to receiving visitors, which is the one task for which they're both still suited. "The President even sent word that he wanted to visit me in my home, you know," Wallace once told me. "But how could I invite him when there is no security? The road is right there, on the other side of the door. Any crazy person could try to hurt him." And then, with a reluctant resignation, he added, "No, he can't come here."

One need not look too deeply to understand that Wallace's battle over his house has nothing to do with a symbol of status or even a place to receive guests. Rather, I believe his battle is one of belonging.

Wallace did more than dedicate his life to ministry in Haiti—he found his life in Haiti. Wallace found the home he'd never had as a child. He found home in the huts scattered along the mountains like freckles on the face of an old woman. He found home in the hymns sung by the light of kerosene lanterns, their black smoke rising like incense. He found home in the heady scent of jasmine billowing across the garden; in the cry of his whistle summoning the tradesmen to work; in the saltiness of fried pork, the bristles scratchy on his tongue.

• • •

Now 90 years old, Wallace stood on a cement block and swung his leg over the wooden saddle of his mount: a scraggly mule, tinted reddish brown like the dirt of the mountains that enveloped them both. A two-day journey to and from Portino lay ahead. He had never visited Portino—which in and of itself was noteworthy, for he had traveled nearly every stitch of these crumpled patchwork blankets. At one point, he thought he might never get to visit this growing community of believers who had scrimped and labored to build a place where they could worship. It wasn't difficult for him to say yes.

Together Wallace and beast would travel up and down the winding mountain path, trusting in one another—for a plunge to the valley below lay waiting in a single misstep, in a weight shifted abruptly, in a stone unseen.

Wallace had lost count of how many times he'd done this before. Alone. With his wife. With his children. With strangers. For a marriage perhaps. For a funeral. For those who lay buried in a landslide. For those they left behind. For the Sunday service. For the Tuesday market. How many times? Looking out over the mountains stretching in all directions, there was one thing he did know: he was at peace if this was the last time. Home lay draped around him, in the wrinkled quilt of the summits and ravines, in the touch of those he loved, in the prayers of those who loved him.

For photographs of Wallace Turnbull and his work in Haiti, visit lightmessages.com/wallace-turnbull.

ACKNOWLEDGMENTS

THERE ARE MANY THANKS TO BE GIVEN to those who came before me, who made Wallace the man he is, who served alongside him, who served him, who allowed him to serve them. Without you, there would be no story to tell.

I am indebted also to a community of individuals without whom this project would have never been completed. I give thanks especially to my grandparents for their willingness to share so openly about their lives and for trusting me with their story. To Uncle Sandy for driving Wallace and Eleanor back and forth from Alabama, for fielding questions, for unearthing facts long forgotten. To my parents, Wally and Betty Turnbull, for more than could ever be listed here, but which includes their incredible support, their many hours of research assistance, and their redirection when I veered off path. To my dearest friend Kezia McKeague for being my very first reader of this project and for her insightful feedback, and to her brilliant husband Eric Gettig for historical context and research advice. To Courtney Harrington for tracking down the name of Madeleine Le Genissel, the wife of the French Ambassador to Haiti. To Mary Ann Hester Pittman for helping me locate a Gujarati translation service. To Rebecca Brewster Stevenson for her tenacious editing and relentless encouragement, and especially for helping me to break down those long sentences. This book is stronger because of her work. To Margaret Williams for her careful proofreading and for teaching me to write so many years ago. Lastly, I give thanks to my beloved husband Roberto for giving me space to write, for understanding when my body was present but my mind was wandering a mountain trail far away.

ABOUT THE AUTHOR

ELIŻABETH TURNBULL was born and raised in Haiti where she grew up surrounded by the people and landscapes of *Say to These Mountains*. After graduating from Quisqueya Christian School in Port-au-Prince, Elizabeth went on to study Spanish and Journalism at Wake Forest University and received her MA in Latin American and Caribbean Studies from Florida International University. Today, she is the Senior Editor for Light Messages Publishing where she is grateful to immerse herself in new stories every day. Elizabeth is also the author of two children's books about Haiti: *Janjak and Freda Go to the Iron Market* and *Bonnwit Kabrit (Goodnight Goat)*. Elizabeth lives on a budding farm in Hillsborough, NC, with her husband, Roberto.

Visit Elizabeth at lightmessages.com/elizabeth-turnbull. Follow her on Twitter, Pinterest, and Instagram @ejturnbull.

If you liked
SAY TO THESE MOUNTAINS
you might also enjoy these other titles about Haiti

Those Who Passed By:
Stories from 60 years at the Mission on the Kenscoff Road
Eleanor Turnbull

God is No Stranger
Sandra Burdick and Eleanor Turnbull

Hidden Meanings: Truth and Secret in Haitian Proverbs
Wally Turnbull

Kite kè m pale (Let My Heart Speak)
Poems in Krèyol
Jacques Pierre

Janjak and Freda Go to the Iron Market
Elizabeth Turnbull

Bonnwit Kabrit (Goodnight Goat)
Elizabeth Turnbull